MY ANGEL'S NAME IS FRED

MY ANGEL'S NAME IS FRED

Tales of Growing Up Catholic

THOMAS BYRNES

1817

HARPER & ROW, PUBLISHERS, SAN FRANCISCO

Cambridge, Hagerstown, New York, Philadelphia, Washington
London, Mexico City, São Paulo, Singapore, Sydney

Selections from this book have appeared in *Catholic Digest* (College of St. Thomas) between 1981 and 1986.

FIRST EDITION

Library of Congress Cataloging-in-Publication Data

Byrnes, Thomas.
  My angel's name is Fred.

  1. Byrnes, Thomas—Childhood and youth.   2. Catholics
—Illinois—Chicago—Biography.   3. Chicago (Ill.)—
Biography.   I. Title.
BX4705.B996A3   1987   282'.092'4   [B]   86-45801
ISBN 0-06-061272-X

87 88 89 90 91 RRD 10 9 8 7 6 5 4 3 2 1

To Ginny

Contents

Preface

One of my milder idiosyncrasies is that I keep on hand a store of ingenuous answers to candid questions that I feel people will ask me sooner or later, though they haven't as yet got around to it. But when they do, I'll be ready.

Sample answer: "We never cared that much for each other."

The unspoken question: "How come you didn't marry Mary Bernice McCafferty?"

Another sample rejoinder: "Because we like kids, that's why."
The question: "How come you had so many kids?"

The question that I feel comes closest to being asked (I can sense when people are *thinking* of asking it) is "Weren't you simply miserable growing up in the restrictive atmosphere of a Catholic home and school?"

The question might be expressed in more particular ways:

"Weren't you simply miserable growing up at a time when the final word in all matters was what 'Sister says,' when anything Sister couldn't explain had to be 'taken on faith,' and when one of the surest ways of losing that faith was to ask too many questions?" (Sister would let you know when you were asking too many questions.)

Let us forge on. "Weren't you simply miserable growing up at a time . . .

" . . . when no mortal was considered capable of getting from one end of the week to the other without committing a sin and you spent the better part of every Saturday afternoon in the long line outside the confessional waiting to get rid of it, and your only diversion, after you had carefully examined your conscience, was to see how slowly you could pass a finger through the flame of any votive candle within reach. . . .

" . . . when if you missed Saturday afternoon confession

(or broke your fast by inadvertently swallowing some of the rinse water when you brushed your teeth), you sat alone in your pew on Sunday morning, shamefaced and scarcely breathing, while your classmates, smug and self-righteous but spotless, shuffled past you on their way to the Communion rail. . . .

" . . . when the hymns to be sung at the eight o'clock children's Mass invariably included 'Come Holy Ghost'. . . .

" . . . when no matter how hard you tried to keep up with your Latin-English missal, the *sanctus* bell always rang out at least two pages before you were ready for it. . . .

" . . . when the intensity of your devotional zeal was measured by the force with which you thumped your chest while chanting, 'Through my fault,' et cetera. . . .

" . . . when the girls' entrance to the school was so carefully insulated from the boys' that it might as well have been in another parish. . . .

" . . . when proper attire included scapulars around the neck and rosary beads in purse or pocket, and standard equipment for a baseball game included a miraculous medal and you blessed yourself every time you came to bat. . . .

" . . . when a sure-fire way of being marked for special handling by the nuns was to start a rumor that you were seriously thinking of becoming a priest."

Per omnia saecula saeculorum.

Those are the questions—at least some of them. But in every case the answer would be the same: "I had a happy childhood."

The stories in this book have appeared over a five-year period in Catholic Digest. I think they explain that happy childhood. The Digest editors believe me. So do their readers. I hope you will, too.

And maybe they'll bring to mind some happy memories of your own.

I. FIRST STEPS

Christmas, Do You Remember?

There is a true Christmas story of long ago that I wish I could make happen again. Unfortunately, the plot requires certain elements that, for me, at least, are forever gone. But you, if you're young enough, may have at hand exactly the kind of characters and setting needed to make the old wonder glow anew.

You need parents, grandparents, two unmarried aunts, and an unmarried uncle—unmarried because they are still quite young (in their late teens and early twenties) and they know they still have time. It is important, too, that uncle, aunts, and grandparents live above you in an old two-family house. And the story must begin on Christmas Eve, about midnight, when a certain five-year-old boy (yourself) is thought to be asleep.

But you have heard laughter and the tinkling of tiny bells. Because you have no idea of the time, you decide to leave your bedroom and investigate. You steal up the long hallway toward the dining room and glimpse, incredulously, a partly decorated tree in the living room beyond. Your cherished belief that Santa brings the tree is saved from extinction by the frantic flapping of Aunt Addie's skirt, held out in front of you like a huge, inverted fan, while she stage-whispers, "Santa's gone for another load! Get into bed quick or he won't come back!"

You scurry into bed at once, not even pausing for a second look or to wonder why the grown-ups are not in bed, too.

A little later the door opens just a crack; you see a figure peering in, but you're not sure whether it's your father or Santa Claus. Yes, it *is* Santa Claus, else why that sound outside your window of reindeers impatiently shaking their bells? So with deep, deliberate breaths you feign slumber, and the rhythm of your breathing soon tricks you into sleep.

Before you know it, you drop with a start into that pool of half-wakefulness where you wonder for a blink or two what day this is; then, in a flash of joy, your mind is flooded with images of gifts, ornaments, songs, candles, and the laughing faces of your family. You notice a slash of early light at the edge of the window shade, and you know that the day you thought would never come has come at last. You explode in a rapturous shout and leap from the bed.

"It's Christmas! It's Christmas!"

You hear your parents in the bedroom next to yours getting into their robes and slippers and your mother asking, "For heaven's sake, what time is it?"

For a moment the scene in the living room is yours alone—the tree in a full bloom of ornaments and tinsel, the tumble of beribboned boxes, then the railroad track, the locomotive and cars. And—no, is it possible?—the train is not just a wind-up, it's electric, with three dry-cell batteries to prove it!

You do not begin playing with your train right now, nor do you open your other presents. First things first in this old Christmas; no gifts may be exchanged until after church. So you try to concentrate on your oatmeal your mother cooks for you. "You can't go out on an empty stomach," she insists. (In this family of yours, the worst thing that could happen to you is to have an empty stomach.) Then you wash and dress and go back to the train after promising you'll only look at it.

You have heard people stirring overhead, and now, on the front porch, you join Grandma and Grandpa, Aunt Addie, Aunt Laura, and Uncle Billy. In a chorus of "Merry Christmas! Merry Christmas!" the noisy company troops through the snow to yet another wonderland.

The strains of "Away in a Manger" drift through the opening and closing doors of the church as you trudge up the steps. Inside there is a glory of light and music and trees. You marvel that anything as big as the towering evergreens that bower the main altar could have been brought through the doors. In front of a side altar, a stable houses the mystery of Christ's birth. The figures are as real to you as the people in the pews ahead.

Your thoughts drift like the incense. You wonder what Santa Claus is doing now. Is he sad because, for him, the excitement of Christmas is over? You put this question to your mother, on your left. She says, "Shh, I'll tell you later." You put it to your grandmother, on your right. She says, "Don't worry about *him*. He's having the time of his life planning for *next* year." Of course.

You bring yourself back to the movements of priests and acolytes. You feel the rolling thunder of the *Kyrie* and *Gloria* in your stomach. But now there is a pause, and without warning, a tiny electric locomotive begins pulling a string of cars along the top of the altar rail.

You race home with your young aunts and uncle. How fast you are! Try as they might, they can't keep up with you, not even Uncle Billy, who slips and falls and cries, "Junior! Give me a hand! Hurry!" You run to his side. With a terrifying yowl he pulls you down and rolls you over and over in a storm of snow and laughter. He is up first and beats you home. But you don't mind. Everything is just as it should be.

"Breakfast will be ready in no time at all," says your mother. "Shall we wait till afterwards to open the presents?"

Your loud "No, no!" is echoed by your aunts and uncle. "We can eat any old time! Let's open the presents!"

Grandpa chides your mother good-naturedly. "One of these years, Mae, you'll stop asking that silly question."

That's the signal to turn on the transformer of your train. But nothing happens. Immediately your father, grandfather, and Uncle Billy are on their knees beside you, advising each other on what to do. Grandpa discovers that the wires are hooked up wrong and reconnects them correctly. The train whizzes around the track. It even has a tiny headlight!

Ribbons and wrapping, so carefully tied, pop open like firecrackers, and the cast-off paper rises in a colorful flood around chairs and tables. "Oh, it's just beautiful!...Just what I've always wanted!...I've never seen anything so lovely!...Merry Christmas!...Thank you!"

These are the "gifts down here"—from Santa and your parents to you and the others. Under another tree are the "gifts up there"—from Santa and the others to you and your parents, waiting for the afternoon, when everyone will stream upstairs for a feast that Grandma and her girls began planning weeks ago.

Now your mother and her sisters are announcing that breakfast is ready, and will you all please come to the dining room table? "Bless us, O Lord, and these Thy gifts...."

After the grapefruit, oranges, grapes, blueberry muffins, coffee cake, honey, jam, basted eggs, bacon, sausages, coffee, and cocoa, and after your grandfather, going for seconds, reminds everyone that breakfast is the most important meal of the day, and after your father tells how, as a boy in Ireland, he helped hunt the wren on St. Stephen's Day, you all return to the living room to sing carols, with Aunt Addie at the piano, and to look again at the presents—and each other.

Aunt Laura lies on her back on the floor and, with her eyes closed, inches her head farther and farther back under the tree until it touches the metal stand that holds the trunk. You're quick to follow.

"Now open your eyes!" she commands.

Above you, the tree soars through an infinity of branches, dark, towering, and mysterious, the enchanted woodland world of all the old tales that begin, "Once upon a time, deep in the forest..." You are the firstborn child of the greenwood, reaching for light through the ancient conifers.

"It's snowing again," says Uncle Billy. "Let's all go out for a run!"

Everyone bundles up except Grandma and your mother,

who insist on doing the breakfast dishes. You have a new sled. Grandpa has filed the runners clean of paint so they'll slip across the snow like a shadow. You belly-flop ahead of the others, then back to them, around them, and away from them, until your legs seem to be made of wood. Then Uncle Billy pulls you with a rope he has remembered to bring, and so do the others, all taking turns.

What an unreal world it is with everything hushed in frosty, Christmas-card stillness! For the first time, you see Mrs. Thorne's delicatessen closed and dark. Far ahead, a trolley clangs its way across the end of your street, and you feel sorry for the motorman who has to work on Christmas Day. You resolve that you will never be a trolley car motorman.

You and the family are opening the upstairs presents now. Aunt Addie's fiancé and Aunt Laura's beau have been invited to dinner, so there is a gift for each of them and gifts from them in return. The tree looks different from yours because the ornaments, for the most part, are handmade of papier-mâché, cardboard, ribbons, and sequins, delicately designed and colored—the work of Aunt Laura's facile fingers, the same fingers that have filled your home and others with a wealth of beautifully hand-painted china and have learned, without lessons, to play the violin.

Aunt Laura passes you a large box, explaining, "I was going to ask Santa Claus to bring you an electric train, but then I felt you'd get one anyway, and you did."

Your hands fall from the box. You stare in disbelief.

"You mean I could have had—?"

Think of it! You could have had *two* trains—could have had *twice* the fun! Aunt Laura reads your face and assures you. "I'm sorry," she says, "but I know you'll like this gift, too." You sigh. Women just don't understand about trains.

You open the box from Aunt Laura and lift the contents out—an ox, a donkey, two sheep, a shepherd, three Wise

Men, and the Holy Family, all in papier-mâché, all hand-painted, and a stable of antiqued wood, filled with straw. Everyone admires Aunt Laura's craftsmanship.

"Junior," your mother whispers in that soft but warning way she has, "what do you *say?*"

You say all the things you know you're supposed to say. You kiss Aunt Laura and hug her. You put the stable on the floor and set the figures in place. And suddenly you have a wonderful idea.

"I know what I'll do," you exclaim. "I'll put the stable next to my track and it can be a station!"

"Was Jesus born in a railroad station?" That's Aunt Addie's fiancé, always being funny.

Although everyone laughs, you feel you've said something wrong. You try to make up for it, but it's Aunt Laura who says, "You just place it wherever you think best."

The afternoon hurries into evening and the evening into night. The dreaded moment comes when at last you're told it's bedtime. The dinner is long over. More songs have been sung, more good times remembered. Grandma has wound up the Victrola and you've listened to Madame Schumann-Heink singing "*Stille Nacht.*" Aunt Laura has played "Star of the East" on her violin. Aunt Addie's fiancé has done tricks with a loop of string—made you think he passed it right through his neck!

But sleep? Then Christmas would be over!

"Come now," says your father, "you'll be so tired you won't fall asleep at all." So downstairs you go—you, your parents, and your presents, trailing a last garland of good-bys. "Wonderful day! Wonderful dinner, Grandma! Merry Christmas, everybody!"

As he helps you into your pajamas, your father comforts you. "Remember, tomorrow you'll have all day to play." And with that promise to hold onto, you roll into bed.

But you don't sleep. You can't let Christmas end so soon. You ask for a drink of water. Your father brings it to you. Your mother enters the room carrying the Christmas stable.

She clears a spot for it on your dresser beyond the foot of your bed and sets it down, carefully arranging the figures around its base. "Something to keep you company," she says.

She covers the lamp shade with a towel so the light is very dim. She kisses you good night. You feel like one of the shepherds of long ago approaching the real manger from a distant hill with songs of angels mounting the shadows. For all you can see in the half-light, the figures could be moving. The Wise Men are arriving at the end of their long quest. Joseph turns to greet them. The ox, the donkey, and the sheep look quietly on, and Mary bends above the Child and softly whispers, "Sleep...."

My Grandmother's Life Was a Love Song

In my harvest of family photographs there is one of a young woman in her seventeenth summer, petite as a moss rose, with a high bubbling of champagne-colored hair above a soft, gentle face that smiles serenely out through sepia mist. Her name is Sarah.

Once, in a forest of bric-a-brac and faded portraits, the picture stood newly taken on an old upright piano top in a modest home in Racine, Wisconsin. The time was somewhere in the 1880s. It was the time when the city of Racine staged a music festival in which the young girl was a featured soprano soloist. Among the guests of honor was a noted director, Theodore Thomas, who was soon to found the Chicago Symphony Orchestra.

So impressed was the maestro with Sarah's performance that, before leaving Racine, he made inquiries and went by carriage to speak his admiration to her parents and to ask about their plans for her future. He was prepared, if need be, to make an offer.

In the tiny parlor, crowded to the walls with father,

mother, younger sisters and brothers—puzzled, uncomfortable, and wary—Thomas told them that Sarah had a voice of such exceptional quality that it would be a great loss not to develop it. Sarah herself sat in glowing silence.

The parents said yes, they knew their daughter could sing; in fact, she had been singing since she was a tot, but lessons would cost money they could ill afford.

Thomas made his offer. He said he would be honored if they would let *him* finance Sarah's musical career. After their initial astonishment, the stern Scots mother, powerless to separate her daughter's talents from the toilsome reality of their lives, decided the matter must be settled quickly and for good. "If Sarah were to spend her time on music," she said, "who would help me with the housework?"

And so Sarah stayed with the housework, and the episode became, in time, another piece of family bric-a-brac to be shown to incredulous friends like a souvenir of a once-in-a-lifetime visit to some exotic land. She stayed with the housework, married her high school sweetheart, moved to Chicago, bore seven children, and became my maternal grandmother.

By the time I was born, three of her seven children were many years dead from a variety of childhood diseases; another, at eighteen, had been killed in a railroad accident. And the family, through a monotony of adversity in which my grandfather's ingenuousness in business matters played a major part, had settled into a penny-watching struggle to keep bills paid and respectability intact. Through it all it was Sarah's indestructible buoyancy that sustained the family morale.

Often during my growing-up years, I heard her children lament what they called the "great tragedy" of their mother's lost opportunity. But never from my grandmother herself did I hear a word of complaint. Like that of so many saints, her response to the demands of her daily life was a way of expressing her love for God. Although she never sang on the stage, she made her whole life a love song for her family. I can still hear the infinite range of its melody.

Though few and modest were her own occasions of self-satisfaction, Sarah compensated by filling each moment of another's achievements with extra measures of rejoicing. For me she was an inexhaustible source of sympathy and understanding. I could always come to her for sure celebration of some childhood triumph, however small, for solace, or for song.

I keep a toddler's memory of her holding me on her lap and weaving stories around the fawns that pranced in twilit frolic across the wallpaper of her dining room.

I remember her string. She saved it not to use it again herself but to spin a great ball for me to play with.

She saved buttons, a big tin can of them, for me to spill out noisily on her kitchen floor and noisily drop back one by one into the can.

When she baked, she gave me scraps of dough to twist into pastries of my own, which she put in the oven beside her loaves. Then she would scoop me up, lower me into a sea of cushions and arm doilies, ballast me down with an enormous book of Civil War lithographs that had been a wedding present, dance across to the piano, and, to the metronome ticking of her grandmother's clock, sing me songs by Stephen Foster while the rooms filled with the warm-bread aroma of security.

During that stretch of my early years when Grandma and Grandpa lived several blocks away, a special treat for me was to stay with them overnight. I would be dropped off by my mother well in advance of Grandpa's return from work. This gave me time to sample the fresh batch of cookies baked for the occasion, bang away on the piano, leaf through the Civil War lithographs, and prepare for the ritual known as "scaring Grandpa."

With a burned cork Grandma would give me a beard and eyebrows as ferocious-looking as those of General J. E. B.

Stuart. At the first sound of Grandpa's step on the stairs, I would hide under the drop-leaf kitchen table and wait till he had entered the room and kissed Grandma. Then with a shriek I would spring out with arms flailing and feet stomping.

Of course, a wink from Grandma had already told him what to expect; but, good actor that he was, he always managed to reel backwards against the wall, one hand at his throat, the other stretched out in a fluttering attempt at self-defense as he cried piteously, "Oh, no, no, no!"

"Did I scare you, Grandpa?"

"I was never so scared in my life!"

Having once again established my unfailing power to terrify Grandpa, I would then accept his peacemaking offer to join him in a dish of ice cream.

At night I sank rapturously into the billowing luxury of the spare bedroom's feather bed. Its carved walnut headboard rose behind me as massively as the main altar at church.

"Read me a story, Grandma."

On the marble-top bedside table was the ever-present Bible, and beside it a book of Bible stories for children, which Grandma had bought for my visits.

"And Ruth said, 'Do not ask me to leave you. Wherever you go, I will go, and where you live, I will live, and your people will be my people and your God my God. . . . ' "

Later, when my grandparents lived upstairs from us, I was an almost daily visitor in their home. "Let's sing something," Grandma would say, and with her at the piano we'd duet our way through "Smile the While," "My Old Kentucky Home," "With Someone Like You," and other favorites, which we repeated with undiminished enthusiasm performance after performance.

Or she would ask, as if for the first time, "How about reciting 'Sheridan's Ride'?"

Feet planted firmly apart for emphasis, I would take my

stand in a favorite corner and furiously declaim the stirring verse celebrating General Phil Sheridan's battle-saving gallop from Winchester to the bloody field where his troops had been falling back. By the time I reached the closing lines,

> Be it said in letters both bold and bright,
> Here is the steed that saved the day
> By carrying Sheridan into the fight
> From Winchester twenty miles away!

I was almost speechless with emotion, and so were she and my grandfather.

"Tomorrow night," I might say as I left, "I'll give you 'The Men of the Alamo.' "

"Oh, do do!" Grandma would exclaim. "Or 'The Children's Hour.' That's my favorite."

"Maybe you'd like to hear it now."

"Oh, that would be wonderful!"

"All right. I'll think of something else for tomorrow."

In high school I was a member of the debating team, which about once a month competed with teams from other schools across the city. Subjects ranged, as I recall, from "Resolved: that the sixteen-inch naval gun is a menace to world peace and should be internationally outlawed" to "Resolved: that the McNary-Haugen Farm Relief Bill should be enacted." Which side of the question you spoke for was of little concern. You were rehearsed to debate with equal conviction affirmatively or negatively. But whatever the subject and whatever the side our team was assigned, there was always one constant—the presence of my parents and grandparents.

After a string of wins, which my supporters applauded with embarrassing enthusiasm, we finally met a team captained by a tall, spindly youth whose appearance reminded everyone of the young Abe Lincoln. What's more, he had something of the Lincolnian gift for incisive humor. We weren't quite ready then for incisive humor and we lost the decision.

My grandmother, especially, was outraged. "You *deserved* to win," she insisted. "Look how hard you worked. I'll bet those silly old judges were mad because of what *I* did, but I just couldn't help it."

What Grandma had done was jump to her feet after a particularly withering rebuttal by young Abe and yell, "Oh, you be quiet!"

Years later, Sarah made peace with her final sorrows. She was at the deathbed of her husband and soon after at my mother's. "The worst thing that can ever happen to you," she told me once, "is to survive your children." She survived all but two of them.

Well into her eighties, and shortly before she slipped into her final illness, she amazed my two aunts and myself one afternoon by going to the piano. Above her on its top were the old family photographs, including the one of herself taken so long ago. She opened the lid over the aging keys. The tremulous fingers anchored themselves to a few basic chords, and the voice, fragile with time and secrets, sang, "I Dream of Jeannie with the Light Brown Hair."

At last she rested her hands in her lap and looked silently at the yellow keyboard. Then gently she closed the lid, returned to her chair—and smiled at us.

"What then is love?" asks theologian Romano Guardini, and he answers with these words of Pierre de Caussade, "Precisely this: 'to do what is to be done in the present moment, because it is exactly that which fulfills the will of God. And to do it as charity should be performed, in a spirit of purity and good will.' "

Or to sum it up in the words of an old plaque that once hung in Sarah's home, "Bloom where you are planted."

My Father and the Six O'Clock Mass

Years ago many parishes had a six o'clock morning Mass on Sunday. For my father it was the *only* Mass on Sunday. He judged the temperature of your faith not by your attendance or nonattendance at Mass but by *what* Mass you attended.

Were you a six o'clock regular? Good. That meant you were a staunch, militant Catholic, assured of a nonstop passage to Paradise the minute you died. Did you prefer the eight o'clock Mass? Well, that wasn't *too* serious, but it did indicate a slight character flaw, a spiritual ennui, if you will, and the sooner you came to grips with it, the better.

Or perhaps you stayed in bed until time to dress for the ten o'clock Mass? Ah, things were getting pretty much out of hand by now, and there was no telling what you might do next.

What you usually did next was start going to the twelve noon Mass. By then, nothing could save you short of a novena to St. Jude, patron of hopeless causes.

The only exemptions from this religious timetable were my mother and my sister, who steadfastly refused to budge from the house on Sunday before eight. My mother asked once, "If everyone in this parish went to the six o'clock, where in the world would you put them all?" But my father's faith was not about to be tempted by the blandishments of higher mathematics. "What a marvelous problem to be confronted with" was all he'd say.

So dedicated was my father to early-morning worship that I used to imagine, in a very irreverent way, that on those rare occasions when, through no fault of his own, he had to forego the six o'clock in favor of a later service, he immediately got himself to confession.

"Bless me, Father, for I have sinned. I missed the six o'clock Mass last Sunday and had to settle for the twelve."

I knew this confession might baffle a younger priest, but my father never went to the younger priests. He went to the pastor, and the older he was the better, for in those days the older pastors were notorious early birds, too. In our parish the six o'clock was the pastor's Mass; no assistant dared covet it.

So I had no trouble imagining the old pastor with his nose to the grill, saying sternly, "So—you missed the six o'clock Mass, my son. Well, well, well, well, well, well, well!" (How the quality of the spiritual advice you get in confession has declined over the years!)

Then the question that has rattled the walls of confessionals and the souls of penitents over countless generations: "How many *times*, my son? What do you mean *only* once? Did Adam have to eat a bushel of apples to be driven from Eden, eh? Now, for your penance, say five Our Fathers and five Hail Marys and make a good Act of Contrition."

Of course, I didn't suppose it ever happened that way, but I was sure it could have.

My father was always the first one up on Sunday morning—or any other morning, for that matter. In bathrobe and slippers he would march to the kitchen to start the coffee. Then he would kneel on the seat of a kitchen chair and say his morning prayers.

He prayed in a loud stage whisper that I was sure could be heard a block away. And he prayed in a somber, almost tragic monotone, the kind some poets use when quoting from their own works. My mother told him, "You sound like a dying archbishop."

The coffee ready and his prayers finished, both at the same moment, my father would come to the door of my room and in a softer whisper would ask, "Junior, would you like to come with me to the six o'clock Mass?"

My father could ask the simplest question and make it sound like Moses delivering the Ten Commandments. But he asked this one in a gentle way that seemed to say, "Trust me, I know what's best." And I can tell you there were times when his words sounded like an invitation from one of the original Twelve to a place at the original table.

And so the two of us would start out—on foot, for our church was within walking distance of our home. This doesn't mean that our church at that time was anywhere near our home (we had moved by then to another parish); it's just that my father considered anything inside Cook County to be within walking distance. And although the morning might be bitter cold, I was always warmed by my father's repeated insistence that this was by far the best time of the day, and wasn't it a shame that so many people missed it?

I look back now and I see the two of them, the man and the boy, bound in priceless intimacy, like the two disciples on the road to Emmaus, except that in our case we knew beforehand that we would soon be meeting Himself.

I used to wonder at my father's fondness for worship at dawn, and one day when I was much older I asked him, "Why?"

"It seems to me," he said, "if we are to listen to Christ's invitation, 'Come to me,' the same invitation He extended to Peter across the troubled waters of Genesaret, then the sooner we come the better. Especially," he added with a smile, "if you're an early riser."

When Grandpa Fixed the Convent Door

Someone once said there's nothing louder than two Irishmen arguing with each other unless it's two Irishmen agreeing with each other.

In my preschool years I had many opportunities to witness the truth of that observation in the relationship between my maternal grandfather and our pastor at the time, Father Sullivan.

In those days, the convent of St. Lawrence parish was next door across a field of tall grass. Living so close to the nuns meant that if you were six years old and about to start school, their habits, which some children found frightening at first, were as familiar to you as your living room curtains. It also meant that on a lazy summer afternoon, if there was nothing to do at home, you could always take yourself and your collie pup to the convent and be sure of a warm welcome, cookies and milk, and a good half hour's fun, with yourself and the younger nuns sitting on the parlor floor playing with the dog.

The nuns were the best neighbors anyone could have had. In the old-fashioned tradition of neighborliness there was a constant, reciprocal flow of felicitations and impromptu gifts—flowers and vegetables from my grandfather's garden, holy cards, medals, scapulars, rosary beads, and prayers from the sisters. There were rides through the park for the nuns in our family car and small favors my grandfather would do for them. It was one of these that one day brought him into critical confrontation with Father Sullivan.

The convent had a front screen door no younger than the ancient frame building itself. The door had a distressing habit of sagging, then catching on the threshold, to be freed only by a nun's well-placed kick on its bottom panel. It might then burst outwards with such force that first-time visitors were often sent reeling backwards. Regular callers like myself learned to stand well back until the door was fully open.

At last, however, the patience of Sister Agnes, the mother superior, was exhausted. She phoned Father Sullivan and told him the problem. The pastor, a dedicated do-it-yourselfer, said he'd be happy to fix it, but since he was about to leave on a priests' retreat, he'd send Joe Dooley, a neighborhood handyman, around.

My grandfather saw Dooley working on the door and immediately called Sister Agnes.

"Sister," he scolded, "why didn't you ask *me* to fix that door? Dooley will cost you a fortune."

"Thank you, Patrick," said Sister Agnes, "but Mr. Dooley was Father Sullivan's idea."

One afternoon soon after, my grandfather and I brought a bushel basket of vegetables to the sisters. I rang the bell and stood back. In a moment Sister Agnes appeared out of the hallway shadows inside and unhooked the catch. She pushed. She pushed again. My grandfather set the basket down and with an expert lifting motion pulled the door free.

"You see, Sister," he said, "that fellow Dooley didn't know what he was doing. All he did was use bigger screws in the hinges. See here, Junior," he said to me, pointing to the door's inner frame, "the wood's too soft to hold the screws tight." I was flattered to be included in his diagnosis, but that's the way it always was with Grandpa and me.

"Don't worry about it, Patrick," said Sister. "Father Sullivan's back now, and he said he'd take care of it himself this evening. And thank you *so* much for the vegetables."

On the short walk home, my grandfather snorted contemptuously. "A fine job *he'll* do," he muttered.

"Who, Grandpa?"

"Father Sullivan. He thinks because he was raised on a farm in Ireland he can fix anything. All he ever did over there was milk cows."

Father Sullivan's direct descent from the "island of saints and scholars," as he was fond of putting it, was a sore point with Grandpa. In their frequent arguments about the "trouble" in Ireland, Father always assumed a superior air, as if my grandfather's birth in Racine, Wisconsin, a generation removed from the old sod, made his lineage less saintly and his knowledge less scholarly than his pastor's. The truth is, Grandpa was an ardent reader who claimed he knew every bump and turn in the long road of Anglo-Irish relations. But Father Sullivan had a way of bringing every battle to what he, at least, considered an unassailable close. "Pat," he would say solemnly, "you forget—I was *born* there." Which Grandpa always claimed was a low blow.

Most of these engagements took place directly above our heads in my grandparents' living room, where Father Sullivan was a frequent visitor simply because the two old men liked each other immensely and showed it—except when certain volatile subjects came up. Most other times, they were in harmony, a condition, however, not always easy to recognize from down below. Sometimes we'd hear a thunderous slap on a table, and my mother would sigh, "They're at it again." But then we'd hear Father Sullivan shouting, "Pat, you're right! Absolutely right!" or "I can't argue with that, Pat! You hit the nail right on the head!" and Grandpa replying with another bang on the table, "It's the only way to look at it! Exactly as you say!"

After such sessions, my grandfather might remark, "I had a fine talk with Father Sullivan today. He's a very sensible man."

Grandpa's opinion of Father Sullivan's manual dexterity was another matter. He felt it suffered by comparison with his own record as a superior craftsman. A master boiler-maker in his earlier years, Grandpa was a man of infinite patience and care. He was the exact opposite of his pastor, who believed that the sooner you get a job done the better, so you can go on to something else. Grandpa's ethic was to do it right no matter *how* long it took. That is why the problem of the screen door continued to irk him.

To verify his suspicions that Father Sullivan had botched the job, Grandpa gathered up another basket of vegetables one day and the two of us went back to the convent. Again the door stuck. Again my grandfather commented scathingly on the folly of trying to fix it with larger screws. "It's like putting screws in butter," he told Sister Agnes.

"Junior," he said to me on the way home, "you and I have some work to do."

Early next morning, Grandpa and I stopped once more

at the convent but without alerting the sisters. He took a tape measure from his pocket and said, "Now help me do the measuring." Of course, he could have taken the measurements himself, and a lot faster than with me helping, but I didn't know that then. So with my thumb holding the tip of the tape at each spot where he placed it, Grandpa and I measured our needs.

"Going to make a new door, Grandpa?"

"Almost but not quite. Now let's get the lumber."

We walked the three blocks to the lumberyard. He selected the smallest piece, about three feet long, and showed me how to carry it balanced perfectly on my right shoulder. He swung the other pieces to his own shoulder and tucked a roll of screening under his left arm, and back we went to the convent. He told me to watch the lumber while he went home for his toolbox.

I was sitting on the top step waiting when Sister Agnes came to the door, saw the lumber, then saw me.

"Junior!" she exclaimed. "What in the world are you *doing?*"

"Waiting for Grandpa. He's going to fix your door *right.*"

"But all that lumber! Is he going to rebuild the convent?"

"No, Sister, just the screen door."

Sister Agnes's hands fluttered nervously about her wimple.

"Does Father Sullivan know about this?"

"I don't think so," I said.

"Oh, my goodness, oh, my goodness! I'd better phone him."

"I don't think Grandpa needs him," I called after her, but she was gone.

In a few minutes she came back, more worried than ever.

"Father's out on a sick call," she said. "Oh, my goodness!"

When my grandfather returned with his tools, he assured Sister Agnes, now flanked by several other nuns, all exclaiming, "Oh, my goodness!" that the sensible thing to do was to fix the door with or without Father Sullivan's permission.

"He'll be delighted," Grandpa said, and he promptly set to work.

I helped, of course. Grandpa saw to that. "Steady the board for me, Junior. That's the boy" (the board was already as steady as an oak). "Hand me that hammer, Junior" (the hammer was well within his own reach). "Give an extra turn to that screw like a good boy" (Hercules couldn't have given it another turn).

At intervals Sister Agnes came to the door, guessing she ought to give Father Sullivan another call—which she did several times but without response.

At one point, for what reason I can't imagine, Sister called my mother, who came right over but had tact enough not to comment within Grandpa's hearing. Mrs. Thorne, who ran a small grocery store across the street, also came over. The mailman stopped by and offered some suggestions, which were ignored. Some neighborhood kids drifted up and sat on the grass, watching. And through it all my grandfather measured, sawed, planed, fitted, and nailed as imperturbably as a combine moving through a field of grain.

By noontime the door was finished, fitted, and hung. My grandfather opened it wide and let it close. It settled into the doorjamb as comfortably as a robin sinking into her nest. "I'll paint it tomorrow," said Grandpa.

"Oh, I don't know how to thank you," said Sister Agnes. "Really, Pat, it's a beautiful job. I'm sure that Father Sul—"

"*Pat!*"

There came a bellow that echoed like thunder behind us in the street. Everyone—except Grandpa—spun around like members of a drill team. Even in turning around, Grandpa took his time and did it right.

At the foot of the walk stood Father Sullivan, imposing as one of the prophets, hands on his hips, his large, raw-boned face glowering from beneath the brim of his Panama hat. He looked at Sister Agnes, who trembled. He looked at my grandfather, who looked steadily back. Then, as silent as the church after Sunday Benediction, he climbed the convent steps, opened and closed the door several times, examined the hinges, tested the spring—and raised his hat in a high salute. There was another bellow. "Pat," he cried, "you're a living saint!" He laughed. He roared. And so did everyone else, at last.

"It was the only sensible thing to do—rebuild it," shouted my grandfather, his voice rising in agreement.

"You're right, Pat! Those screws couldn't have held a butterfly in place! You're absolutely right!" He gave Grandpa a fist on the chest that would have toppled a lesser man. "You're a genius! That's what you are, Pat, a genius!"

"This way it'll last for years," yelled my grandfather.

Father Sullivan doubled up, gasping for breath. "Why, Pat," he finally managed, "it'll outlast the convent itself!"

On the way home, his pipe lighted, his blue eyes dancing, my grandfather allowed himself one last critical remark.

"I'll bet that even in Ireland he never did what you and I just did." He patted my head.

As I say, Grandpa always took his time and did things right—including the job of being a grandfather.

How Father Curran Won the Fireworks War

The greatest summer treat of my early schoolboy years was to be invited with my parents and baby sister to spend the Fourth of July with my great-aunt Kate.

No one I know celebrated the Fourth with as much gusto as she. Ancient but indestructible, dignified and proper, almost Victorian in her dress and decorum, Aunt Kate nevertheless harbored a patriotic fervor so strong that once a year it exploded in a fireworks display many called the glory of their town's night sky.

Her feelings sprang, however, from her own singular interpretation of American history. In Aunt Kate's blue Irish eyes the Revolution had been not so much a colonial revolt against British misrule as a punishment that God visited on England for her historic maltreatment of Ireland. For my aunt the Declaration of Independence was the Almighty's wrathful answer to the plunderings of Cromwell's army of invasion, the Battle of the Boyne, the Penal Laws, and absentee landlordism.

Aunt Kate lived a two-hour journey on the interurban from our home in Chicago. We always arrived the day before the Fourth and stayed for two or three days after. She would meet us at the station dressed as usual in a black silk dress, high lace choke collar, and high feathered hat quilled with sinister looking hatpins that I once thought passed right through her head.

She sat like a queen at the steering bar of her elegant electric automobile, the only one left in town and, for all I know, in the world.

Then came the stately ride through the narrow streets at the car's top speed of little more than a trot while the line of frustrated motorists trapped behind us grew to parade proportions. Alerted by the blaring of horns, pedestrians would pause to wave at the regal leader of this triumphant procession. Kate always smiled and waved back.

Finally we were there—rolling up DeKoven Boulevard to the red brick colonial house, a *grand dame* in its own right, skirted with white verandas and filled with rooms and attics and passages that waited for me to explore them anew.

I will never forget our next-to-last Fourth of July visit.

"Come on, Junior," said Aunt Kate as she brought the electric to a gentle stop. "I'll show you the fireworks. We have more this year than ever before."

As gleeful as a small child showing off a litter of new

kittens, she led me to the enormous kitchen pantry, still cluttered with bins, boxes, and kettles from the days when her husband was alive and her children, now married and gone, clustered around her table.

On the floor along one wall was her arsenal: bag after bag of firecrackers, pinwheels, skyrockets, and Roman candles—enough firepower to restage the Battle of Bunker Hill.

"I have a new one this year called the Vesuvius Volcano," she said, giving my hand a squeeze. "I can hardly wait to try it."

"What about the Penway Smiths?" I asked.

Aunt Kate grimaced. "Never mind," she said. "We'll show *them* a thing or two."

Then she brightened. "Father Curran, our new pastor, will be here for dinner tomorrow and to see our display. Isn't that nice?"

I agreed it would be nice to have Father Curran, but I still wondered about the Penway Smiths.

The Smiths were an elderly couple who lived next door. Several generations removed from their English background, they had settled in the neighborhood a few years ago shortly after converting to Catholicism—and promptly faced in Aunt Kate the first serious test of their newfound faith.

To them the exuberance of my aunt's annual celebration of Independence Day was an Irish impertinence, an unneighborly and unchristian affront to their English heritage.

With the banging and blazing of each successive Fourth, communication between my aunt and her neighbors deteriorated to the frostiest of nods, delivered as infrequently as possible over the hedge that separated the two properties. Even this meager recognition became less and less frequent as Aunt Kate, whose hedge it was, let it grow to an untrimmed height of seven feet.

"I'll be blessed if I'll stand on a ladder just to nod to *them,*" she'd say with a smirk.

Nowhere was this mutual enmity more visible than in

parish activities. Both Mrs. Smith and my aunt were tireless workers at church bazaars, bake sales, rummage sales, corned beef dinners, and the rest. But they always took up positions as far from each other as possible and managed somehow never to let their eyes meet.

Dissension of such magnitude between two such prominent parishioners was bound eventually to divide much of the parish into opposing camps. You were on the side of Tessie Smith or on the side of Kate Carroll; there was no middle ground.

It was not a healthy situation, but in time old Father McQuade, the pastor, came to accept it as he did his arthritis—painful but incurable.

This was the state of affairs (I learned as I grew up) when, before our next-to-last Fourth with Aunt Kate, Father McQuade retired and young Father Curran took over. It wasn't long before he discovered that he had inherited a house divided. A dedicated, energetic young priest, he vowed that he would bring this festering feud to an end. All it needed, he was sure, was some small incident that would break the ice between these two stubborn people. But what? Neither one on her own would make the first move.

A solution did not suggest itself until the memorable night when he joined us for dinner and the fireworks display that followed.

Mealtime was marked by Aunt Kate's diligent efforts to equate the American Revolution with the cause for Irish independence—and by Father Curran's equally diligent efforts to change the subject. He knew why my aunt had invited him—to show the neighbors that in all future tensions the Irish would stick together—and he didn't like it. But he was a peaceful man at heart and was content to bide his time.

After dinner we brought Aunt Kate's Regina music box to the front veranda to play background music. Almost as big as a washing machine, the Regina plucked its melodies from large, perforated platters of metal that moved slowly on a turntable. For this evening my aunt had chosen Sousa's "Stars and Stripes Forever" and "Semper Fidelis" and, for good measure, Thomas Moore's "The Minstrel Boy."

For a while everything went peaceably enough. Pinwheels spun in centrifugal splendor, fountains burbled their cascades of sparks, Roman candles poof-poofed their brilliant puff balls into the night's shadows, and rockets lifted their proud starbursts above the treetops.

Then Aunt Kate said, "We have a special treat tonight— a brand new firework called the Vesuvius Volcano—and I ask our guest, Father Curran, to set off the first one."

Father Curran, who was enjoying himself immensely, struck a match, lit the fuse, and backed away.

A choking sulphurous cloud of red smoke boiled upward from the cone of the Volcano sitting on the grass and was followed by a screeching fireball that soared magnificently toward heaven.

But heaven was not its destination. Suddenly, for no apparent reason, it veered from its course and headed straight for the neighbor's house.

In a blinding flash it exploded just outside their dining room bay window, lighting up the interior as if it were on fire. Though miraculously the glass held, the figures of the two terrified occupants could be seen fleeing from their dining room table, convinced no doubt that Aunt Kate had them under siege.

"God's mercy!" cried Father Curran, horrified, "what have I done?"

He left for the Smiths on the run. "I must apologize," he called back to us. "Oh, those poor souls!" he added as he plunged through the hedge.

He was gone a long time. We held off on the remaining fireworks and let the music box unwind into silence.

When he finally returned, he was still on the run. He quickly gathered up an armload of Aunt Kate's biggest rockets and started back. After a few steps, he paused.

"Kate," he called, "you are about to do a great work of charity. God will bless you for it." And then he was gone.

Within minutes the sky was once more ablaze with rocket fire—but this time it came from the *other* side of the hedge.

The story of what had happened between the priest and the Smiths has filtered down through many tellings and re-tellings at countless family gatherings, but I'm sure that a flavor of truth still remains.

Amazed that our neighbors had no fireworks of their own, Father Curran—after profuse apologies for his errant fireball—asked spiritedly, "Why aren't you celebrating? Who in the world do you think won us our independence? The Irish? No! Englishmen! English colonials! You should be proud. You should be out there blazing away with the rest of us. Your name is Smith," he continued recklessly. "If I remember my history, wasn't there a Colonel Smith in Washington's army who distinguished himself at the Battle of Trenton? I'm sure there was. Why, you might even be related! So celebrate!"

Then, divinely inspired, he added, "Mrs. Carroll agrees with me a hundred percent. She'd *love* to see this silly feud come to an end, and so would I. As a matter of fact, she has a present for you. I'll run and get it."

With that he went back to Aunt Kate's for the rockets. After helping the Smiths shoot them off, he insisted they join our group for a bang-up conclusion to the Fourth.

Mrs. Smith thanked Aunt Kate profusely for her gift of the rockets. Under Father Curran's fiery eye, my aunt could do nothing but extend her hospitality.

Before the evening ended, the young priest had another brilliant idea. "Next Fourth of July," he said, "we'll have a parish picnic, fireworks and all. And I'm depending on you two ladies to be in charge of it."

With that he shot off the last of the fireworks. Everyone cheered.

Our last visit to Aunt Kate's, a few months before she died, was to attend her church's picnic and watch the magnificent display that she and Tessie Smith had put together. I can best describe the new relationship between the two women by reporting that the hedge separating their houses had been cut back to its original height of four feet.

Although the colonial English may have won the decisive battles of the War for Independence, I like to remember (no doubt because of my ancestry) that it took an Irishman to win the Battle of DeKoven Boulevard.

The Irish Setter in Noah's Ark

On drowsy summer afternoons, when other diversions left our spirits becalmed, Jimsey Biddle and I knew there was always Sister Martha's Noah's ark. Visiting the ark never failed to restore our faith in the world's ability to keep two six-year-olds entertained.

"Think she'll mind?" one of us would ask.

"Naw, she won't mind."

This brief exchange was in deference to our parents' warning not to wear out our welcome. That taken care of, off we'd go to the convent—up the broad gravel pathway between the sisters' home and the school to the gate of the convent yard. "Afternoon, Sister!" we'd call.

Outside or in, Sister Martha always heard us. We made sure of that. "Oh, come in, come in!" she'd reply, as if she had been waiting all day for our arrival. We'd open the gate, and our afternoon adventure would begin.

Sister Martha was cook and housekeeper for the nuns of St. Lawrence parish. The convent stood next door to the two-family home of my parents and grandparents, with only Grandpa's vegetable garden in between. We regarded the sisters as wonderfully friendly neighbors, as well as holy women.

Older by several years than my mother but as spirited as a blue jay, Sister Martha took it as her duty to feed not just the convent nuns but all the wildlife that entered the convent's back yard. "Love the animals," she said once, "because God loves them. If He didn't, He wouldn't have commanded Noah to bring them with him on the ark. And aren't we all descendants of Noah?"

Born and raised on a farm, Sister understood better than most the full implications of Noah's God-given responsibilities: "Of every living thing of all flesh, two of every sort, shalt thou bring into the ark to keep them alive with thee!"

"To keep them alive," she'd remind us. "Oh, the Bible makes it look so simple, but think of it! All those animals! Poor Noah! He not only had to round them up and get them into the ark (imagine the trouble the mules gave him!), but he also had to keep them alive! That meant feeding them, grooming them, exercising them, breaking up their fights, training them to accept one another, and cleaning out their cages and stalls. Just think of it!"

Jimsey and I would think of it—and bless the divine plan that had put us in *this* century and not in Noah's.

To help her keep the animals of her refuge alive, Sister decided one spring that the yard needed an all-purpose feeder, one with separate compartments for the various foods she set out—nuts and peanut butter for the squirrels, graham crackers for the chipmunks, small seeds and crumbs for the smaller birds, sunflower seeds for the cardinals, suet for any bird with a taste for it, sugar water in a bottlelike container for the hummingbirds, and small twigs and dried grass cuttings for nest building and repair.

She mentioned this to my grandfather, who had already built her several birdhouses. "But of course," she added, "that would be a terribly big project, and I wouldn't dream of asking you to become involved."

After Grandpa built the feeder, he and I set it up on four sturdy legs in the center of the yard, about three feet off the ground. "Patrick," Sister Martha thanked him, "you must be the greatest carpenter since Saint Joseph!"

To make access easier for the chipmunks, we tilted a board against the feeder's side. With its ramp, its many compartments, and its peaked roof, the feeder looked like nothing so much as Noah's ark, and Sister so named it.

The middle of the afternoon, as far as Sister was concerned, was the best time for our visits. Luncheon for the nuns was over; preparations for the evening meal were not yet started. This, she said, was her "quiet hour," her time to replenish the feeder and, from a bench in the shade of a hawthorn tree, watch her backyard guests come to table.

She had pet names for many of them: Smudge for a roguish dark gray squirrel who looked as if he might have just come out of someone's chimney; Topper for a blue jay, in tribute to its handsome crest; Richelieu for an imperious-looking cardinal; Mike and Ike for a pair of impish chipmunks.

Once a field mouse scampered up the ramp. Memories of my mother flailing wildly with a broom whenever one of these tiny creatures paid us a visit prompted me to yell, "A mouse!" as if a marauding lion were on the loose.

"Junior!" Sister scolded me. "Calm down! That's Abelard! Thank heaven he's back!"

A moment later, another mouse joined Abelard. "Heloise!" Sister cried delightedly. "She's back, too!"

Where Abelard and Heloïse had been we had no idea.

"Be very quiet now," she whispered as she picked some bread crumbs from a bowl beside her. Extending one hand close to the ground, she bent forward.

The mice paused on the ramp, held a brief conference, then with many starts and stops made their way to Sister's hand, where they quickly ate the crumbs. "If I'd known you were coming," she said softly, "I'd have brought some cheese.

But do come back tomorrow." After a few exploratory sniffs around her fingers, the mice were gone.

That was the most fun—tempting the animals to eat out of our hands. In time the squirrels and chipmunks, as well as Abelard and Heloise, would climb up on the bench and even sit on our laps while we fed them. Often I saw Sister stand up slowly and, still as a statute, coax a chickadee to take thistle seeds from her outstretched palm. "Noah did this all the time," she would say, as if there was nothing unusual about her performance.

Equally bold were several pigeons whose home was the belfry of the church nearby. Father Sullivan had tried unsuccessfully to get rid of them. He said their cooing was a distraction during Sunday Mass. Grandpa's view was that our pastor resented the competition they gave him during his sermons. Sister Martha insisted they were merely supplying a musical accompaniment.

On several occasions Father had none too gently suggested that, instead of feeding them, Sister chase them away. She promised to do her best, but it was obvious that her best was tempered by her conviction that Noah had welcomed pigeons to his ark.

A few times, when Father Sullivan came near the yard, I noticed that if the pigeons were around, Sister would busy herself with her flower garden. Father would glare at the birds, wave his arms, and cry, "Shoosh!" The pigeons would flap to the edge of the convent roof and wait patiently for him to leave. "Can't have these birds around here, Sister," he'd say. "They're a nuisance!"

"I'm doing my best, Father."

Father would throw a sour look in the direction of the ark, but he stopped short of telling Sister to get rid of it. As soon as he was gone, the pigeons would return to the yard, and Sister would leave her flowers. But you could tell that Father's attitude bothered her. "If Father only understood

Noah better," she'd sigh. It was clear that she had read more into Genesis 6:19–22 than he had.

This was our "peaceable kingdom," serene, undisturbed except by the occasional visits of our pastor—until the day we heard a sudden crashing in the bushes and looked up to see a strange dog bearing down on us.

I must explain that the convent yard was protected in back and on the side nearest my home by a high board fence. Between the convent and the schoolyard next door was a hedge of white lilacs, as there was between the school and the church and between the church and the rectory. Anyone, man or beast, could cross from one building to the other through any of several openings in the bushes.

The dog was an Irish setter. He had the rich mahogany coat and exuberant disposition of that popular breed. Close on his heels came the tall, angular figure of Father Sullivan. His face was almost as red as the dog's, but his disposition at the moment was anything but exuberant.

"Paddy!" Father commanded, as if exorcising an evil spirit.

Paddy had no time for exorcists. He was still celebrating his recent graduation from puppyhood and couldn't understand why the rest of the world wasn't celebrating with him—an oversight he seemed determined to rectify.

Roaring a joyous greeting to us all, he circled the yard at a full gallop. He sent the squirrels and chipmunks scurrying and the birds rising in protesting circles of indignation. He stopped long enough at the feeder to sample the peanut butter, then washed it down with a drink from the birdbath. At last, panting magnificently, he dropped himself into Sister's flower bed. There! he laughed, how was *that* for an entrance!

Jimsey and I were sure Sister would be furious. Instead she clapped her hands and cried, "Isn't he *beautiful!*"

Taking the clapping for well-deserved applause, the dog got up and trotted over to Sister to extend his thanks.

"Paddy!" Father Sullivan cried again.

"Father," said Sister politely but firmly, "*do* please sit down."

Reluctantly Father sat down on the bench. Sister Martha ruffled the hair behind Paddy's ears and told him again and again what a handsome fellow he was—but I noticed that one of her hands had slipped down to his collar, which she now held in a firm grip. Still talking in her quiet, soothing way, she said to me, "Junior, there's some clothesline under the back porch steps. Quietly now, quietly, bring it to me."

Soon Paddy was securely tethered to a clothes post.

"I can't do a thing with him," Father Sullivan complained, stating the obvious.

Paddy, he explained, had been given to him yesterday by a well-meaning friend to take the place of Mugsie, his phlegmatic old basset hound. A month before, as he put it, Mugsie had gone off to join his ancestors in canine heaven.

"Mugsie was a gem," Father said. "No trouble at all. But this one! He races from one end of the rectory to the other, up and down stairs, scattering rugs and knocking things off tables. A few minutes ago I opened the front door to get the mail and he went by me like a shot!"

I felt that Sister Martha was asking herself a question: How would Noah have handled this?

"It's obvious," she said at last, "the poor lad hasn't had a moment's training."

"Training!" Father Sullivan snorted. "How do you train a whirlwind?" He stood up to go. "Sister, if I may borrow your clothesline till I get home, I'll be much obliged."

"Keep the line short," Sister advised as she handed the dog over. "Make him walk beside you. If you let him get out in front of you, he'll pull you off your feet."

Father Sullivan thanked Sister for her help. Paddy thanked her for her obvious love of animals. He did it by jumping up and trying to lick her chin.

"Down!" Sister ordered—and without a moment's hesitation slapped a foot on one of the dog's hind paws. Paddy returned to earth, startled but willing to forgive. "Do that every time he jumps up on you, Father," she advised. "Then praise him for staying put. He'll soon get the message."

As he turned to leave, Father Sullivan sighed. "I don't know. I'm not much at dog training. He's a beautiful beast, but I'm afraid I may have to give him back."

"Oh, no," Sister whispered under her breath. Again I knew what she was thinking. Would Noah do that?

If Noah could have seen what happened in the next few weeks, he would have been proud of his descendant Sister Martha. He would have seen Jimsey and myself, every afternoon (according to Sister's plan), ring the rectory doorbell and tell Mrs. Corbett, the housekeeper, that we had come to take Paddy for his afternoon walk—an arrangement that Father Sullivan had thankfully agreed to.

And Noah would have seen us bring the dog immediately to the convent yard, where a onetime farm girl, now in a nun's habit, taught it the essential behavior expected of a canine gentleman.

She trained Paddy to sit, holding her right hand under his throat to support his head, pressing his hindquarters down with her left hand while commanding, "Sit!" and then rewarding him, at first with a scrap from her kitchen and later with praise alone.

Similarly, she trained him to lie down, to heel and halt, to remain in one position, and to live peaceably with the other animals. Over those many summer afternoons, Jimsey and I watched the dog almost miraculously change into an easily manageable and congenial companion.

And then came the afternoon when Sister showed Father Sullivan all the commands she had taught Paddy—and how to make sure the dog continued to obey them.

"Just remember, Father," Sister said. "A trained dog is a happier dog." She might well have added, "And a priest with a trained dog is a happier priest." But the priest could already see that.

Father never mentioned the pigeons again. They came to the ark as always and cooed their musical accompaniment to his Sunday sermons.

Noah, Sister was sure, would have liked that.

My Angel's Name Is Fred

Guardian angels don't seem to be getting the attention these days that they did in my early years. At that time they were as much a part of daily living as the Mass schedule of St. Lawrence parish.

Your angel was more than a security blanket; he was a security *guard,* whose only concern was your spiritual and even your physical welfare. He was God's answer to your plea, "Lead us not into temptation but deliver us from evil."

In your waking hours you brought him your problems, including the most trivial. He was always a sympathetic listener, a wise counselor, a pleasant companion. And he kept a closer eye on you than did your mother.

When you went to bed, did he doze off too? Never, to my knowledge. Wide awake, he perched on your headboard and maintained unceasing vigil through the hours of the night.

He was right there when you woke up in the morning, when you bathed, dressed, ate your breakfast, and went out to play. He was beside you when you rode the back step of the iceman's wagon in summer, when you belly-flopped on your sled in winter. And for all this attention he asked nothing in return except that you be a good boy and not forget who had created you.

I met my guardian angel through my grandmother. Of course, he had always been with me, but it was she who first called my attention to that fact.

One Sunday, when I was not quite four, Grandma and Grandpa, who lived upstairs, took me with them to Sunday Mass. As sometimes happened, Father Sullivan, our pastor, was having difficulty that day finding a suitable ending for his sermon. As he tried one after another, I became more and more restless. To keep me occupied, Grandma went to her prayer book, which also served as a depository for countless holy cards that she had collected over many prayerful years. "Here," she said, handing me a full deck, "look at the pretty pictures."

I looked—and was immediately stunned. The very first card showed a towering angel with overpowering wings hovering just above a golden-haired little girl. Judging from the child's carefree smile, she had no idea she was being followed.

I had seen pictures of angels before, but always they were cherubic little creatures with tiny w ings, dreamy eyes, and heads haloed in ringlets; they were doing nothing more sanguinary than watching the clouds roll by. But here was an angel taller than Grandpa and with wings like an eagle's. What his intentions were I couldn't be sure, but he seemed to be in an excellent position to swoop down on the unsuspecting youngster and make off with her. But *why?* This was a matter that cried out for clarification.

"Grandma," I whispered, "why is the angel—"

"Shhh! Later, dear."

"But, Grandma—"

"Later!"

So I was left, like Jacob, to wrestle alone with the angel.

After Mass, Grandma retrieved her holy cards and, as expertly as a cook filing recipes, nested them comfortably among the epistles and gospels of her overstuffed prayer book.

"The angel on the holy card," she explained on the walk home, "is a guardian angel."

"But what's he *doing?*"

"Protecting the little girl from harm," said Grandma.

"Protecting her?"

"Exactly."

Grandma went on to inform me that I, too, had a guardian angel who protected *me*. In fact, everyone had a guardian angel.

"But why can't we *see* them?"

"We just can't. They're pure spirits. They're like the wind; you can't see the wind, but it's there."

Well! So all this time I had had a special friend right beside me; a kind and loving friend, a tall, strong, winged friend, who, as Grandma said, kept a hand always on my right shoulder. I found this very exciting.

"What's my angel's name?" I asked. (If you're going to have a friend like that for the rest of your life, you should at least know what to call him.)

Grandma considered my question for a long time. Finally she looked to Grandpa for help.

"I think," said Grandpa, "he'll accept whatever name you'd like to give him."

Too young to know that the Church frowns on assigning names to angels beyond those mentioned in Scripture, I promptly christened my angel Fred. He raised no objection. In fact, I was sure he smiled.

I named him Fred after my special neighborhood hero, Fred Palmer, a ten-year-old who often gave me rides on the handlebar of his bicycle and taught me how to swing his baseball bat—which wasn't easy, because every time I swung, I tipped over. But Fred Palmer never lost patience. He was a true friend.

I took Fred, my guardian angel, home and introduced him to my parents. They were delighted to meet him, and he seemed pleased to meet them. I was glad. It's nice not to have friction between your parents and your friends.

I showed Fred my room, my clothes closet, my box of toys, and my guppies. He was intensely interested.

At dinner that afternoon I sat as far over to one side of my chair as I could without falling off.

"Why are you sitting like that?" my father asked.

"To make room for Fred. He's as big as Grandpa."

My mother, as usual, was equal to the problem. "Don't worry, dear," she said. "Angels prefer to stand." That made sense. If Fred sat down, where would he put his wings?

One question remained, however: What did this guardian of mine look like? Like the one on Grandma's holy card? Or do angels have faces all their own? I decided that they do. Else how could they tell each other apart? I pretended that my spirit friend had red hair, freckles, and a friendly smile, like the other Fred. And I also felt that sooner or later he would reveal himself to me so I could be sure.

Not long afterward, in one blinding moment, I was certain that he had.

At the age of almost four, my freedom of movement was limited mostly to the backyard—except when Fred Palmer took me riding on his bike. If I ventured out front on my own, I was not to cross the street and not to go beyond Mrs. Grimes's bungalow in one direction and the nearby convent in the other.

For a long time I had felt that these parental restrictions showed an unflattering lack of trust in my navigational skills. Some day I'd show my parents that I was meant for more distant horizons—like the forbidden territory of Seventy-fifth Street, a full block away; that's where the action was.

Now more than ever I was sure that my parents had nothing to fear. Wasn't Fred at my side? Wouldn't he see to it that I'd never be harmed?

One soft summer afternoon I was sitting on our front steps gazing, as usual, toward Seventy-fifth Street. I could see scores of cars and trucks and an occasional trolley crossing the busy intersection. I could hear the happy cries of older children calling to one another from their bicycles. Then suddenly I heard the sound of a fire engine gong—and a red streak cut through the blur of the distant traffic.

I stood up.

"Shall we?" I asked, taking a deep breath.

"Why not?" I was sure Fred answered.

Halfway down the block, my absence as yet undetected by my mother, I broke into a trot. Another fire engine roared past. I began to run.

By the time I reached the corner, the fire engines were out of sight, though I could still hear the far clanging of their gongs. "We'd better hurry," I told Fred.

We continued west on Seventy-fifth Street, but my legs were getting tired, and the sound of the fire gongs had slipped beneath the surface of the traffic noise. If it's any kind of fire, I told myself, it will still be there when Fred and I arrive. I sat down on a city trash box near the curb and watched some boys do fancy turns on their roller skates.

We resumed our journey westward, but only halfheartedly; there were other attractions more immediate than a far-off fire.

Like Foley's Department Store. I must show Fred the traveling baskets and the escalator.

On previous trips to the store with my mother, I had been fascinated by the wire baskets, about the size of a shoe box, that traveled on overhead wires from the main counters to a cashier's cage, which hung like an oriole's nest from the high ceiling in the rear. At the conclusion of a sale, the clerk would put the customer's money and the sales slip in a basket, yank a pull-rope, and—*zing!*—send it soaring to the cashier. A moment later it would coast back down with the customer's change and the receipt. (I think now that most of the fun went out of retailing with the disappearance of the overhead basket.)

Next, we rode the escalator to the third floor, which was the end of the line, and another one back down. We did this several times, until a man with shiny black hair and a flower in his buttonhole asked me where my mother was.

"She's home," I said, proud to let him know I was on my own.

"Then you'd better get home too, kid," he replied gruffly. "Go on now, get outta here!" (It took me a long time to get over my antipathy toward men with shiny black hair and flowers in their buttonholes.)

Out in the sunshine again, Fred and I decided not to bother looking for the fire. There were still other wonders closer at hand.

Like the woman in white sitting at a table in the window of a candy store. In front of her sat a pan of walnuts and, next to it, a larger pan of melted chocolate. In a gesture as sure and constant as the swinging of our mantel clock's pendulum, she dipped nut after nut in the chocolate, set them on a tray, and then topped each one off with a swirl of her chocolaty fingers, so it looked like a tiny brown minaret. Other kids and grown-ups paused to watch for a few moments, then moved on. I stayed. At last the woman looked up, smiled, beckoned me inside, and gave me a piece of the candy.

"Where's your mother, dear?" she asked. (Did everyone have to ask that question?)

Wiser now, I answered, "Not far away."

"You'd better find her then. Don't get lost." She was a nice lady. (To this day I am partial to ladies with chocolaty fingers.)

And there was the jewelry store where a real Indian sat in his window making bracelets of silver and jade.

And the hardware store window with a model of a Great Lakes steamship.

And the shoemaker in his window banging away with his odd-looking hammer, his mouth full of tiny nails, which, miraculously, he never swallowed.

And finally, a few more blocks away, the overpass and adjoining embankments of the Illinois Central's main line to New Orleans.

Trains! Was there anything in the world of childhood more awesome, more mesmerizing? The giant steam locomotive in all its black-iron, high-wheeled, piston-driven, smoke-belching majesty; the rumbling roar of its thunderous passing; the engineer, as self-assured as Vulcan at his forge, waving at you from the window of his cab—all this had thrilled me from my earliest memories.

Along the base of the embankment ran the remains of a rusty wire fence. It had long ago been retired from active duty and was lying half-hidden among weeds and wild sumac.

I stepped over the wire and scrambled up the cinder-coated slope. I paused as a freight train whistled by, then resumed my climb. I would move up to the track and see what was coming next.

I had just gained the rails when a hand gripped my right shoulder. I trembled as I thought, Fred is finally showing me what he looks like!

The hand whirled me around—and there was my angel!

I was amazed to see that he bore a striking resemblance to Father Sullivan!

"In the name of all that's holy," Father exploded, as a train from the other direction roared by. "What are you trying to do—get yourself killed?"

That, I thought, was a strange question, coming from a man who must have believed in guardian angels as fervently as I did.

"The whole neighborhood's looking for you!" he shouted, not waiting for my answer. "Your mother even called the police!"

She had also, I learned later, called the convent, where I was a frequent and welcome visitor, and the nuns had called Father Sullivan. In those days, whatever the crisis, you called your pastor. And, no doubt, *my* guardian angel had called *his* guardian angel and told him where to look for me.

I suppose I began to cry. In any case, Father's attitude softened. "Come now," he said, leading me to his car, "I'll take you home. Thank God you're safe!"

Thank God—or Fred? Or both? It was a question I was

too tired to pursue. I told Father I did what I did because Fred was with me and would protect me.

"Where's this Fred now?" the priest demanded, looking around for the wretch who would abandon a small child on a railroad right-of-way.

"He's right *here*," I answered. "Fred's my guardian angel!"

In spite of himself, Father Sullivan began to smile. "Lord knows," he murmured, "he *must* be here!"

As we approached my home, he said, "You have to understand one important thing. This guardian angel business works both ways. Fred is a dear friend, one of the dearest friends you will ever have. So why make his job difficult? If you truly love a friend, you want everything to be as easy as possible for him, right?"

"Yes, Father."

"Don't make him rush into traffic to save you from being run over. Don't make him burn his fingers putting out matches you've lighted. Don't make him climb railroad embankments to keep you from being killed by a train. If you really love your angel—and the God who gave him to you—you'll be as kind and considerate as you can. Understand?"

"Yes, Father."

I may not think of Fred as much as I used to—except sometimes when the warning lights flash and the gates go down or a long freight rumbles across an overpass.

But now the locomotive is a diesel. It hums in the smug monotone of modern efficiency. No more thunder and lightning on the rails, no more shaking of the earth under your feet, no more white trails of smoke streaming like Cyrano's plume along the car tops.

It's just not the same any more.

I'm sure Fred agrees.

The Furnace
That Kept the Peace

A memorable feature of my childhood home was the building's furnace. You may think it odd that something as mundane as a furnace should take root in a child's fancy, but this was not your chaste, compact heating unit of today, sheathed in featureless panels of unadorned steel. Ancient as the house itself, it crouched in a cavernous corner like a brooding octopus, spreading the giant tentacles of its huge hot-air ducts into the dim, coal-dusty reaches of the basement.

Encrusting its surface like barnacles were blowers, dampers, drafts, chains, dials, and levers—a chaos to anyone but my father, who understood its moods and ministered to its needs with deft and knowledgeable care. His mastery of this fiery-eyed monster made him, to me, a giant among men.

Two of my earliest intimations of what it means to have a loving and providing parent were the sound at dawn of my father below, shaking the grate and shoveling coal while I lay snug in my bed savoring the delicious prospect of another hour under the blankets, and, at the end of the day, the all's-well evening sound of the fire being banked for the night.

The furnace served me in another way, too. With its fire door open, it gave me a vivid picture of what our pastor, Father Sullivan, was talking about when he preached on the "inextinguishable fires of hell, reserved for impenitents."

I wasn't sure who or what impenitents were. I thought they might be like the Democrats, about whom my father, a Republican, had nothing good to say, or the Republicans, about whom my grandfather, a Democrat, had even fewer good things to say. The four-letter word for the nether regions was no stranger to their political arguments.

If I was present when my father, returning from work,

suggested we check the furnace, I would peer into the firebox and imagine I saw the faces of Democrats, Republicans, and impenitents staring back at me through the sulfurous flames. The memory of that inferno may not have kept me in later years from voting Democratic or, in some elections, Republican, but it still helps keep me from being an impenitent—and for that I am truly grateful.

At times the furnace could be quite temperamental. For reasons that not even my father fully understood, it would occasionally draw a deep sigh, as if bored with its circumscribed labors, then exhale with a loud and rebellious WHOOMPF! Immediately clouds of smoke would rise through the registers in the rooms above. Mother would quickly open all windows to the saving air of winter and rush my sister and myself upstairs to Grandma's apartment, which, luckily, was never affected.

For me these sudden evacuations were great fun. They meant cookies, cake, and hot cocoa and another opportunity to wander through the pages of Grandma's enormous picture book on the Civil War.

Meanwhile, my father, joined by Grandpa, would be in the basement. To the frantic rattling of drafts and dampers and the shouting of contradictory orders, they would finally coax the furnace out of its tantrum.

"I keep telling you, Tom," Grandpa would yell, "you've got to burn a harder coal!"

"Nonsense, Pat," Dad would reply. "The coal's all right. It's a sudden shift in the wind that does it."

"So change the wind," Grandpa would retort sarcastically.

When the barrage of arguments echoing up through the registers finally subsided, we refugees knew the crisis was over.

My father often vowed that he would replace "that blasted furnace" if it was the last thing he did—and the furnace, chastened perhaps by his threat, would perform like a trained seal for at least another month.

But I knew Dad never really intended to get rid of it, partly because a more modern heating plant would not provide the same stimulating challenge to his engineering skill, but mostly because of something our pastor, Father Sullivan, said about it one memorable Sunday.

Our upstairs and downstairs families were a happy, congenial, and spirited unit—except on those occasions when the spirit got out of hand and caused someone's feelings to be hurt.

My mother, for example, exercising an older sister's prerogatives, might voice disapproval of the length of Aunt Laura's new dress. Or Grandpa, in my mother's presence, might remark that nobody could cook an omelet like Aunt Addie. Or my father might ruffle Grandma's protective instincts with a critical though well-intended remark about Aunt Laura's violin playing or Uncle Billy's performance in a recent football game. Then a sudden frost would descend on our relationships. Visits would cease. Greetings, when unavoidable, would become terse, and faces would be swept clear of smiles.

When these tiffs coincided with a particularly heated political debate between my father and grandfather, the chill became almost unbearable, especially for me. My world suddenly seemed split in two.

Fortunately, such periods were short-lived. After a day or two, Grandma, unsuited by nature for cold-war diplomacy, would bake some loaves of cinnamon bread (a favorite of my father) and bring one downstairs. Or my mother, equally supportive of free trade, would bake a chocolate cake (a favorite of my grandfather) and send me upstairs with it.

There would be hugs and kisses all around and promises not to let these silly misunderstandings occur again. But heaven on earth, that blessed place where promises made are never broken, was still a ways off.

One November a candidate supported by my father se-verely trounced a candidate of my grandfather's for some national post. Or maybe it was the other way around. At any rate, the fireworks of the preelection campaign were nothing compared to those Dad and Grandpa blasted off. The coun-try, according to one or the other of them, was about to go to the dogs.

Then came the inevitable chill—a chill that extended through a Friday, Saturday, and Sunday and promised to go on indefinitely.

Complicating matters was the fact that Mother had pre-viously invited her family to that Sunday's dinner, where Father Sullivan, an old friend of both camps, was also to be a guest.

When Father arrived, he was understandably disap-pointed to find that the upstairs family was absent—and would remain absent.

"They all seem to have bad colds," my mother fibbed. She was about as adept at telling a lie, even a small one, as the saint for whom she had been named—Mary.

Father Sullivan saw through her immediately but, gentle-man that he was, knew there was nothing he could do without calling the "bad colds" excuse into question. A cold is a cold and needs time to work itself out.

After what seemed to me a strained and interminable period of small talk, we finally sat down to dinner.

Dad was placing a beef roast on the table (enough for two families, as Father Sullivan observed) when our guest suddenly exclaimed, "What in thunder was *that?*"

We had heard it, too—a sigh as mournful and profound as the sigh of a wounded leviathan in its final travail. Then WHOOMPF! and Mother was flying to the windows and Dad was on his way to the basement. "Nothing serious!" he called back through the smoke. "I'll have it fixed in no time at all!"

Father Sullivan was on his feet, shivering, coughing, and wiping his eyes with his handkerchief. "Enough of this!" he exclaimed at last. "Bad colds or no bad colds, we're moving this meal upstairs!"

With that he picked up the platter of roast beef and made for the door. There was nothing for Mother to do but follow after—with bowls of potatoes, squash, and peas cradled in her arms. I took charge of my sister and the salad bowl and joined the exodus.

There was seldom a situation so tense in our family that a sense of the ludicrous wasn't lurking somewhere within it, waiting to be spotted by a good-natured eye. The sight of our tall, dignified pastor bursting into their home unannounced and carrying a platter of roast beef as if it were the Book of Kells, followed by my mother with her armload of cooked vegetables and myself with the salad—this was too much for my young aunts. They began to giggle, then laugh. They laughed so hard they doubled over, as did the others. Grandpa roared. So did Father Sullivan. "I try never to come empty-handed," the priest gasped.

"I must go down and help Tom," Grandpa managed after he caught his breath. And down he went.

Once more the storm of orders and counterorders boiled up through the registers. And once more, when it subsided, we knew that all was well. By then Grandma's table was set.

It was a reconciliation I will never forget. When the dinner and long visit afterward were over at last, my father and I accompanied Father Sullivan to the main entrance downstairs.

"I'm going to replace that blasted furnace if it's the last thing I do," Dad vowed.

Father Sullivan paused at the step. "Tom," he said, "if you're wise, you'll keep that furnace for as long as your two families are under the same roof. Remember the Beatitudes."

"The Beatitudes?"

Father Sullivan tapped my father's chest with a long, bony forefinger. "Blessed," he said, "are the peacemakers, for they shall be called the children of God."

But he had time for one more shot. Partway down the

walk he turned once more. "Be sure to tell the folks upstairs how happy I am that their colds are better."

"I'll do that," my father promised.

Grandma's Guess What?

My grandmother was a confirmed guess-whater. Seldom if ever did she announce a bit of news in a flat-out, declarative statement; there was always the dramatic buildup.

"Guess what?" she'd exclaim, her eyes dancing in anticipation of your reaction.

"What?" you'd ask, right on cue.

After a suitable pause, Grandma would then deliver the bulletin of the moment. "Mrs. Madigan's cat had six little kittens this morning!"

"No!" you'd exclaim, as if loath to believe that such a thing could be possible. Whether your astonishment was genuine or feigned, you responded with great vigor. This was the ultimate compliment to Grandma's news-gathering prowess and an accepted part of her guess-what ritual. You would no more have omitted it than you would the "Amen" after blessing yourself.

There were variations, of course. If Grandma deemed the news to be of headline proportions, she'd open with "You'll *never* guess...." (You'll *never* guess...Bridie Bemis's boy—the wild one—is going to study for the priesthood!")

If the event was of the "Extra! Extra!" variety, she'd pin you down with "You'll *never guess in a million years....*" ("...Nancy McIntyre is getting married again, and her late husband dead for less than a year, may God be good to him!") She did this, I feel now, not so much to draw attention to herself as to enliven the days of those around her—as the ancient storytellers, spinning tales beside the herdsmen's fire, sought to lift one nomadic moment above the rest.

Grandpa was treated to more of Grandma's guess whats

than anyone else. Each evening she had one ready for him, like a cocktail, when he returned from his work as a boiler inspector for the city of Chicago. From the dullest day's experience she was always able to cull *something* of interest that would revive his flagging spirits. Many of her reports involved me, and I was often on hand to witness their effect on my grandfather.

"Guess what happened today, Pat."

"What?"

"Junior wrote me a letter—*all by himself!*"

"*No!*"

What did it matter that the letter merely said, "Thank you for the crayons, Grandma. I like them," or that it had to travel only from the first floor to the floor above? A good story, she knew, depends a lot on how you tell it.

Invariably, Grandpa's response was everything Grandma could hope for. His "What?" was a masterpiece of unbearable anticipation, his "No!" an explosive cry of incredulous wonderment. My grandparents, incidentally, had a long and happy marriage.

And yet it was Grandpa who found it necessary one day to warn me, "Beware the Great Guess What!" (as he called it). "In the wrong hands it can be a snare and a delusion. It's not for everyone," he said, "only people of the strongest moral fiber. It tempts you to look to your imagination for the facts, and that can be dangerous. Some people would call it lying. Besides," he added darkly, "it's highly addictive."

I didn't understand all his words, but I knew exactly what he meant and why he was warning me.

A month or so earlier, I had entered the strange new world of first grade—strange because now things had to be done in concert with others and at Sister Marie's discretion, not my own. Happily, however, it was also a fertile source of stories worth taking home and relating to my family, especially when dressed up with a few guess whats.

"Guess what happened today!"

"What?"

"I got a gold star on my drawing of a horse!"

"*No!*"

I shall never forget their faces, so full of expectation, so bright with undiluted attention! Their hands, busy one moment, then frozen the next in midair above a newspaper, a sewing machine, a pan of potato peelings! I was Marc Antony in full possession of all the ears of Rome. I was Father Sullivan in his Sunday pulpit about to reveal the consequences of breaking the Fourth Commandment. For me— me alone—the world was standing still—and listening!

In short, I was hopelessly hooked on the Great Guess What.

For the first few weeks the supply of first-grade story material seemed inexhaustible. But then it began gradually to thin out. In fact, there were times when Sister Marie and my classmates stubbornly refused to do anything memorable.

Homeward bound, I would pause before climbing our front steps to wonder, "What in the world can I tell them tonight?" Young as I was, I knew that repeating a previous story would mean I had peaked out. An outright fabrication would have destroyed my credibility—if discovered.

Ah! *If* discovered . . .

I began to improvise—cautiously at first, then, as I gained confidence, with abandon. Before long, I made the storyteller's awesome discovery that improvisations can often be more exciting then facts.

The guess whats multiplied like Jimmy Deedy's gerbils.

"Guess what! I'm now in charge of the blackboard erasers!" (Fact: Marjory Gerlichman was in charge of the blackboard erasers.)

"Guess what happened today! I had to sit with Marty Mulligan and help him do his numbers!" (Fact: Marty Mulligan had sat with *me* and helped me do *my* numbers.)

And so it went for several days. Then, hopelessly caught up in my own creative momentum and exhilarated by the adulation heaped on me at home, I went too far. I made the mistake of involving a saint in my designs of duplicity—and the patron saint of young Catholic students, at that!

"Guess what happened today, Grandma!"

"What, what?"

"I won a religious medal!"

"No!"

"Yep, I sure did."

"Whatever for?"

"I won a drawing contest. I drew a castle with a king and queen and knights on horseback. It was the best in the whole class."

"Well, then, where's the medal?"

"Sister hasn't given it out yet."

That part was true. Sister hadn't given it out yet, and for the excellent reason that she hadn't yet decided who deserved it.

But I was sure I'd win. All the kids who sat near me in class said my drawing was the best.

True also was the fact that the prize was a medal inscribed to St. Aloysius. Sister had shown it to us when she had announced the contest a few days earlier. Like a halo around the saint's head were the words "St. Aloysius, pray for us." It was the most beautiful religious medal I had ever seen.

The medal's beauty, my confidence in my drawing, and the fact that the preceding days were what the press calls "slow news day" all prodded me to take my chances and claim victory without delay.

I don't know why Sister took so long to make up her mind. Another day went by, then another and another.

"When are you ever going to show us your medal?" my family would ask each evening.

"Gosh," I'd say, snapping my fingers, "I forgot it again! But I'll show it to you tomorrow for sure!"

Did I detect a look of suspicion on their faces? I did.

Soon, however, it became clear that I'd never be able to show it. Evelyn Walsh was showing it to *her* parents. Evelyn had drawn a picture of Jonah in the whale's belly. She had him sitting comfortably in an easy chair reading a newspaper account of his recent shipwreck. Sister said Evelyn showed unusual imagination.

I now had to strain *my* imagination more than ever. What excuse could I possibly give them? I thought of praying to St. Aloysius, but I had a vague feeling he'd want no part of this deception.

At last, one afternoon, while searching my desk for a lost eraser, I found not the eraser but the answer to my problem. That evening at home I sadly announced that I'd lost my medal.

Did I detect a look of *intensified* suspicion on their faces? I did. At odd moments I would catch them staring at me as if wondering what kind of person I'd grow up to be, cer-tainly not one of Grandpa's "people of the strongest moral fiber."

Father Sullivan, our pastor, didn't help matters either. Wouldn't you know, his sermon the following Sunday was on the devastating effects of lying.

"The lie is an insult to yourself, your fellow men, and God!" he thundered. "Whoever tells a lie, like him who steals, must set matters straight before he can expect God's forgiveness!"

I was desperate. What would St. Aloysius have done in the same circumstances—confess and clear his conscience once and for all? But then, I thought, he wouldn't have told the lie in the first place. So much for St. Aloysius.

I must insist, however, that one morning, after a long and restless night, I did resolve to admit my transgression and ask my family's forgiveness. I would do this tomorrow for sure. Or the next day, at the very latest.

Then suddenly it was too late.

That afternoon my mother was walking my baby sister in

her buggy, and—guess what—who should she meet but Sister Marie and a companion!

There were the usual comments about how cute the baby was, and then Mother said, "How disappointed we all are that Junior lost his medal."

"Medal?" said the puzzled sister. "What medal?"

I prefer to leave the rest of that conversation unrecorded. Even now I am uncomfortable thinking of my mother's shame when the truth finally came out.

That evening she had a long talk with me. So did my father. So did Grandma. They all drew copiously on Father Sullivan's sermon on lying. How could I have done such a thing? Would my mother ever have done such a thing (asked my father)? Would my father ever have done such a thing (asked my mother)? Would Uncle Ed and Uncle Dan (both priests) ever have done such a thing? A few close friends were also mentioned. They would never have done such a thing, either.

Sister Marie was more comforting. "I think St. Aloysius prayed for you."

"He did?"

"He prayed that this trouble would soon end and leave you with a clear conscience."

No wonder St. Aloysius is the patron saint of young Catholic students.

But it was Grandpa who put his finger directly on the "worm in the bud." "Beware," he had said, "beware of the Great Guess What! It's not for everyone—only people of the strongest moral fiber."

I am still in a quandary. Must I someday decide whether to go on being a writer—someone who often looks to his imagination for the facts—or become a person of the strongest moral fiber?

I think I will put off my decision for the time being because right now I am remembering the time when, according to Grandma, even God Himself used the Great Guess What.

One day (she said) God turned to His good friend, the archangel Michael, and exclaimed, "Guess what I just did!"

And Michael asked, "What, Lord?"

And God said, "I made the world!"

And Michael, who could hardly believe his ears, whispered, "*No!*"

Then God smiled a heavenly smile and replied, "Oh, yes, Michael, I really did—all the seas, the land, and all the people. I made them, every one."

And Michael believed Him.

And so do I.

The Day
I Betrayed Arley

In that time of wonder when I was first allowed to explore the world beyond my backyard, I was given a protective blanket of admonitions by my parents: stay on your own block; don't cross Seventy-fifth Street; don't speak to strangers.

And don't make fun of Arley.

Arley, the wheelbarrow man, was a fixture of our neighborhood, as ageless as the spires of St. Lawrence Church, the odors of Jensen's Fish Market, and the stubby little "tea kettle" steam engines that pulled the Illinois Central commuter trains into downtown Chicago.

Tall and narrow-shouldered as a cornstalk, slightly stooped in a graceful sort of way, Arley pushed his wooden flat-bed wheelbarrow along our sidewalks with the steady rise-and-fall gait of an old but tireless swayback horse.

And yet we never thought of him as old. We never thought of him as young, either. We thought of him as eternal.

His smile seemed eternal, too. Whatever his mood, it

never left his face; it expressed joy, apprehension, serenity, the hurt of rejection, the pain of ridicule, the hope of acceptance.

Arley was dressed always in the gray-striped overalls and cap and red bandana of a railroad engineer. In a breast pocket, anchored to a buttonhole by a heavy gold chain, he kept a railroad man's watch. Its snap-open cover was elaborately engraved with the image of an early wood-burning locomotive. He showed it to us often with great pride. It had been his father's.

Arley was never without his wheelbarrow, which was usually empty. You might meet him in the morning or late in the afternoon, loping purposefully along the sidewalk, and you might ask, "Where y'goin', Arley?"

"Gotta make my run," he'd say, broadening his grin. "Southwest Division today. I'm running a little late." His voice was deep and as soft as buttermilk; his speech was slow and deliberate.

Arley's wheelbarrow was the locomotive and cars of his train. Weather permitting, it ran six days a week. Neither Arley nor wheelbarrow appeared on Sunday.

He lived with his mother in a small bungalow not far from my home. His father, once an engineer on the Illinois Central, had been killed in a crash when Arley was a youngster. His mother supported her son and herself by working as a stenographer in the railroad's main office downtown.

Nothing pleased Arley more than to have you ask for a ride. Upon such a request he would become a conductor. He would set the wheelbarrow down and take a small square of colored paper from a pocket. "Here's your ticket," he'd say. "All aboard!" Once you were settled, he'd call, "Tickets, please!" You'd hand him the tiny piece of paper, which he'd examine carefully, then punch with a conductor's ticket punch. "Hold on to this now," he'd say. "That ticket's good for any stop on the line."

The wheelbarrow could accommodate as many as three

passengers at a time—one in the center, feet up, and one on each side, feet hanging overboard. Only when your legs grew so long that your shoes touched the sidewalk as you rode did you become ineligible to board the train. Arley simply considered you too big to be seen in a wheelbarrow.

The ride was like that of no other vehicle. It was a bone-jarring mélange of every motion known to science. The old, bare iron wheel, grating and growling its way down the sidewalk, crushing small stones and bounding defiantly over larger ones, produced an erratic but relentless vibration like that of an ailing jackhammer. In addition, the axle, worn thin over many years, gave the wheel a freedom of lateral movement it thoroughly exploited, pitching you from side to side as it wobbled capriciously along. This discord of sound and movement was cradled beguilingly in a pattern of steady up-and-down motion—like that of a rowboat on a swelling sea—generated by Arley's peculiar bob-and-dip walk. Only kids with strong stomachs were able to survive the ride for very long. The others became seasick and, as best they could, found their own way home. Their mothers promptly forbade them to ride with Arley again.

In a small box fastened to one of the shafts, Arley kept an oil can and rag. When alerted by a high-frequency squeak, audible only to himself and the neighborhood dogs, he would pull over on the parkway grass—a siding, he called it—and oil the wheel. After carefully wiping the spokes clean, he would back out of the siding and resume his journey.

At intersections he would pause long enough to check his watch and consult a timetable—a dog-eared, finger-stained fold of paper that in meticulous hand lettering listed departure times from imaginary stations. He might murmur, "Right on time" or "Running a little late" and be off again.

Occasional strangers to the neighborhood, walking toward Arley on a direct collision course, were nonplussed to discover that the wheelbarrow refused to move over to make room. They had to walk around it. "Sorry," Arley would smile as he chugged past, "gotta keep 'er on the track." To his passengers he'd mutter, "Folks shouldn't be up here on the right-of-way." Local residents, including the nuns from St. Lawrence and the policeman on the beat, knew enough to step aside for the Arley Express.

On different days he covered different routes of several blocks each that represented the various divisions of his railroad. He made four or five trips each day. You could get on or off at any point along any route or stay until he brought you back, possibly an hour later, to where you had boarded his train. After he took a brief rest, you were welcome to go with him on his next run. Although your parents instructed you not to stray beyond your own block, you were free to go anywhere with Arley. At least I was.

His call "Back to the roundhouse!" signaled the end of the day's operations. His smile would become apologetic as he said good-by. Two or three times, as he moved farther and farther away from you, he'd set the wheelbarrow down and turn to see if you were still watching him. If you were, he'd wave another good-by.

The inevitable day came at last when my own legs were no longer short enough to keep my shoes clear of the sidewalk. I was sitting, feet down, on one side of the wheelbarrow, balancing the weight of a friend on the other when I felt a sudden scrape of leather against concrete. I slipped both hands under my legs just behind my knees to raise my feet higher, but it was no use. The gesture was all too familiar to Arley. He stopped the train.

"I'm sorry," he said. "You're too big now, you're too heavy. And it doesn't look right." His smile became wistful, apologetic, and sad. It was the smile of a beloved professor saying good-by to a favorite student at graduation.

We were both aware of the significance of this moment. It was a turning point in our relationship, and it could have dark consequences. I had a decision to make and Arley knew it. The next few days would show him what that decision was.

I have sketched only one side of Arley's story—the happier side. There was another. I will introduce it with a question: How can a grown man, wearing a perpetual smile and pushing a wheelbarrow day after day for no practical purpose, escape the cruel mischief that broods in so many of us and vents itself so readily on the defenseless?

When we were small enough to cadge rides from Arley, we were his friends, and we harbored no thoughts of ridicule. But once our feet began to touch the sidewalk, we crossed into another world that burdened us with a choice: to go on (as some did) being a friend of Arley's, though no longer his passenger, or to become the friend of certain older boys, the "real guys" of the neighborhood, and to prove our loyalty to them by joining in their bedevilment of the wheelbarrow man.

Echoing, in many cases, intolerant attitudes they had picked up at home, they expressed their budding, lopsided masculinity by calling out within Arley's hearing: "Dingdong, ding-dong, Arley is a ding-dong!" or a couplet that went

> Arley is a choo-choo train,
> Arley's crazy in the brain!

To gain admission to the elite inner circle of "real guys," you had to be willing to hurl some such insult at Arley as your new friends watched from nearby cover to make sure you didn't chicken out. That was the initiation rite.

I, too, coveted the respect of the older boys. Kids who stayed friends with Arley were called sissy-britches and pantywaists, to be ignored unless desperately needed to fill out the lineup for a softball game.

Was I a sissy-britches, a pantywaist? Not on your life. I could be as tough as the best of them. I agreed to insult Arley.

"Arley is a choo-choo—" I started to yell, but the rest of the words wouldn't come. Behind me, hidden under a front porch, was the jury of older boys. I began again. "Arley is a choo-choo train!"

Across the street, pushing his empty wheelbarrow, Arley looked up, startled. He slowed down. The smile wavered, almost flickered out, but held on—with inexpressible sadness. "You, too," it seemed to say.

I wish I could report that I took a deep breath, squared my shoulders, and resolutely walked over to Arley and apologized. But I can't—simply because the matter was suddenly taken out of my hands. I had failed to notice that, a few houses away, my father had come out on our front porch to summon me for dinner. He had heard it all.

"Junior!" he called, as only my father could call. "*Come here!*" He was standing now at the bottom of the steps.

My friends, astonished by this interruption, popped their heads out of hiding to get a better look. My father spotted them immediately. "You," he roared, "*all* of you! Come here!" I think if they had been Attila the Hun's army, they would have come. "Right *here!*" my father repeated, not moving an inch. "And hurry up!"

They hurried up, every one of them. "Now," said my father, his eyes like two saber points, "I want each one of you boys to apologize to Arley, you hear? Be quick about it! Tell him you're sorry and you'll never do it again."

Arley, as amazed as the kids, crossed the street to within speaking distance, still pushing his wheelbarrow.

"Go on," my father prompted. One by one, myself included, we apologized to Arley.

His smile showed embarrassment, then joy—and complete forgiveness. Arley shook hands with all of us, including my father. After a moment, he fumbled for his watch, snapped it open, and said, "I'm afraid I'm running a little late." He recrossed the street, set the wheelbarrow down, and waved to us. We waved back.

My father looked each one of us in the eye. With a fine disregard for legal consequences, he said, "If I ever catch any of you insulting that man again, I'll knock your blocks off!"

The persecution of Arley did not stop immediately. But day by day it diminished, until after a week or two it sputtered out completely. We began to accept Arley again as one of the ageless—and respectable—features of our neighborhood.

I still think of Arley now and then. His image and his smile become especially vivid in that sorrowing season before Eastertide, when the words of St. Luke are read describing the awesome moment in the high priest's house when Christ gazed upon Peter after the denial and, in the light of the courtyard fire, stamped him forever with his look of infinite love.

And God Created Dorchester Avenue

There was a time in my early preschool years when I firmly believed that my childhood neighborhood and its familiar cast of characters had been part of God's original act of creation. It had always been there and would be there forever.

I can't pretend that I gave this matter much thought. I simply took it for granted.

I knew that God had made my parents, my grandparents, and myself. My grandfather, the oldest and therefore wisest member of our family, had told me so. Furthermore, I knew they would never grow older. They would all look the same tomorrow because they all looked the same today as they did yesterday. I myself would eventually grow up, but the rest of my family would remain unchanged.

God had made everyone else in the neighborhood, too,

their houses and their shops. This I learned one day on a visit to my grandparents' home upstairs.

"Did God make Mr. Hanson, Grandpa?" I asked.

"He did indeed," said my grandfather, trying to light his pipe.

"Did He make Mrs. Thorne?"

"Definitely," said Grandpa, lighting his pipe again.

"Did He make Mr. Hendry?"

At this rate Grandpa would never get his pipe lighted. "Junior," he said, pointing the pipe stem at my middle, "God made *every*body! Understand? Everybody!"

"Did He make—"

"And every*thing!*" Grandpa concluded with a sweep of his arm that took in the old Victrola, the potted fern in the front window, and the vast world beyond.

Next Sunday in church I was happy to hear Father Sullivan support my grandfather's views. "In the beginning," said our pastor, obviously quoting from an even higher authority, "God created the heaven and the earth."

So there I had it. Heaven *and* earth. Was there any doubt about who had built Hanson's Grocery and Meat Market, Mrs. Thorne's Delicatessen, and Hendry's Dry Goods Store?

And God had made the convent at the end of our block, and He had made the nuns, who often took me with them when they went for a walk.

He had made the neat rows of comfortable homes on Dorchester Avenue, where I lived, including the bungalow of Minnie Mitt.

Minnie (Elmina Smith to grown-ups) was a widow who lived alone a few doors away. She was my very special friend. Whenever I wandered in her direction (which I did with delightful regularity), she would rap on her front window, where she always sat, fragile as a dandelion puffball, and beckon me inside. A moment later I would be sitting cross-legged on her living room floor, ginger snaps and milk beside me, lost in Gustave Doré's brooding illustrations for Dante's *Inferno*.

Close to the front of Minnie's house was a forest of plants she called elephant ears. Their broad, wide-spreading, high-reaching leaves formed a secluded hideaway where a small boy, full of cookies and milk and beset by dreams of a secret place all his own, could build mud castles while a phantom-like lady watched from her window and nodded approval.

Why God had made Minnie Mitt so old to begin with was a question that troubled me for a time until Grandpa explained that He had a special liking for old folks because they seemed to pay more attention to Him.

God had also made some people Catholic, some not; some Irish, some not. But all this was God's business and I was not to worry about it. Hadn't Father Sullivan in that same sermon said, "God saw that it was good"? If it was good enough for God, should I complain?

For me it was very good indeed—all of it—a friendly, secure, easily explored little world of my own, and it would never be disturbed.

But it was disturbed. Surprisingly enough, it was disturbed by my gentle old friend, Minnie Mitt. She disturbed it by dying.

"What does it mean to die, Grandpa?"

"It means that God, who created you, wants you back living with Him."

"Won't I ever see Minnie Mitt again?"

"You'll see her some day in heaven."

A tiny pinprick of fear became an icy chill that spread into every corner of my body as the implications of Grandpa's words sank in.

"Will Daddy and Mommy die? Will you and Grandma die?" I asked in a rush.

Grandpa, touched perhaps by some distant memory, did

his best to cheer me up. "Not for a long, long time," he said. "So don't you worry."

But I did worry, especially in the dark, intimate hours of the night. I had nightmares of unthinkable landscapes like those of the *Inferno,* over which I wandered in endless search of lost parents and grandparents. How soon would God take them away from me? In spite of Grandpa's words, I had the awful feeling that it could happen at any moment and nothing could stop it. Some mornings I had a difficult time explaining to my mother why my pillow was damp and my eyes were so red.

Once I went to look at Minnie's deserted bungalow. Its shades were drawn; its windows reflected nothing but empty sky. Rain had washed away the last of the mud castles under the elephant ears. I promised myself I would never walk that way again.

Eventually, however, after repeated assurances from my parents that they were not about to die—in fact, they weren't even *thinking* of dying—I slipped back into my old familiar world of contentment, as secure as it was eternal.

Then one day, shocked and angry, I brought my mother the news that "Some new people are moving into Minnie Mitt's house."

"You didn't expect it to stand empty, did you, dear?"

"But I don't *like* them!"

"Have you seen them?" she asked.

Yes, I had seen them. I had seen the big van pull up in front of the bungalow. I had seen a thin little man with bushy black hair and a ferocious-looking mustache run out of the house and start giving orders to the moving men. He also gave orders to a much younger man he called Aldo. Aldo also had lots of black hair and a fierce mustache. And there was a stout woman Aldo called Mama, who kept appearing on the front steps to give orders of her own. She too had jet-black hair, but hers was drawn into a tight bun at the back of her head.

No, I didn't like them. They were intruders. This house was not really theirs. God had made it for Minnie Mitt.

They were destroyers, too. Within a week they had dug up the elephant ears and replaced them with prickly, low-growing evergreens. You can't build mud castles under prickly, low-growing evergreens. Oh, wouldn't Minnie Mitt have been furious!

No, I would not go near them. I would not be friendly toward them. If I met them on the street, I would not even speak to them. I would pretend to be watching a worm crossing the sidewalk.

"Well now, how are *you* today, Junior?" asked a familiar voice one day.

I looked up from my search for a four-leaf clover in our front lawn.

"Afternoon, Sister. Afternoon, Sister," I said, careful to include both Sister Margaret and Sister Celeste. Good friends of mine, they were also wonderful walking companions.

I particularly liked Sister Celeste. She was young and had dark eyes, a smiling mouth, and a look that said, "You are the most interesting person I have met all day."

"Would you like to take a walk?" asked Sister Celeste.

"Oh, you bet, Sister!"

"Good. Run tell your mother. We'll wait."

Permission granted, I raced back to the sisters.

"We have a surprise for you today," said Sister Celeste.

"What kind of a surprise?"

"You'll see."

We began walking. Rather, the nuns walked; I hopped and skipped around them and brought them up to date on everything that had happened to me since I saw them last.

Before I knew it, we were in front of the bungalow. Sister Celeste paused long enough to take my hand.

"There are some very special people I want you to meet," she said.

Too surprised to resist, I let myself be led up the walk toward Minnie Mitt's home. We had scarcely reached the steps when the front door was flung open and Mama rushed forward to greet us.

"*Carissima!*" she cried to Sister Celeste.

"*Mamma mia!*" cried Sister.

The two embraced.

"Papa!" Sister Celeste exclaimed as the thin little man with the bushy hair and the ferocious mustache appeared in the doorway, followed by Aldo.

"*Carissima!* . . . *Cara mia!* . . . *Tanta Caro!*"

The scene was a giant, living halo of arms, embraces, laughter, exclamations, mustaches, and gleaming white teeth beneath them.

The halo moved into the old, familiar living room.

"*Piccino!* So you are the little boy down the street," said Mama, giving my face a squeeze. I decided this was no time to look for a worm crossing a sidewalk. I smiled at her. What else can you do when a jolly, laughing lady is holding your face in her hand?

"Why had you never come to visit us?" she demanded with feigned vexation. How could I tell her why?

"Ah," she said. "Bashful. But no more, you hear?"

She stepped back, studied me for a moment, then declared, "You're starving!"

Soon I was sitting cross-legged on the floor beside a whatnot stand just like my grandmother's. In front of me were a glass of milk and a plate of strange-tasting cookies.

"I hope you like anise," said Mama. I liked it better with each bite.

"I was dying to come sooner," Sister Celeste scolded her mother, "but you wouldn't let me."

"I told you," said Mama. "The house wasn't ready. How could you bring a friend like Sister Margaret if the house wasn't ready? What kind of housekeeper would she think I am?"

The whatnot stand, I felt, was worth a closer look. On its highly polished shelves were miniature vases holding clusters of delicate china flowers, a silver box inlaid with brilliant stones, and a large photograph of two very solemn-looking children, a boy and a girl, seated on the sofa holding hands. Where are *they* today? I wondered.

"You must think all this grown-up talk is silly," Mama said to me. "I have something I know you'll like."

She turned to a glass-covered bookcase, selected a large volume, and placed it on my lap. "The fountains of Rome," she said. "Aren't they beautiful?"

They *were* beautiful, I admitted to myself; they were sparkling and joyful, not at all like the somber pictures in Dante's *Inferno.*

Now Papa was in the middle of the room playing a violin. It must have been a dance, because he turned, dipped, and side-stepped as he made the bow flash across the strings. When he finished, everyone clapped and cried, *"Bene!"* I clapped and cried, *"Bene!"* too.

Then Aldo played a song on his accordion and everyone sang. I had to keep silent because I had never heard words like these before. But I could tell they were merry words.

On the way home I asked Sister Celeste where the children I had seen in the photograph were.

"They're in heaven," she answered.

"They died? When they were little?"

"A long time ago," said Sister. "Do you know who they are? My brother and sister—Arturo and Angelina. They were very sick and God took them back with Him."

I looked closely for signs of a tear, but her face was as serene and smiling as ever. Grandpa, I'm afraid, had looked a little bit sad when he talked to me about people dying.

"And you'll never see them again?"

"Oh, but indeed I will!" she exclaimed. "That's the wonderful thing about heaven. It's the place—the only place—where we will all be together and never be apart again!"

It was hard to believe, but there it was. Sister Celeste could smile and be happy when talking about her little brother and sister in heaven. And her parents—how could they have been so joyous if they didn't really *know* that some day they would be with their children again? Heaven must be quite a place after all.

The pinprick of fear that had touched me for a moment was gone.

Yes, God had made it all. He had made the convent and He had made my friends the nuns. He had made the neat rows of comfortable homes on Dorchester Avenue, where I lived, including the bungalow of the Bondino family.

And I'm sure that, as Father Sullivan had said, He looked down and saw that it was good.

Grandpa's Garden Goes On Forever

As a youngster I was sure that if death claimed someone very special in my life—like my beloved grandfather—someone else just like him would eventually be found, and the remembered good times would roll again.

Only when I was much older did I understand that life has something more constructive to do with old memories than rerun them with stand-ins.

My fondness for my maternal grandfather was enlivened by our shared enthusiasm for such important things as ice-cream sodas, peanut brittle and popcorn, Saturday afternoons at the movies, building a coaster wagon, and visiting the engine room of a Great Lakes steamship.

Grandpa Pat Duffey had been a boilermaker. "One of the best," my grandmother told me proudly. "He was ambidextrous—he could swing the riveter's hammer equally well in either hand." It was a talent that greatly facilitated his work in the cramped quarters of some boiler rooms, especially those in ships, and, according to Grandma, made him a legend in his own time.

Once, as an off-day treat, he took me on a shipboard visit to a chief engineer he had come to know well.

"The *Star of Duluth* docked this morning," Grandpa had told me the night before. "How would you like to see the engine room of the biggest freighter on the Lakes?"

Like Dante descending into his inferno, we followed the chief engineer down the iron-black web of stairways and ladders into the clanking, hissing, steam-hot, oil-smelling depths of the great vessel. I swallowed hard to keep the excitement from choking me and marveled that Grandpa could look so calm and unafraid in this awesome confusion of giant pipes, valves, gauges, pistons, and flywheels.

A furnace door was opened so that I could peer inside. Though the fire was partially banked, I felt overwhelmed by the enormous ball of heat that forced me back. But Grandpa stood his ground, surveying the furnace interior with the critical eye of one who knows all its manifest strengths and secret weaknesses.

As knowledgeable as if he had built the ship himself, he explained how it generated its vast power—how water entered the boilers to become steam, which passed into the steam chests to move the pistons, which turned the drive shafts, which turned the propellers. He was determined that I should understand everything I saw.

"Maybe some day," the friendly chief said to me, "you'll be a great boiler man like your grandfather."

I could have wished for nothing more.

On the train ride home, I thought sadly, Why are the good times over so soon? How do you make them go on and on? I knew Grandpa sympathized with my mood, though he said nothing. That was another thing about Grandpa and me: we could understand each other through silence.

Arriving home from work on Friday evenings, Grandpa would pause long enough at our downstairs back door to call in, "Junior, don't forget tomorrow!"

I would forget Christmas sooner than tomorrow.

Almost every Saturday afternoon the two of us would board a Stony Island Avenue streetcar at Seventy-fifth Street and ride up front with the motorman to Sixty-seventh—and Brubaker's Candy Shop. Provisioned with a large bag of peanut brittle, we would settle down in our seats in the theater next door. Between mouthfuls of candy we roared with laughter at the antics of Charlie Chaplin, the Keystone Cops, or Fatty Arbuckle—or gasped in terror at the plight of Pearl White in "The Perils of Pauline."

After the show we both tacitly agreed that no such outing should end without a chocolate soda at the corner drugstore before the ride home.

The forlorn slurp-slurp of my straw at the bottom of the empty glass betrayed my reluctance to let the lovely afternoon slip away.

"Cheer up," Grandpa might say. "We can do it again next Saturday."

But next Saturday was always light-years away.

There were lazy afternoon visits to Jackson Park, where a few landmarks of Chicago's Columbian Exposition still lingered—the Arts Palace, later to become a museum; a Japanese teahouse; and the beautiful tree-shored lagoons, on which you could take rides in a wheezy old motor launch.

Grandpa had seen the Exhibition with his own children when they were growing up. Now, as much for himself as for me, he retold the glories of the great fair—the incomparable Ferris wheel, imported all the way from Europe; the Yerkes telescope, which brought the farthest stars down to the tip of your nose; the brilliant network of incandescent lighting; the telephone hookup over which you could hear concerts from New York. Wonder after wonder, their images floated through the treetops as my grandfather brought them back to life.

Again the chocolate soda before returning home. Again the forlorn slurp-slurp of my straw in the bottom of the glass.

"When can we come again, Grandpa?"

"Soon, Junior, real soon."

I think I felt closest to Grandpa when I was working with him in his garden, which took up most of an adjacent lot owned by my father. I remember the garden best because it was here that Grandpa found the perfect answer to my boyhood complaints about the impermanence of life's pleasures. It was an answer, however, that I did not fully understand until years later.

But I must begin with the evenings early each spring when he would come downstairs, pencil and paper in hand, and say, "Junior, it's time you and I started planning our garden."

What shall we grow this time? Each year he thought of making the garden smaller and easier to care for, but after a few minutes at the kitchen table among dreams of giant tomatoes ripening on their vines, cabbages and cauliflowers forming ranks, onions raising their greening blades in salute to the sun, we would agree that we couldn't do without carrots, beets, lettuce, turnips, and parsnips, too. And if we couldn't do without these, how could we do without eggplants or beans or a few rows of corn? And what about squash and cucumbers? What about the thrill of fishing with your hand under the sealike surface of broad green leaves and suddenly discovering that you had landed a leviathan?

All male members of the family and a few friends were

recruited for the initial spading of the garden: Grandpa and myself, of course; my father, Uncle Billy, and Mr. Deedy from across the street, who had been raised on a farm and welcomed this opportunity, he said, "to get back to the land." And the surest way for any beau of Aunt Addie or Aunt Laura to prove the seriousness of his intent was to volunteer for several hours of digging.

It was usually finished in a day, a day highlighted at noon by a farmer's feast prepared by Grandma, my mother, and her sisters and spread out on blankets under the maple trees of our backyard.

Grandma would survey the digging done so far and remark, "For heaven's sake, Pat, you'll have enough food to feed an army."

But Grandpa wasn't worried about what he would *do* with the food. His satisfaction was in *growing* it—his personal celebration of life. What vegetables we couldn't use he would give away—and that, too, was one of his special joys.

After days of patient waiting, I would at last bring Grandpa the exciting news that "the onions and radishes are coming up!" Together we would rush out to the garden to verify this annual phenomenon. And would you believe, in the time it had taken me to run upstairs and back, the first lettuce would also have announced its presence.

To Grandpa the garden was as exciting as a miracle, perhaps more so. More truly than if a tomato plant were suddenly to bear grapefruit or a corn stalk to grow heavy with apples, the very predictability of the garden testified to God's goodness.

"Think of it," he would say. "Every year the same carrot seeds, planted anywhere around the world, will still produce the same carrots. I think that's exciting, don't you?"

It was indeed, even if only because Grandpa said it was.

Working in the garden was fun; Grandpa made it so. When we cultivated, he hitched me up with a clothesline to his one-wheel cultivator so I could pretend I was a horse pulling it, while he pushed and guided it from behind.

I became a horse again as successive crops of vegetables came to harvest. After setting aside enough for our family, we divided the rest into separate baskets for special friends and neighbors, loaded them onto my coaster wagon, and, with me pulling, began our rounds.

Often more than one trip was necessary, but always the first stop was the parish convent. The sisters' thanks were as numerous as the beads of the huge rosaries that hung from their waists. "Patrick, you're a wonder. . . . How do you grow tomatoes so perfect? . . . We've never seen such cabbages. . . . You must have a special devotion to St. Fiacre, patron saint of gardeners."

Then to the rectory, where Mrs. Corbett, Father Sullivan's housekeeper, insisted that Grandpa could become a millionaire overnight if he'd turn to farming.

Mr. Deedy, the former farm boy, was equally complimentary, though only after a critical examination of random samples to show that he really knew what he was talking about.

Among the stops was one at the house of the Reverend Elwood Peabody, rector of the local Episcopal church. Grandpa had counted him a friend since the day they had shared a streetcar seat and discovered that their views on the "trouble" in Ireland were the same. Grandma and my mother clucked occasionally over the propriety of such ecumenical generosity, but Grandpa retorted that men of such broadminded intelligence were hard to find and should be treasured.

The day would come at last when Grandpa and I, looking out across our garden, could see no further signs of growth— only the topsoil turning grey, only the squash vines curling into dust.

There was a chilling hint of autumn in the air, and in me a sad and unexplainable sense that the old relationship would soon be different somehow. He was growing older; more to the point, so was I. I would still love and respect him, but would it still be in the same blind-trusting, hero-worshiping way of childhood innocence?

Grandpa sighed as if he knew exactly what I was thinking. "We'd best look at it this way," he said. "The vegetables are gone. We can't do anything about that. But something *can* be done about the garden. It can still be planted each year by *someone*. The garden can go on forever."

Now it is many years later. A young grandson has asked me, "Grandpa, *when* are we going to build the coaster wagon?"

I assure him that we will go to the lumberyard tomorrow without fail. His eyes brighten with the gladness of springtime blossoms.

A young friend is with him. The friend asks incredulously, "You're going to *make* your own coaster wagon?"

"Sure," says my grandson proudly. "My grandfather can do *anything!*"

I am suddenly aware that there is something far more satisfying than holding on to old memories; it's the making of new ones for someone else. Grandpa was right. The harvest changes from year to year, but the garden can go on forever.

The Boy
Who Asked Questions

Willie the Wanderbug first appeared at our kitchen door one afternoon in my seventh summer. My mother and I could see he was plainly another of "those poor unfortunates," as my parents called them, who came by from time to time for food or money.

Younger-looking than my father and not quite as tall, he was dressed in wrinkled gray trousers, a faded blue shirt, and well-worn shoes. Under his arm he carried a small brown-paper parcel tied with string.

But Willie was different. His black hair was neatly combed. His trousers, though old and wrinkled, were clean, and so was his shirt. His face looked freshly shaven. His manner was pleasantly polite, not ingratiating.

"I wonder," he said, "if you folks might have any work I could do around the house."

Work? The others had never asked for work. "Well now," my mother said, taken aback by this approach. "Let me see." I knew she was noticing the same things about this stranger I had noticed.

"Any kind of work," he went on. "Washing windows, cutting grass, cleaning the basement—anything."

"All right," my mother said finally. "What would you charge for beating some small rugs?"

"Whatever you think is right, ma'am."

Mother named an amount that the stranger said was "fine with me." But she had noticed something else. "Before you start," she said, "you'd better have a bite to eat."

"I'll be much obliged to you, ma'am," he replied gratefully. "And my name is Willie."

Another difference: the others had all been nameless.

At my mother's invitation, Willie sat down on the back steps. I sat two steps below him, watching his hunger fade with every bite of the thick roast-beef sandwich and with every swallow of the coffee that Mother brought him.

"My name is Junior," I volunteered.

"Junior," said Willie, solemnly extending his hand. "I'm pleased to make your acquaintance."

None of the others had ever offered to shake hands. I felt that the first steps toward a more personal relationship had been taken.

"You live near here?" I asked.

"Near and far, here and there," Willie responded. "Wherever the wind blows fairest. I'm a wanderbug, Junior, born to travel—and travel light. No worldly possessions to weight me down—except what I can carry." He nodded toward his small parcel, beside him on the steps.

"But where do you *live?*" I persisted, certain that no one could survive without a permanent home.

"For the time being," Willie laughed, "I live in Paradise. No, no, that's just a poor joke," he hurried to explain. "For the time being, I live in the Paradise Hotel downtown. It's not as heavenly as it sounds, but it suits me fine."

Why had he stressed "For the time being"? This certainly suggested further questions, but Mother, meanwhile, had brought the rugs and the rug beater to the back door.

"Junior," she admonished me, "it's not polite to pry."

I helped Willie gather up the rugs and spread them on the grass. "First," he said, "you beat them on the ground to loosen the dirt. Then you hang them on the clothesline and beat them some more. That blows the dirt away."

Seeing that I was about to explode from the pressure of unasked questions, he smiled and said, "Go ahead, Junior, talk. I don't mind."

But it was Willie—between strokes of the beater—who did most of the talking, filling me with tales of the wonders he had seen in his faraway wanderings: the underground river in a great Kentucky cave with waters so dark that the fish had long ago lost their eyesight; the geysers of Yellowstone that spewed water higher than our church steeple; the mountains of ice in Alaska that actually *moved!* Willie had seen them all! I wished that we had rugs enough to keep him beating and talking for the rest of the day.

All too soon the work was finished, and he brought the rugs, neatly folded, to my mother, who thanked him, gave him his money, and wished him good luck.

But instead of leaving, Willie asked her if she had a pair of clippers handy. The lilac bushes at the back of the yard needed pruning, he said, and he'd be happy to do it for what she had already paid him. Scarcely believing what she had heard, Mother accepted Willie's offer but insisted that he take another sandwich and some fruit with him when he left.

The pruning finished, he picked up his paper parcel and said, "Back to Paradise." I asked him when he'd return. There were many more stories that he had only hinted at.

"Hard to say," he answered, his face growing strangely solemn. "I don't like to be tied down to times and places. Willie the Wanderbug, that's me."

He told me how much he had enjoyed my company, and we shook hands as he said good-by. I was sure I would never see him again.

"The poor unfortunate" who had insisted on doing more work than he was paid for immediately became a prime topic of family conversation. That evening my mother told my father, who said, "I didn't think they made 'em like that any more." She told my grandmother, who said, "Will wonders never cease?"

A week later Grandma said, "Wonders *will* never cease." Willie had returned and, after being paid for cutting the grass, had insisted on weeding the flower garden.

Another few days and he got paid for painting the alley fence and then washed the basement windows. Five days later he washed the first floor windows, got paid, and straightened up the basement. He said he enjoyed working— and talking to "young Junior."

By now the story of Willie's generosity had spread beyond the family. Mother told her good friends the nuns of our parish convent, who said, "The poor dear man, we must remember him in our prayers."

My father told Father Sullivan, our pastor, who said, "Isn't it strange? We are always so amazed when we find someone who takes the Sermon on the Mount to heart. Remember? 'Whosoever shall compel thee to go with him a mile, go with him two.'" Father added that when we ran out of jobs for Willie, we should send him directly to the rectory. "I can keep him busy," he promised.

I don't think we would ever have run out of jobs for Willie, but one evening our pastor phoned to ask if we'd be willing to share him with our church, at least for a few days.

Matt O'Toole, the parish's aging custodian, was looking forward to retiring as soon as a good replacement could be found.

"Tell Willie it's just for a week," Father said. "That'll give me a chance to look him over. We'll go on from there."

My parents promised to send Willie to the rectory, if and when he came again.

It took some talking on my mother's part to persuade Willie, when he again showed up, to work for Father Sullivan. The idea of steady employment, even for a few days, troubled him. "I like to keep my time loose," he said with a frown.

Nevertheless Mother finally talked him into it, and with me along for company, he reported to the rectory.

Our pastor had a gift for making people feel at ease with him at once, mostly, I suppose, because he felt so at ease with them. I knew from that first meeting that the two men would get along. Father gave Willie a list of jobs to be done, mostly around the school, but told him to work at his own pace and if he got hungry between meals to see Mrs. Corbett, the housekeeper.

Although the rectory was only a block from our house, well within my travel limits, my mother insisted I keep my visits short and infrequent so as not to "get in the way."

"Willie's working for Father Sullivan now," she said. "He won't have time for telling you stories."

I saw Willie only briefly over the next few days but, unhappily, I sensed a change. Though still friendly, he seemed less inclined to talk, to make jokes and laugh. I felt he would just as soon I didn't ask so many questions. After a while I stayed away altogether.

Then one evening Father Sullivan came to our house visibly upset and worried.

"Has Willie been here today?" he asked without sitting down.

The answer was no.

"Then," said Father with a great sorrow in his voice, "I'm afraid I've lost him."

He dropped into a chair and lowered his chin to his fingertips, peaked like the church roof.

"Maybe I reached for too much too soon," he murmured.

"Oh well," said my father, trying to console him. "Willie, after all, is a born wanderer, always in search of greener pastures."

Father's head never moved, but the piercing blue eyes shot upward and held onto my father. "Did it ever occur to you," he said, "that a man of his caliber might not be searching for something new but that he might be running *away* from something he already knows?"

"From what then?" asked my parents together.

"From God," said our pastor softly. "From the Great Pursuer of men, from the Hound of Heaven, as one poet called him."

Piece by piece Father laid out the sad mosaic of Willie's life. "The minute I spoke to him, the minute he answered me, I knew he was a Catholic—or had been one once."

"How could you tell?" my mother had to ask.

"The way he said, 'Yes, Father' or 'Good morning, Father' or 'Good-by, Father'—as natural and easy as if he'd been addressing priests all his life. You can spot it every time." Father sighed. "I *had* to know if this man was a lost sheep. It was my priestly duty to know. So day by day I encouraged him to confide in me. Ah, the poor man."

Our pastor laid his head back and closed his eyes. "They had been married a year," he said softly, "himself and Maureen. They had great plans for the future. They wanted a child and were soon expecting. He lost them both—mother and son—in childbirth. That was seven years ago, and Willie has been running ever since. Seven-year-old Junior here may have slowed him down a bit, but now he'll be off and running again."

My mother shook her head, not yet comprehending how running away could solve anything. "Why?" she whispered.

"Because Willie blamed God for what happened. 'If there is a just God ...' You've heard the rest. He thought that

keeping away from God would be his revenge, his one consolation. He knew that if he ever stood still for long, God
would catch up with him. He almost did. Today I was to
hear Willie's confession."

Father Sullivan stood up and exclaimed, "If I only
knew where he's staying, I'd take up God's chase and go
after him!"

This was my hour! I became dizzy with the importance
of it—me, the kid who was often shushed for asking too
many questions.

"*I know where he lives!*" I shouted.

"*Where?*" Father Sullivan shouted back.

I almost said "in Paradise," as Willie had often jokingly
said, but I caught myself in time. "The Paradise Hotel
downtown!"

"I'll find it!" Father Sullivan was still shouting. "God bless
you!" he cried as he laid his hands on my head. "God
bless you!"

I was a frequent companion of Willie's after that. Upon
the retirement of Matt O'Toole he became parish custodian.
He called me his chief assistant.

But now that I think of it, all I ever did was ask more
questions.

How Mother Cleaned Up the Neighborhood

We all admire the fast decision maker who, in even the most
intense situations, can correctly decide yea or nay with the
will and snap of a horse biting into an apple. In fact, the
more speedily the decision is made, the more it seems to
signify uncommon wisdom and courage.

Admiral Farragut, by all accounts, was a fast decider.

"Damn the torpedoes!" he said. "Full steam ahead!" And in no time at all, so to speak, he had won the Battle of Mobile Bay. Later that evening, he no doubt wrote home to his wife, "What did I tell you? He who hesitates is lost!"

On the other hand, make a fast *wrong* decision and your critics are ready with such hardy apothegms as "Look before you leap" and "Haste makes waste." Or, worse, some poet might do for you what Tennyson did for the bungling British command at the Battle of Balaklava—perpetuate the blunder in verse. Remember *The Charge of the Light Brigade?*

I know a man who bought a new house for his family without his wife and children having seen it first. I hasten to add that he wasn't being capricious or inconsiderate; it's just that he had to be very practical. But how *brave* he was—much braver than I would have been under the same circumstances.

This man and his family lived in a part of the country far from the state of Michigan, where he had just bought a commercial fruit farm. Remembering the old Chinese adage "The footsteps of the master are the best fertilizer for the garden," he decided, with full family approval, that Michigan must now be their new home. And so, because his children, for the moment, couldn't afford to miss school and because his wife couldn't afford to be away from the children, he set out alone to find a suitable dwelling. When his family finally saw it, they loved it. By latest reports they're all living happily ever after.

I stand in awe of a man like that, a man who not only makes fast decisions but fast decisions that turn out *right*.

Not that I'm a man of *in*decision. Some mornings, for example, I choose my tie for the day without so much as a word to my wife. Later, when her pained look tells me that I've locked her out of another sharing experience, I may feel remorse. But a man *has* to stand on his own two feet now and then—providing, of course, that he doesn't overindulge. And I don't. Many mornings I'll say something like "I think

I'll try the blue tie with the little fleur-de-lis today, dear. What do you think?"

"Not with *that* shirt," she might say.

You see? It never hurts to ask around.

I guess your ability to make big decisions quickly and on your own depends a lot on your upbringing. Mine was a decision-making family through and through. By that I mean that anytime one member made a decision, you could be sure most of the others had had a big hand in it. By "others" I mean my grandparents, my mother's unmarried sisters, Addie and Laura, and her brother, Bill—all of whom lived upstairs. In addition, there were my parents and my father's brothers, Uncle Ed and Uncle Dan, both priests. Father Ed helped with the run-of-the-mill decisions whenever he could. Uncle Dan was a monsignor; we saved the *big* ones for him.

We relished family decision making just as we relished Sunday dinners together, walks to church together, evenings on the front porch together, rides through Jackson Park together in my father's Overland. We were a "together" family simply because we enjoyed each other's company.

Did Grandma and Grandpa decide to look for a new couch for their living room? Whoever else was free at the moment went along. Whoever wasn't went later. The final purchase was always delayed until everyone available had had a chance to form an opinion. This doesn't mean that the final decision had to be unanimous. It was rarely that. It simply meant that each of us felt more important, more needed, for having participated in it.

The only unanimous decision I can remember involved a stereopticon machine, which my mother bought for my birthday—with full family agreement. You slipped a postcard or photograph into a slot in back, turned on its light, and, wonder of wonders, there was the picture projected life-size on a bed sheet hung against a wall. If, after a while, attention lagged, you woke everyone up by projecting an image upside down. Seeing Aunt Laura at the last family picnic standing on her head and pouring lemonade uphill was always good for a few guffaws. It didn't take much in those days.

Did Mother go shopping for a new dress? Not without Grandma, Addie, and Laura. Did Dad go shopping for a new winter overcoat? Then everyone went—men, women, and children. It was common knowledge that no man could be trusted to choose the right overcoat for himself.

One of the most agonizing buying decisions of my parents' young lives involved an electric vacuum cleaner. It was not a matter of choosing one brand over another; it was a matter of choosing (for the first time) between an electric machine and another Bissell carpet sweeper.

The vacuum cleaner was called the Ohio. It looked somewhat like a carpet sweeper except for an electric motor about the size of a quart jar of pickles on top of its chrome housing and a large cloth dust bag attached to its handle. I would peg the noise it made when running somewhere between insufferable and unbearable— but impressive.

Both parents sensed, I feel now, that a decision to buy the Ohio would hurl them precipitously into a whole new age—the Age of Electricity—in which unfamiliar gadgets, foretold in the more sensational Sunday supplements, would replace the old tried-and-true implements that had served their parents and grandparents so loyally for so long. What woman in her right mind, for instance, would trust her hair, much less her life, to a hair curler heated by electricity? I was told that one of the features my parents like best about our house when they bought it was that the electric light fixtures also had gas jets—just in case.

We didn't go looking for the Ohio. The Ohio came looking for us. Sitting on our front porch late one hot Friday afternoon, my parents and I watched it zigzag toward us from a block away. It was being carried by a door-to-door salesman, who would knock on two or three doors on one side of the street, then cross over and knock on two or three on the other side.

"Wonder why he doesn't come straight down one side and then back up the other," my father mused.

"Maybe he doesn't want to end up where he started," my mother suggested. "Maybe that could be bad for a saleman's morale."

Eventually the machine reached the foot of our porch steps. The salesman looked as if he couldn't carry it another foot.

"My oh my," he sighed, "but it's hot!"

He was a pleasant-looking man of sixty or more, short, overheated, and worn out. "Yessir," he said, "a real scorcher."

"It *is* hot," my father agreed. "Why don't you rest yourself for a while?"

Grateful for the invitation, the other man sat on the steps and fanned himself with his straw hat.

"My name's Pat Clohissy," he said, not forgetting his mission, "and I wouldn't be here today if I couldn't guarantee that this wonderful machine will cut your housework in half."

My father was a salesman, too—in the wholesale furniture business—and he had a singular compassion for others in the brotherhood, especially those in the tough, mean door-to-door bottom end of it.

"How would you like a glass of beer, Mr. Clohissy?" he asked.

"Oh, *my!*" exclaimed Mr. Clohissy. "That would really hit the spot!" He added quickly that ordinarily he didn't drink while working but, the day being so hot and himself so tired, he just might make this stop his last of the afternoon.

When my father returned with the beer, our caller thanked him, studied him for a long moment, and said, "You know, you're a dead ringer for a dear friend of mine."

"Well now," said my father.

"By any chance," Mr. Clohissy asked, "do you know Father Ed Byrnes of St. Sebastian's?"

"I should think so," said my father. "He's my brother."

"Your brother and my pastor!" Mr. Clohissy bubbled. "Imagine that!" He was as pleased as if this made them blood relatives. "What a rare coincidence!"

Yes, one of those blessed coincidences arranged by the saints themselves exclusively for their favorite Irishmen. "How long have you been in Ed's parish?" "Twenty years, not a day less. Didn't Father Ed marry my daughters, Peg and Maureen?" "I think I may have seen you at one of my brother's bazaars." "And why not? Don't I work the bingo game for every one of them? Twenty years working the bingo game!" "And what part of the old country are you from?" "From Wicklow, and yourself from Tipperary; I know, the Father told me." "Will you have another glass of beer?" "And why not—the day being so hot and this being my last call. And bless you for your hospitality."

I'll say this for Pat Clohissy: he was a true salesman right to the end of his visit. Sometime shortly after his second beer, he managed to get the Ohio into our living room. He turned it on and did a fine job of vacuuming the big center rug. I was impressed by the casual way he took a handful of sawdust from a bag in his pocket and scattered it at his feet and then turned the Ohio loose on it.

"Well now, think of that," said my mother.

"It must be a powerful machine," said my father.

But I could tell there was still a heavy cloud of doubt lingering in their minds, probably blown there by the windy carpet sweeper salesman who had stopped by two weeks ago. I could still hear him bad-mouthing electric vacuum cleaners in general.

"For one thing, they'll ruin your fine rugs. All that concentrated suction pulls the nap right out by the roots! If there's a loose floorboard underneath, watch out! Worst of all, if there's a toddler around who can't get his fingers out of the way in time—"

"Oh, no!" My mother almost fainted.

The new electric vacuum cleaner had a lot going for it—and a lot going against it.

Mr. Clohissy had sworn testimonials to answer all objections from satisfied Ohio users. Their carpets, their floorboards, and their children's fingers were still intact, he assured us.

At any rate, he finally had to admit that this was not a decision to be made in one afternoon. (He must have been from a "together" family, too.)

"Tell you what," he said. "I usually don't do this, but it's been a long, hot week. Why don't I leave the Ohio with you over the weekend, and I'll drop back Monday?" His manner became conspiratorial. "Feel free to use it all you want, but I would appreciate it, Mrs. Byrnes, if you kept it in your own home." He nodded and winked to seal the arrangement.

I thought that when he departed he seemed relieved to be leaving the Ohio behind him.

It proved to be a very busy weekend. As soon as our caller was gone, Mother invited Grandma, Grandpa, and her sisters and brother down to see the cleaner in action. They each had a turn pushing it—through the living room, dining room, hallway, and bedrooms.

Grandma asked if she could see how it worked upstairs on *her* rugs. Mother guessed it would be all right, provided Grandma would never mention it if she bumped into Mr. Clohissy.

Well, it worked just fine on Grandma's rugs—and everybody had a turn guiding it across Grandma's floors.

Aunt Addie and Aunt Laura made supper for everybody, and we sat around the table afterwards talking and talking about vacuum cleaners versus sweepers until I fell asleep. I woke up long enough to find my father helping me into my pajamas down in my own bedroom.

Apparently no definite decision had been reached that night, because next morning Grandma came downstairs with a wonderful idea calculated to break the logjam.

"Why don't we take it over to Mary Kate?"

Mary Kate Corbett was Father Sullivan's housekeeper and one of Grandma's dearest friends. Besides, she had "a good head on her shoulders," and she'd be able to spot the strengths and weaknesses of the Ohio in no time at all.

"I don't know," my mother worried. "I promised Mr. Clohissy I wouldn't let it out of the house."

"What you meant was," said Grandma, "you wouldn't let it out of your sight. Didn't you? Of course you did. So come along and watch Mary Kate try it out. You owe it to yourself, Mae. After all, you're not buying lollipops."

"I love it!" said Mary Kate. She admired the way it sailed across the big rug in the rectory's main parlor and across the rugs in the reception room as well. It also did a fine job in the dining room, in Father Sullivan's study, and in one or two bedrooms. Not once did it pull up the nap by the roots.

"I'm going to keep after Father Sullivan until he gets me one," vowed Mary Kate when she finished.

We were halfway down the rectory steps on our way home when Mary Kate, at the door, had another idea.

"D'you know who would *really* appreciate a machine like this? Sister Martha! I'll go with you!" Mary Kate and Farragut.

Sister Martha was the housekeeper and cook for the convent, halfway down the block—not too long a distance for three women and small boy to carry a vacuum cleaner.

But Sister Martha preferred to be cautious. She disliked being pushed by what some people called progress. I gathered she had only recently come around to accepting the Bissel carpet sweeper. The good old reliable broom had always been her favorite—that and the O'Cedar floor mop. "I don't know," was all she'd say, shaking her head. "I just don't know."

This indecision of Sister Martha's was much less than Mother had hoped for. If Sister had said, "*Go* with it!" I feel

Mother would have decided to buy the Ohio on the spot. But now she wasn't sure. She felt she needed another opinion.

We were passing Mrs. Thorne's delicatessen and candy shop.

"Mabel has a good head on her shoulders," said my grandmother, obviously a dedicated connoisseur of heads. We brought the Ohio in and showed it to Mabel Thorne.

An hour later, we were back home, the Ohio somewhat heavier because of the assorted gum and candy wrappers and the snippets of cheese, smoked sausage, and salami it had picked up at Mrs. Thorne's.

Sunday was a day of rest—for the Ohio as well as for my family. We just sat around and looked at it.

On Monday Mr. Clohissy appeared again, considerably refreshed by his weekend away from his machine.

Mother, however, was still not sure. "I understand," she said, stalling, "that some people around here like the Whirlaway."

Mr. Clohissy smiled the easy, confident smile of the seasoned salesman and bingo caller. "Ah, yes," he said. "The Whirlaway. Dangerously overpowered. It pulls up the nap of your rugs by the roots. And if a small child should get his fingers in its way—" He shuddered and reached for the Ohio. "Not at all like the positive but safe vacuum action of *this* machine." He switched it on. It started, sputtered, and choked.

"Good Lord," the salesman exclaimed. "Look at that poor bag!"

My mother had either forgotten about emptying the bag or perhaps thought it wasn't full enough to need attention.

"Feel it," Mr. Clohissy said, turning pale.

Mother felt it. We all felt it. I couldn't think what to compare it to then, but I can now—a sack of potatoes.

Mr. Clohissy spread newspapers on the floor, onto which he would empty the bag. "Stand back," he commanded. "This bag looks pretty full." He was being kind. The bag looked ready to explode.

As a child I had seen huge dump trucks unload their landslides of sand, gravel, or good black soil, and I was impressed. But not any more impressed than I was by the avalanche of dirt, dust, and debris that poured from the Ohio's bag—feathers, hairpins, buttons, pennies, crumbs of sausage, cheese and crackers, chewing gum and candy wrappers, a tattered holy card, bits and pieces of the parish bulletin, and a shredded Mass schedule.

Mr. Clohissy stared at the pile as Father Hennepin must have stared at Niagara Falls when he discovered it in 1678. "Mrs. Byrnes," he said, the old salesman in him finally taking over, "I'll bet you had no idea how much hidden dirt this machine would pick up around your home."

Without hesitation my mother turned to my father and said, "I really think we should buy it, don't you?"

My father promptly agreed.

The decisions in my family were seldom fast—nothing like Farragut's at Mobile Bay. Considering my upbringing, if I had been in the Admiral's boots, I would have shot off the following message to all members, including Uncle Dan (this would certainly have been one for the monsignor):

TORPEDOES DEAD AHEAD. SHALL I CHANCE IT—OR WHAT? TALK IT OVER AND GET BACK TO ME AT YOUR EARLIEST. LOVE TO ALL. ADMIRAL BYRNES.

Not the best way to conduct a naval engagement, you say? But let me tell you something. If my family had been running things back then, we would probably never have gotten around to a Civil War in the first place.

How Father Sullivan Saved St. Patrick's Day

Recently I came across some statistics on the increasing incidence of U.S. families dining out. If my mother had ever seen them, her final moments would have been much less serene than they were. By 1990, according to the figures, nearly half of our food dollars will be spent away from home.

Mother would have taken such a trend as a personal affront, a wanton revolt against "Mom's home cooking," and evidence of the kind of moral decay that led to the fall of the Roman Empire. Had the dining-out trend in *my* family ever been plotted, the chart line, except for a few little bumps, would have remained as flat as a tennis court base line.

I grew up in a time when only in religion could you find anything more sacred than home cooking. Few distinctions were more treasured by a homemaker of those days than to be known as a good cook. Her kitchen was a culinary sanctuary, and she was its high priestess. The odors and vapors that rose from the assorted pots on her stove or exploded like a divine revelation when the oven door was opened were the domestic incense with which she blessed her family's togetherness. In our home the final benediction came when my father, with freshly honed carving knife in hand and all of us watching, sliced a medallion from the top of a sizzling roast and declared rapturously, "Mae, it's *just right!*" It was enough to keep my mother smiling for days.

In this hallowed atmosphere of home cookery, going out to eat was like going to the zoo on Sunday morning instead of to Mass.

For one thing, Mother considered restaurants an extravagance; seldom did she read a menu without clucking disapprovingly over the prices. She also felt there were serious risks involved:

"Those people in the kitchen are perfect strangers to us," she'd say. "How do we know how carefully they wash the tableware—or, for that matter, their hands?"

Of equal concern was the question of whether the breads, rolls, pies, pastries, and cakes were homemade. If they were, Mother found it easier to relax. If not, she went through her meal slowly, cautiously, like a minesweeper moving through enemy waters. It was bad enough having your food prepared by "perfect strangers" in a kitchen only a few feet away, but to her those unknowns who cooked it in big, impersonal factories, located "only God knows where," might as well have been unfriendly Martians.

The Abramsons, who lived across the street, went out for dinner "all the time," as Mother put it (actually a couple of times a month). The conclusion was that Mrs. Abramson was a poor cook or simply didn't give a collapsed soufflé for the needs of her family.

"Look at that poor man," my mother would say. "Thin as a rail. What he needs is more good home cooking."

According to Dad, my mother firmly believed that when our Lord enjoined Peter to "feed my lambs," He was really looking over the apostle's shoulder directly at *her*.

Oh, to be sure, we went out, but only for very special occasions and only after my father, with great difficulty, convinced my mother that it was not because we were tired of her cooking but because she deserved a rest.

We went out whenever my great-aunt Kate made one of her rare visits, but only because when we visited her in Racine, Wisconsin, she took us to dinner at the Racine Hotel. We went out the day my parents bought their first car, an Overland. We went out the day Grandpa retired from his job as a boiler inspector for the city of Chicago.

And one memorable St. Patrick's Day that fell on a Sunday, my parents and grandparents and I went out for corned beef and cabbage with Father Patrick Sullivan, our pastor, and his widowed sister, Mary Kate Corbett, who kept house for him.

The decision to go out was not easily made. First, there was my mother insisting that we have the corned beef and cabbage at *her* table. Then there was my grandmother insisting it be served at *her* table upstairs. Then there was Dad, sensing an unpleasant argument ahead over who should have the privilege of "cooking for Father," suggesting, "Let's all go *out* for dinner."

Both my mother and grandmother stopped contending long enough to agree that Dad's idea was preposterous.

"On Saint Patrick's Day?" my mother exclaimed. The idea was not only preposterous; it was sacrilegious.

"How can we be sure of getting corned beef and cabbage?" my grandmother wanted to know.

"And even if we do," my mother chimed in, "the meat will probably be tough as nails. Corned beef has to be cooked *just right!*"

Grandma nodded her head, as if only the two of them in the whole world knew how to cook corned beef.

After this brief meeting of the minds, the tug-of-war between upstairs and downstairs resumed.

At last my exasperated father put his foot down. "Look," he said, "we're getting nowhere and here it is Saturday already. Can't you see? This is a very special occasion. We're honoring Saint Patrick *and* Father Sullivan; it's his feast day, too, remember."

At last it was settled. I think my mother and grandmother were relieved to have the argument over with, even though each by now had a fine brisket of corned beef in her ice box. (We continued honoring St. Patrick and Father Sullivan well into the next week.)

Our pastor rode with my parents and me in our Overland. Mary Kate rode with my grandparents in their Model T. Our destination was the Parkview, a graciously aging *grande dame* of a hotel, built at a time when our corner of Chicago had been expected to reach its cultural maturity a lot sooner than it did. My parents had eaten there once before I was born and before Mother had had time to rack up her impressive record as a cook. My father, who said he still fondly remembered the occasion, was sure the Parkview would have corned beef and cabbage if anyone did. Did he make a reservation? my mother asked. No, he forgot. But the dining room was so large there'd be plenty of room.

We parked the two cars, closed ranks, and pressed on through the Parkview's huge gilt-bronze doors. We crossed the spacious lobby and continued down a long avenue of potted palms toward the dining room. At its entrance was a sign. It said the room was closed for remodeling and would reopen June first.

After a stunned silence, Father Sullivan observed, "That's a long time to wait—even for corned beef and cabbage."

We about-faced and walked out.

"If we'd eat out oftener," my father grumbled, "we'd know what's going on in the neighborhood."

"Don't worry," Father Sullivan assured him, "we'll think of another place."

He paused before getting into the car. "Since this outing is in honor of my patron saint, I'll ask *him* where he'd like us to go." He winked at me and closed his eyes with an exaggerated look of concentration. "Saint Patrick says, 'Try the Pickwick.' "

The Pickwick was another, though smaller, hotel on the other side of the parish. Father recalled that the Holy Name Society had once held a dinner-dance there a few years back.

The rest of us stayed in the cars while my father went into the hotel to make sure corned beef and cabbage were on its menu. The grim look on his face when he returned told it all. No corned beef and cabbage. "In fact," my father sputtered, "I'll bet they've never even heard of Saint Patrick!"

"I'll try my patron again," said Father Sullivan, refusing

to be discouraged. He winked and closed his eyes once more.

Almost immediately, his sister, Mary Kate, called from the other car, "I seem to remember a place named Sweeney's." She said she had had a lovely dinner there some time ago and thought it was up on Stony Island Avenue, "somewhere between Sixty-third and Sixty-seventh."

"Well now, doesn't a name like that sound promising?" said Father Sullivan. I was sure that this time he was being answered.

Our caravan crossed the parish once more and began a slow cruise up and down Stony Island Avenue.

"I'm so hungry," my father said at one point, "I think I'd settle for a peanut butter sandwich."

But not at Sweeney's. Sweeney's was nowhere to be found.

We parked to regroup. A streetcar conductor on his way to work walked by, and my father asked him if he knew where Sweeney's Restaurant was. The conductor said the only Sweeney's he ever heard of was in South Bend, Indiana, where his wife's folks lived. We held another council beside the Model T.

I think it was Grandma who noticed it first. "Merciful heavens!" she exclaimed. "*There's* a restaurant!" She pointed to a building a few doors up the street.

At first glance it looked like a scaled-down medieval fortress, but it was a restaurant, all right. A sign on top said so—Ristorante Lucia.

We looked at the sign, then at each other. A big question hung in the air: Corned beef and cabbage? For me there was a second question: What kind of game is St. Patrick playing?

We checked a copy of Ristorante Lucia's menu that was fixed to the door. No corned beef and cabbage. The frustration and the mounting hunger were evident on everyone's face—except Father Sullivan's. Determined to keep our spirits up, he snapped his fingers and said, "I think I see what Saint Patrick is getting at." His face had the private smile of a storyteller who has just thought of the perfect ending for a long, tall tale.

"It has something to do with the Communion of Saints," he continued. "In this case, communion between the saints themselves. I see Saint Patrick having a chat with Saint Joseph, whose feast is the day after tomorrow, and Saint Joseph says, 'Patrick, if I weren't a saint, I'd be envious of you. The whole world goes bang on your feast day. Shamrocks everywhere. Carnations are stained green. So are rivers and, in some places, beer. But as for me, I rely mostly on the Italians for the big celebrations, and I must say, they've been wonderful. But would it disturb you if more of *your* friends remembered me with the same enthusiasm they remember you?'

"And Saint Patrick replies, 'I'll get to work on it right away.'

"And he did. And so here we are, exactly where he wants us to be!"

We laughed and applauded. Thanks to our guest of honor, we were going to have a good time after all.

"Inside, then," said Father Sullivan, "for a fine Italian dinner in honor of Saint Joseph!"

Later that evening, Mother said, "We must go back there again soon."

I know why she said it. Everything—the antipasto, the minestrone, the pasta, the sauces, the zabaglione—all of it was homemade!

II. FULL STRIDE

The Great Pony Raffle

Whenever someone asked me during my early childhood years, "Where do you live?" I would answer promptly, "St. Lawrence's parish." A few years later, when we moved from the south to the north side of Chicago, my answer to that question was just as unfailingly, "Our Lady of Lourdes." I might mention my street address later but only as an afterthought.

For me and for most Catholics of those days, the parish was the primal homeland. Loyalty to it came as naturally as loyalty to our families and their traditions—and at no time was that loyalty more exuberantly manifest than at the parish bazaar. We would as soon have missed our Easter Duty as one of those great annual reunions, where needed funds were raised and parish spirit was renewed.

My parents, however, had an equally strong attachment to another parish, St. Sebastian's, just a few miles away. The reason: my father's brother, Uncle Ed, was its pastor.

Rarely did we miss any of St. Sebastian's major activities—First Communions, Confirmations, and eighth-grade graduations—and we *never* missed its bazaars. In fact, every year my father and I helped set up the booths in the schoolyard, hang decorations, and string lights. In time we got to know Uncle Ed's congregation almost as well as we knew our own.

Two of his parishioners in particular stand out in my memory, simply because they stood out so noticeably in the parish itself—Michael Dolan, who was a prosperous furniture dealer in the neighborhood, and Paddy O'Dwyer, who owned a livery stable near the bridle paths of Lincoln Park.

The two men had been born in the same county in Ireland. Their coming to the New World may have put the Atlantic Ocean between themselves and their native heaths,

but a brooding rivalry, spawned in some ancient family dis-
pute and perpetuated in political controversy and the great
hurling matches of their youth, had also booked passage to
America. It settled down with them in St. Sebastian's parish
and became as permanent a feature of the neighborhood as
the Clark Street car line. As Uncle Ed, who had known them
in Ireland, once said, "They probably couldn't live without
it."

My uncle's attitude became less tolerant, however, when
Sister Veronica, superior of his grade school, complained that
the contentiousness of Dolan and O'Dwyer was becoming
more and more strongly reflected in the behavior of their
numerous offspring.

"Some days," she said, "I feel that I'm caught up in the
old feud between the Hatfields and the McCoys. I shudder to
think what it could lead to as they grow older."

Conferences with the parents helped—but only for short
periods. A more enduring solution was needed, and, as Sister
Veronica felt, it would have to begin with the children—
something healing and of mutual interest to both factions.

"That's what I pray for daily," she told Uncle Ed.

I don't think even Sister Veronica dreamed that a parish
bazaar would provide the answer.

Each year's event gave Dolan and O'Dwyer a highly visible arena for their incompatability. They became fiercely
competitive in their efforts to raise raffle money for their
church.

For a long time Dolan, the furniture man, maintained an
edge. His generosity in donating raffle prizes was impressive—one year a pair of end tables, the next a china cabinet,
followed by an easy chair with ottoman.

What O'Dwyer's efforts lacked in variety they made up
for in personal involvement. He supplied a pony from his
livery stable and gave pony rides; that is, he charged ten
cents for a circuit of the schoolyard with himself or one of

his stable boys at the pony's head and turned all proceeds over to the parish.

He began with one pony. Later, he supplied two, then three ponies and more stable hands. He dressed his animals in ever more elaborate saddles, blankets, bridles, and pompoms. He eventually upped the price to fifteen cents.

One year he added music. Near the fence rail where he tied his ponies between rides, he set up a gramophone, which he had to wind and rewind to keep going. Over and over it played a four-piece repertory of "Camp Town Races," "Pony Boy," "The Old Grey Mare," and "Dapple Gray"— tunes that O'Dwyer felt would stir the blood and open the pocketbooks of all true horse and pony lovers.

After a few hours of this, Dolan suggested he shut the "racket" off or buy some new records; people were getting tired of the repetition. To this O'Dwyer replied, "What's wrong with repetition? Do we change the numbers on the bingo wheel?"

Still, when each bazaar was over and the proceeds were counted, it appeared that Dolan's donation had inspired the most profitable response.

Then one year, the year that Dolan provided a magnificent library table with its own lamp, O'Dwyer had what he called "an inspiration from above." He would not only offer pony rides for this bazaar, he would donate one of his ponies *to be raffled off!*

The bazaar committee, including Uncle Ed, thanked him profusely but insisted the idea was impractical. In this modest neighborhood, made up, for the most part, of small homes, smaller yards, and one-car garages, who in his right mind would buy chances on a *pony?* Where in the world would the winner *keep* it?

O'Dwyer was ready with the answer. "If he doesn't have room for it himself, he can keep it in my livery stable—one year's board free!" Who could resist such a generous offer?

And so in the end O'Dwyer won out. "It'll be a glorious success," he promised.

And he was right.

The novelty of the idea attracted and intrigued. Advance publicity also helped. Well before the bazaar, one of the more enterprising committee members sent notice of the raffle to the neighborhood and diocesan newspapers. Both ran the story, which included a statement from O'Dwyer that "every child should have a pony."

Not only parishioners but people from all over the area apparently agreed. Never before had a St. Sebastian bazaar enjoyed such attendance.

From the outset it was obvious to everyone—including the flabbergasted Dolan—that the pony was a hit. "Absolute nonsense!" the furniture man maintained. He vowed he would not even go *near* the animal, much less buy chances on it. (His children, I learned later, felt otherwise.)

O'Dwyer, the born promoter, set up card tables and chairs near his pony station. He reasoned that if people are comfortable when writing their names on tickets, the more tickets they'll buy. He was right again.

I was *very* comfortable writing in *my* name. My father had advanced me two weeks of my weekly allowance to spend as I wished. I spent it all on the pony.

Even though my parents pointed out that we really had no room for the animal (and O'Dwyer's stable was several miles away from our house), I continued to picture myself galloping through our neighborhood streets with all the Wild West bravado of William S. Hart "heading 'em off at the pass."

Once I saw Uncle Ed writing away at one of O'Dwyer's tables.

"Are *you* trying to win the pony?" I asked incredulously.

"Lord, no," he laughed. "I'm writing in the name of a dear friend of mine."

More than that he wouldn't tell me. But he didn't have to. I knew his "dear friend" had to be his dear nephew.

The popularity of the pony raffle continued to grow

throughout Saturday afternoon and evening. Although Dolan threw in a pair of bookends and a volume of *Irish Folklore* between them, the pony continued to run the legs off the library table.

At last, well into Sunday evening, Uncle Ed announced that the drawings for the major prizes would now be held. Father Michaels, the assistant pastor, would be in charge. Father took up his post on top of a large picnic table in the center of the yard. I stayed next to my uncle and parents on the edge of the crowd.

The depository boxes were brought up to the table. Two men from the bazaar committee made an impressive show of shaking each of them to insure a thorough mix of tickets. The first box was then opened slightly and handed up to Father Michaels.

"This drawing," he announced in his Sunday-best voice, "is for the girl's bicycle so generously donated by our dear friends at Emerson's Hardware!"

A great cheer rose from the yard. "God bless the Emersons!" an elderly woman behind me said.

Assuring the crowd that his eyes were closed tight, and to the good-natured cries of "No peeking, Father!" the priest plunged a hand into the box.

What a showman he was! I remember him still, standing there with the winning ticket in his hand, pausing after saying, "The winner is—," pretending he was having trouble making out the name, then finally bellowing, "Katie Muldoon!"

The crowd roared its approval. What matter that Katie Muldoon was eighty-six years old? She had been president of the Altar and Rosary Society three times; no one could launder an altar cloth more beautifully than she. "God bless Katie," said the woman behind me. "It's high time she got some recognition."

And so it went through the roll call of prizes won—a coaster wagon, framed paintings, towels, linens, roasting pans, chinaware, radios, a rocking horse—each gift seeming to take on a special luminescence as if reflecting its donor's generosity.

"And now," said Father Michaels at last, "who will win the magnificent library table donated by that great and good parishioner, Mike Dolan?"

In the past, the drawing for Dolan's offering had been the climax of each bazaar. But not this time. Grim-faced, the "great and good parishioner" looked as he might have years ago in Ireland watching O'Dwyer send the hurling ball whistling past him toward the goal posts.

The winner of the library table was a pretty young woman who ran up to Dolan and kissed him on the cheek. He softened noticeably. I always thought he was a good man at heart.

"And now," said Father Michaels, "the drawing for the grand prize—a live Shetland pony, generously donated by the one and only Paddy O'Dwyer!"

The applause was deafening. My heart was beating like a jackhammer. I glanced at Uncle Ed, still beside me. His expression was noncommittal. He's waiting for my name to be announced, I told myself.

Now Father Michaels was clearing his throat once more. "The winner is—" he began. Then came the climactic bellow—"Michael Dolan!"

In the hurricane of shouts, applause, and laughter, I heard Dolan loudly protesting, "But I never even bought a chance on that nag!"

Uncle Ed's expression was still serenely noncommittal. Why, I wondered, doesn't he look more disappointed that I was not the winner?

"Someone else must've written my name in!" Dolan howled. "It's a low-down Irish trick!"

Soon Dolan was pushed forward to accept ownership of the pony from O'Dwyer. The two men stood glaring at each other. Here was a development that neither had anticipated.

The look on Dolan's face said, "The day I have to accept something from *you*—*!*"

The look on O'Dwyer's face said, "The day I have to turn something over to *you—!*"

For a tense moment it seemed that Dolan was about to refuse his prize, but his children were already clamoring around him, shouting, "We won the pony!"

"What'll I do with it?" their father asked in an agony of indecision.

"Keep it at the livery stable!" Uncle Ed advised. "Your children will bless you for it!"

The Dolan children blessed their father immediately.

"We'll keep it at the livery stable!" they echoed.

Dolan's wife kissed him and cried, "How wonderful for the children!"

The two rivals looked at each other once more—the kind of look that brings all memories of the past into proper focus. Then a sense of the ludicrousness of their old and tired angers—of the foolish rivalry that had kept their relationship on edge for so many years—burst over O'Dwyer like a wave of the Irish Sea. He began to laugh. "Every furniture man should have a pony!" he roared. The crowd responded with approving cries and whistles. He gave Dolan a peacemaking punch on the shoulder. He laughed until he doubled up. I always knew O'Dwyer was a good man at heart.

Dolan at last began to laugh too. "Me, of all people!" he gasped. He returned O'Dwyer's punch and extended his hand. They were both good men at heart.

"God bless Michael Dolan and Paddy O'Dwyer," said the woman behind me.

"Amen," said Uncle Ed.

Weeks later, we learned from my uncle that all was now peaceful between the Dolans and the O'Dwyers. The Dolan children went regularly to the livery stable, where the O'Dwyer children taught them how to ride. They spent many an afternoon together on the bridle paths of Lincoln Park.

Who had written Dolan's name on the winning ticket?

One of his own children, most likely. Maybe his wife or an anonymous friend. Maybe Uncle Ed?

Who cared? Not Sister Veronica. She knew her prayers had been answered—how, it didn't matter. "There are so many beautiful mysteries in the Church," she is reported to have said. "Surely there's room for one more."

As for me, what could I have done with the pony anyway? It wasn't even a member of our parish.

When My Father Worked on Sunday

One of the earliest and most delightful discoveries of my childhood was how strikingly different Sundays were from other days of the week—a difference, I'm afraid, that has eroded substantially over the years.

On a Sunday in those days all stores were closed except Rauschert's Drug Store, Mrs. Thorne's Delicatessen, and Kimberley's Ice Cream Parlor. The milkman, the mailman, the ice man, the "rags-ol'-iron" man, and the scissors grinder never appeared—only the balloon man and the organ grinder with his monkey. On Sunday the very air was different—more luminous, more serene. The sunrise seemed less peremptory in its command to be up and going. Even in the matter of getting to Mass on time, it wasn't the sun that prodded you—it was your father.

In short, Sunday was a day of rest. And it was that way always.

Well, almost.

One evening in the middle of my seventh summer we received the second of two telephone calls in a month from my father's younger brother, my uncle Dan.

The first call had been to tell us that Uncle Dan, a priest, had just been assigned his first pastorate, St. Mary's, in a small but growing rural community about a two-and-a-half-hour drive north of where we lived in Chicago.

The second was to say that he had moved in a couple of days ago, and would we like to drive up and visit him the following Saturday?

"Wouldn't Sunday be more convenient?" my father asked.

"No, Tom, Saturday will be fine."

Before he hung up, however, Uncle Dan said, "Oh, by the way, Tom, bring a hammer and saw if you can."

"What for?" asked my father reasonably enough.

"Oh, that's right," said Uncle Dan with feigned absent-mindedness that didn't fool my father one bit. "I forgot to tell you. I'm building a garage."

"*You're* building it!" My father laughed. "Dan, you never drove a nail in your life."

"Oh, I hired a carpenter to do the actual work," Uncle Dan replied, "but can you believe it, just before he fin-ished—*just* before—he sprained his back. Of course, I *could* look around for another carpenter, but they're all so busy right now."

"Save your money," said my father. "We'll be glad to help."

"God bless you," said Uncle Dan. The way Uncle Dan said, "God bless you," you felt that all nine choirs of angels were fanning you with their wings. "See you Saturday, then."

"Hold on a minute," my father said, suddenly aware that he was in the middle of a mystery story without having read the preceding pages. "Are you telling me the parish has no garage at all?"

"Old Father Cudahy never drove," said Uncle Dan. "All we have is a wagon shed that's ready to fall down."

"But you don't drive either," my father remembered, still working his way back through the mystery.

"Oh, didn't I tell you?" said Uncle Dan. "I just got a Model T. I had to, Tom. This parish is *growing.*"

"All right," my father sighed. "We'll be there bright and early Saturday morning."

Just my father and I made the trip. Convinced that no car—especially our old Overland—was ever meant to survive two and a half hours of steady driving, my mother used my sister's bronchitis as an excuse to stay home.

St. Mary's was a scene that might have set the ghost of Oliver Goldsmith dreaming again of his "Sweet Auburn, loveliest village of the plain"—the old stone church with its four-square belfry set far back from the dusty, elm-lined road; the crosses of the parish graveyard in its shade on one side waiting for another Grey to meditate among them at twilight; on the other side, the rectory, a contented-looking country house with a wide, lazy veranda. All around were the homes of the town on their broad, spacious lawns but with here and there a new construction crowding in.

Well behind the rectory was the garage—that is, what was *going* to be the garage. As it stood now, just big enough for one car, only its frame was in place. A new Model T coupe waited patiently under an apple tree.

In the presence of any but his priestly brother, my father's reaction would have been far more explosive than it was. "Holy Saint Patrick," said he with admirable restraint, "I thought you told me it was almost finished!"

"Surely," said Uncle Dan undaunted, "the worst is over. All that's missing is the siding and roof." He added, "The lumber's in the wagon shed," as if getting the lumber had been a stroke of genius.

Cooling down with a visible effort, my father said grimly, "This will take at least two full days. Can you put us up for the night?"

"Of course I can put you up," said Uncle Dan. "But I wouldn't expect you to work on Sunday."

"Oh, wouldn't you," said my father. "Let's say I'm the fellow in the Bible who had to pull his ox out of the pit on the Sabbath."

"His sheep," Uncle Dan corrected him. "Saint Matthew. But I see your point. It's necessary work—for the good of the parish."

"All right then. Today *and* Sunday."

"After Mass," said Uncle Dan.

One of the more dubious legacies left by old Father Cudahy, the previous pastor—who died, Uncle Dan said, from too much tramping around the parish on foot—was Ellie Moran. Ellie, whose age could have been sixty or eighty, depending on how well her hair stayed up, had the compact, no-nonsense look of a pious aspiration. She had been Father Cudahy's housekeeper and cook, she said, "for ages and ages." At his death she had announced that she would retire simply because "there'll never be another Father Cudahy."

Only after an extended talk with Uncle Dan, in which it was disclosed that Ellie's mother had been born in County Tipperary, home of the Byrnes family, did Ellie consent to stay on—"at least until you're over the hump," as she put it. She was heard to observe later to a friend, "Maybe it won't be too bad working for a Tipperary man."

Tipperary man or not, Uncle Dan soon had his problems with Ellie. Right off, she told him she knew that the ghost of dear Father Cudahy still roamed the house "just to keep an eye on things." In other words, no changes in the daily routine.

Once she wanted to know why Uncle Dan had to spend so much time preparing his Sunday sermon. Father Cudahy could lift you right out of the pew with a sermon he put together between the sacristy and the main altar. "No notes either," she said. "All right out of his head."

Father Cudahy never had anything but buttered toast and tea for breakfast. Uncle Dan wanted something more substantial, like bacon and eggs. "I suppose I can manage," Ellie finally agreed with a sigh.

Father Cudahy was dead set against the automobile—too noisy, too dangerous. "How did he make his sick calls or get around to see his parishoners?" asked Uncle Dan.

"They came and got him—or he walked."

"I'm afraid I'll be moving a little faster than that," said my uncle.

"Father Cudahy always said St. Paul never had a car and look how far *he* traveled."

But it wasn't until Sunday morning when Ellie spotted my father, after Mass, preparing to nail on more siding that we learned of another—and the most inflexible—of Father Cudahy's rules of order: no work on Sunday.

"But this is God's work," Uncle Dan explained.

"Not if it makes you perspire," said Ellie, seeing my father wipe his brow. "Father Cudahy always said if the work makes you sweat then it's profane."

Just at that moment my father hoisted several boards to his shoulder. Ellie looked at Uncle Dan sternly. "You know what the prophet Jeremiah said—'Bear no burden on the Sabbath Day!' "

"I wish," said Uncle Dan, his patience about exhausted, "you'd spend more time reading the *New* Testament."

That was a mistake. No one, not even a man from Tipperary, could question Ellie's choice of Biblical passages. She turned on her heels and stomped into the rectory.

Early that afternoon, after locking herself in her room for an hour, Ellie gave notice. "Go on with your work," she said icily. "I'm going to pack." Nothing Uncle Dan could say, including several more quotes from the New Testament, could change her mind.

Ellie's packing took a surprisingly long time. Three walls of the garage were finished and she was still at it. As board after board went up—Uncle Dan and I holding, Dad hammering—we would catch brief glimpses of her face at a rectory window. But the minute our eyes met, the face would be gone.

At last, late in the afternoon, the garage was "closed in," as my father said, "against the weather." The great moment had come to put the Model T in its stall.

"Want to be part of this great adventure, Junior?" Uncle

Dan asked me—the same question Columbus might have put to some dockside hanger-on at the start of his voyage to the New World. I climbed up on the seat beside him.

After a series of sudden leaps, back-ups, stalls, and re-starts, the Model T was finally lined up with the garage door.

"Plenty of room on this side," my father called from just beyond the right fender.

With his head out the driver's window to make sure he had plenty of room on that side, Uncle Dan began working the Model T's three pedals. "Let's see now," he kept saying, "let's see now." The car lurched forward. He worked the pedals again. The car gained speed.

"Slow down!" my father yelled, backing away.

The rear wall of the garage came toward us like a tidal wave. As a last, desperate maneuver, Uncle Dan blew the horn. To no avail. With a splintering crash the wall parted like the waters of the Red Sea. The engine sputtered out. We suddenly found ourselves motionless with an unobstructed view ahead of the parish graveyard.

Shaken but unhurt, Uncle Dan and I crawled out. The front fenders of the Model T drooped like the wings of a wounded seagull. I thought my father would explode—which he did but, amazingly, in a storm of laughter. "If you could have seen yourselves!" Furious with himself, Uncle Dan at first aired out some of the darker corners of his vocabulary; then when my father cried, "Thank God you had sense enough to blow the horn!" he broke into roars of laughter. "I guess," he managed at last, "there's nothing that can't be fixed. I'll look around for a carpenter tomorrow."

I happened to glance at the rectory. There in a window was Ellie—smiling, triumphant, vindicated. The Lord had spoken. He had punished the stiff-necked for their transgression. All was now right with Ellie's world.

With the air of one who knows what it's like to be on the side of the angels, Ellie came down and announced she would stay on a little longer—"till you're over the hump."

That evening at dinner, a plenteous feast of corned beef and cabbage—which, my father noted, Ellie must have had cooking even while she packed—Uncle Dan asked her if she knew of a good carpenter.

"Indeed I do," she replied airily. "Mrs. Conerty's nephew—she's the president of the Altar and Rosary Society, you'll remember—and he's the best there is."

She helped us to another serving and turned to leave the room. At the door she paused. "There's only one thing," she said firmly.

"What's that, Ellie?" asked Uncle Dan.

"He doesn't work on Sunday."

My First Communion Day

When I was a youngster, the occasion that drew the most members of my family together at one time was a First Communion. More so than a religious feast or a national holiday, a seven-year-old's introduction to the mystery of the Eucharist called for a total mustering of the clan.

Moreover, at no other time were you so exclusively the object of so much loving attention, except, perhaps, the day you were born. But even then, strictly speaking, you shared the honors with someone else—your mother. True, each subsequent birthday was also a cause for a celebration, its size depending on how much advance publicity you had spread around. Unfortunately, your more distant relatives tended to forget the date unless your mother arranged a party for you.

Christmas and Easter were great family days, too. These, however, were everybody's days (one of the reasons they *were* so great, as you'd understand later), but for now you rejoiced that First Communion Day was all yours.

And, you felt, deservedly so. Consider what you had just been through.

There was the period of intense pre-Communion instruction in the second-grade boys' class of Sister Mary Judith. Sister had been preparing boys for their First Communion for many years. To us kids she seemed quite old. Her First Communicants by now must seem quite old, too, but I'm sure that what she taught them is still as fresh in their minds as it is in mine.

It had to be fresh in *everyone's* mind that Friday afternoon before First Communion Sunday when Father Shay, our assistant pastor, conducted the oral examination. He sat at a card table just outside the open door of the classroom. One by one, thirty boys went out to be questioned, each convinced that unless he got the answers right he might *never* reach the altar rail.

"Now then," said Father Shay, his round face glowing with encouragement, "let's see how well you know the Act of Contrition. 'Oh, my God—' " he prompted.

"Oh, my God, I am heartily sorry for having offended Thee, and I detest all my sins because I dread the loss of Heaven and the pains—"

"Very good, that'll do. I can *see* you know the rest. Tell me now, who is it you'll be receiving for the first time next Sunday? Our blessed—?"

"Our blessed Lord, Father."

"Under the appearance of bread and wine. Good. And how long must you fast? From midnight Saturday till after—?"

"Till after First Communion, Father."

"Not even a drink of water, eh?"

"Not even a drink of water, Father."

"Excellent! Excellent!"

Meanwhile Sister Mary Judith nervously paced the aisles between the desks. She was lucky; she could move around. We kids had to sit as still as clams.

At last Father Shay came into the room. "All finished, Sister," he called out heartily. "What a fine group you have this year. My congratulations!"

It was probably the same thing he said every year, the same thing he had said to the girls the day before, but Sister Mary Judith beamed as if hearing it for the first time.

"This is one of the best classes I've ever examined," Father Shay continued, "and, Sister, as a reward for their fine work, perhaps these children could be dismissed fifteen minutes earlier today."

Hurray for Father Shay! He had a good heart. But now, after he had blessed us and left, Sister Mary Judith had the thankless duty of reminding us that since some of us were being met by our mothers at the regular dismissal time, she couldn't possibly turn us loose until the bell rang. "But," she added brightly, "I'll read you a story."

Those of us trusted with finding our own way home groaned. No story in the world could make up for the loss of fifteen minutes of unexpected freedom. Sister Mary Judith, however, ignored us. Her book of Bible stories was already in her hands. So with an effort at resignation we settled back to listen, as I recall, to the old tale of how Joseph had been sold into bondage by his brothers.

But it was the fast that worried us most—that worried everybody most, especially my parents and grandparents.

How could "poor Junior"—after all those years of waking every morning to the aroma of food cooking in the kitchen, after all those hearty breakfasts of milk, orange juice, grapefruit or cantaloupe, of oatmeal, French toast, or scrambled eggs—how could he, poor child, wash and dress and sit through the heat of that long ceremony on an empty stomach?

Many were the family horror stories of children who hadn't quite made it. My Aunt Addie for instance: "I fainted dead away, and it took so long to revive me that I almost missed my First Communion—almost *missed* it—all because of an empty stomach."

The worst thing that could happen to you in my family was to have an empty stomach. It was considered a reflection on the women's cooking skills—which were considerable—and the men's ability to provide. This was also a time when "cleaning your plate" was mandatory; when the fatter children were the better; when a skinny kid signified a mother who didn't like to cook; when (before homogenization) mothers would change dairies for the sake of a deeper cream line. Tell my mother, Grandma, or Aunt Addie that you were hungry and the battle against the empty stomach was promptly rejoined. They went for their utensils as resolutely as Joan of Arc reached for her sword at Orleans.

As Saturday evening approached, the strategies for getting me safely through the fast multiplied like the loaves and fishes. My mother advised my father to give me much more than my customary serving—"to carry him through," as she said.

I rose manfully to the challenge and, as always, cleaned my plate.

Grandma came down from upstairs and said I should be allowed to stay up a little later than usual and fed again before going to bed. Father promised he would wake me up again just before midnight for some cookies and milk.

Neither of these proposals materialized, however, because with my stomach so full I fell sound asleep even *before* my regular bedtime, and my father, who went to bed at 9:30, didn't wake up until dawn.

He was furious with himself. "Hang it all, I slept right through. How do you feel?" he asked me anxiously.

I felt fine. A touch hungry, perhaps, but fine.

My mother brushed my blue serge suit and straightened my tie for the fourth or fifth time. "You'll be all *right,*" she assured me, more for her own comfort than mine.

Grandma appeared and held the back of her hand to my forehead. "He seems a little flushed," she said to my mother.

"He'll be just fine," said my mother.

Grandma took me aside. "Here," she said as she slipped a small, flat parcel into one of my coat pockets.

"What is it, Grandma?"

"A molasses cookie. I made some last night."

"But I can't break my fast!" I protested.

"Of course not," she answered. "You won't have to. But just knowing the cookie is *there* will keep you going. You can eat it right afterwards."

All First Communicants were to report to the school forty-five minutes before Mass so the sisters could check the boys' shoe shines and ties and the girls' veils and coronas of lilies of the valley. We would then process to the church, which was next door.

I had expected to walk to school as I did every day, but my father announced, "I'll drive Junior to school; then I'll come back for the rest of you."

"I can walk," I said.

"Best save your energy," my father replied. "Come now."

"Corpus Domini nostri Jesu Christi custodiat animam tuam in vitam aeternam. Amen."

You heard the words coming closer and closer as the priest moved down the altar rail from kneeling child to kneeling child. You mustn't turn your head to see how near he is. You must wait.

"Corpus Domini nostri . . . "

Suddenly the *corpus* was being offered directly to *you.* You tilted your head back. The last thing you saw before closing your eyes was the host tracing a sign of the cross above the chalice. You opened your mouth, and that strange, new bread—that taste you had never known but would know forever—was resting on your tongue as gently as a prayer.

You marched back to your pew, eyes fixed firmly on the shoes ahead of you. But something was wrong. Your knees went rubbery as you realized that the host was stuck to the roof of your mouth, and you couldn't work it loose with your tongue. You were about to do the unthinkable—free it with a finger—when you recalled Sister Mary Judith's words, "If the host should cling to the roof of your mouth, don't worry. Just let it dissolve."

Afterwards, on the church steps, in a high tide of faces, hugs, pats, and kisses, your grandmother whispered, "You can eat your cookie now."

But you couldn't. "Sister said we should drink some water before we eat anything."

Grandma rolled her eyes heavenward. "Well, I never," she exclaimed. "Come along now," she added quickly. "You must be starving."

Once home, you were promptly fed, of course. Before you dug in, you treated yourself to a moment of self-satisfaction at having survived the fast. But then, so did your fellow Communicants. Holy Mother Church—in her infinite wisdom, as Sister Mary Judith was fond of saying—had probably known all along that you'd make it.

The rooms soon filled with the cheery sounds of arriving relatives, all bearing congratulations and gifts—so many gifts that you wondered what you would do with them all: seven prayer books, five rosaries, three statuettes of the Blessed Mother, two framed pictures of the Sacred Heart, innumerable scapulars, holy cards, and medals.

In time, some of them would disappear, as if by themselves. But others would work their way from the front to the back of dresser drawers to be come upon later, reminding you as you grew older that even on that special day, which you once thought was yours alone, you had shared the honors with someone else.

How Radio Came to Our House

In these days of the "boom box," the VCR, and the home computer, it may be difficult to imagine a time when a youngster's status among the kids of his neighborhood was determined largely by the size and range of his family's radio set. But there *was* such a time, and I remember it well. I remember it because for a while we had no radio at all, and I was hard-pressed to give my friends a reasonable excuse.

"How come you still don't have a radio?" I'd be asked several times a week. Everyone had a radio or was planning to get one. Radio was the miracle of the age.

"My father knows there's a new one coming out soon," I'd lie, "with better reception than *you* guys get."

"Oh yeah?"

"Yeah!"

How could I make them understand something I scarcely understood myself—that my father was reluctant to buy anything new if it involved a shift in loyalty from something similar that we already had? The old hand-pushed lawn mower, the vacuum cleaner, the washing machine, the family car—his fondness for these old friends grew in geometric proportion to their age. Though some of them were in the last stages of mechanical senility, he would no more abandon them for newer models than his Irish farmer ancestors would have abandoned an old hired hand who had served them faithfully and well for most of his life.

Needless to say, my mother did not always share these tender feelings for inanimate objects. She felt they were there for only one reason—to make life more enjoyable. When they failed in that function, she saw no excuse for keeping them around.

My father's sentimental attachment to old possessions also included our ancient Victrola. Hadn't the Victrola given him some of the most delightful evenings of his life? The voice of famed Irish tenor John McCormack, the songs of Stephen Foster, the marches of John Philip Sousa, certain ballads of the Old West—these and more, he felt, would never be played again if we had a radio.

Early one evening, our neighbors the McCourts invited us over to listen to *their* radio. "It's to be a special program of Irish music," Mrs. McCourt told my mother over the phone. "I thought your husband especially would enjoy it."

Hopeful that this experience might persuade Dad to adopt a friendlier attitude toward the airwaves, Mother happily accepted the invitation. Dad said the McCourts were just doing it to show off, but he finally agreed to go.

The McCourts' radio was recognized as the biggest and best set in our neighborhood. My friend Jamie McCourt had often invited me in to see it—not to listen to it but to stand and look at it. Operating it required special skills that only his engineer father possessed. And his father didn't turn it on just any old time.

Jamie had repeatedly told me that the set was a super-heterodyne. He loved big, chewy words that he could roll around in his mouth like a wad of taffy. "Lycoming" was another, and so was "Dusenberg." Someday, he said, he would own a Dusenberg car with a Lycoming engine.

The McCourts' superheterodyne was a dark, mysterious complex of large and small boxes festooned with knobs, switches, dials, coils, and tubes, topped by a speaker as big as a soup tureen. Its many parts were interconnected by a maze of wires that reminded me of a picture I had once seen of the telephone company's main switchboard.

Several other neighbors had also been invited. Mrs. McCourt seated us in a semicircle facing the radio, which sprawled out across a long living-room table. All faces were bright with anticipation except my father's. His expression was one of lightly veiled skepticism.

Mr. McCourt asked for everyone's attention and gave a

short speech outlining the development of wireless communication. He made frequent reference to such things as circuitry, detectors, audions, vacuum tubes, alternators, and Dr. Lee DeForest. It was clear that Jamie's father liked to chew on big words, too.

At last, after a glance at his watch, our host announced that it was about time for the program to begin. With a warning to us all to be very quiet, he flipped the main switch. A soft, pulsating hum filled the room and quickly swelled to an earsplitting roar—somewhat to the surprise of Mr. McCourt.

"Well now," he said. "Let's see."

He moved to one end of the table and twirled a few knobs and dials. The roar became a series of angry squawks and shrill whistles that would have summoned all the dogs in the neighborhood if the windows had been open.

"A little interference tonight, but don't worry," Mr. McCourt assured us. "This ought to do the trick."

He turned several more knobs and, sure enough, we could make out the sound of someone singing, "Ireland, Mother Ireland." This, however, was soon interrupted by a burst of organ music, and immediately the squawks and whistles took over again.

"Must be a flock of canaries on the antenna," said my father. Mother whispered to him to be quiet.

Someone else suggested that maybe the lead-in wire was flapping against a downspout. In spite of Mr. McCourt's insistence that downspouts had nothing to do with the problem, several of the men went out to have a look. In a moment they reported back that the lead-in wire was clear of all downspouts.

By now beads of perspiration were forming on our host's forehead. It seemed to me that his hands were twirling the knobs indiscriminately. "Damnation!" he exclaimed at one point. My father smiled and winked at my mother. She pretended not to notice.

Mrs. McCourt suggested that this might be a good time to serve the coffee and cake she had prepared. Her husband growled that he didn't want any coffee or cake and continued to work on his superheterodyne while the rest of the grown-ups ate, drank, and exchanged the latest gossip. Jamie and I compared baseball trading cards.

Only as we were preparing to leave were Mr. McCourt's efforts rewarded. "And that," said the loudspeaker, "concludes our concert for this evening."

We lived about a half a block from the McCourts. My father laughed all the way home. He said, "I think I'd rather enjoy Irish music right in our own living room. And what's more," he added, "I can listen to it any time I like, not just when somebody tells me I can."

"But we could buy a set that's less complicated, couldn't we?" my mother asked.

"They're all alike," said my father, the expert.

The last sound I heard before dropping off to sleep that night was John McCormack singing "The Tumbledown Shack in Athlone" on the old Victrola.

We'll *never* get a radio now, I mourned.

Evenings I'd come in for dinner with fresh reports of exciting programs heard by our neighbors. Ed McCoy's mother told Ed to tell me to tell my mother that there was an excellent series of cooking programs being broadcast. "My mom followed a new recipe for beef stew last night," Ed informed me, "and was it ever great!"

When I brought this news home, my father, who was listening, said, "Your mother doesn't need any radio to tell her how to cook beef stew. Her beef stew is the best anywhere."

Kids in my fourth-grade class frequently told of radio programs they had listened to the previous evening—after assuring Sister Mary Bridget that they had finished their homework first. One afternoon, when it was my turn to stay and clean the blackboard, Sister asked me if *I* enjoyed the radio. I had to admit that there was no radio in my house. Well enough acquainted with my parents to know they could easily afford one if they wanted it, Sister asked, "What's the reason, then?"

"My father," I said, and I told her about my parent's feelings on the subject of old versus new.

She laughed—a laugh that had first sounded in the hills of Tipperary not far from where my father was born.

"I had a father like that, too," she smiled. "He'd hang on to an old horse so long that some days I was sure he ought to be carrying the animal instead of the other way around."

Sentiment, she said, was the trouble. The Irish were forever getting their hearts mixed up with their brains. As for my problem, the only answer was prayer—"a lot of good, no-nonsense prayers to a favorite saint asking for help in changing your father's mind about radios." Sister believed that the more specific you were, the easier you made it for the saint to pass on the message.

Ordinarily, the favorite of Sister Mary Bridget's heavenly intermediaries was St. Patrick. But this time, considering that she was in charge of the children's choir, of which I was a member, and that music was the staple of most radio shows, she advised me to try St. Cecelia.

I did—and was immediately amazed at how swiftly some saints respond.

From what I could tell, St. Cecelia got in touch with my friend Ollie Johnson, whose parents had just bought a new radio set. She apparently suggested to Ollie that instead of throwing away his old homemade crystal set, as he intended to do, he offer it to Junior Byrnes, who had no set at all. This would be in exchange for a number of Junior Byrnes's best baseball trading cards and any six of his bull's-eye marbles. To me this offer was all the more miraculous because Ollie wasn't even a Catholic. I wondered if St. Cecelia knew that.

The set, which Ollie's father had made for him a year

earlier, consisted of a wood base about a foot square to which were fastened a tiny quartz crystal and a coil of wire with a sliding wire arm for tuning in the stations. There was no loudspeaker, only earphones. But Ollie assured me I'd be able to hear "as clear as anything" once an antenna was up.

With Ollie's help my father and I erected a crude antenna on our roof and connected it with a lead-in wire to the crystal set, which sat on a dining-room serving table.

I will never forget the thrill of putting on the earphones for the first time and hearing someone named Freddie Fox announce that the next number he would play on his "mighty Wurlitzer" would be "The Battle Hymn of the Republic." Ollie was right; the sound came through "as clear as anything."

Although the set was mine, I had to share it with the rest of the family, particularly my little sister, sometimes with stormy results. The one-person-at-a-time headset was obviously going to be a source of continuing problems, which my father was willing to ignore.

One Sunday afternoon I handed him the earphones. John McCormack was singing live. Dad could hardly believe it. "This is John himself!" he kept repeating, refusing to surrender the headset. "He's actually singing right now!" When the concert was over, my father said, "Take good care of this set, Junior. It's a beautiful instrument."

I knew the signs. Father had already fallen in love with the crystal set. It would be a long time, I thought—and so did my mother—before Dad would let a radio with a speaker take its place.

But St. Cecelia had other ideas. About a month later, after more and more arguments over use of the headset, I was able to bring home the news that a local station had invited the children's choir to give a program of old hymns the following Sunday afternoon. What's more, my classmate John Flynn and I would appear as soloists.

My parents were elated—until my mother, always the more practical of the two, remarked to my father, "*You* can use the earphones for the first half of the program; I'll take them for the second half. If Grandma and Grandpa drop over, they can sit and read the funnies."

My father's expression never changed. Without a word he stood up and left the house. Within an hour he was back—with a proper radio under his arm, not a superheterodyne, to be sure, but an efficient-looking, compact unit that had one switch for turning it on, a dial for tuning, a knob for volume—and a speaker.

My mother kissed him. "We'll invite Grandma and Grandpa," she cried excitedly, "and Aunt Laura and Aunt Addie and—"

"And the McCourts," said Dad.

"And the McCourts."

Sentiment. A heart-over-head feeling for all things near and dear. That's what I liked best about my father.

Knuckles Down and No Fudging

There was a time each year in my schoolboy days when, along with the first daffodils, crocuses, tulips, and lilacs, a springtime bloom of varicolored marbles (or mibs or immies) would appear, devotedly tended by young males on their knees. Every year the crop was the same: glassies, realies, aggies, cat's-eyes, steelies, shooters, and laggers.

Each year the soil conditions had to be the same, too: level patches of bare ground on which shots could be made with a fair expectation of accuracy and where a circular or elliptical "pot" could be clearly etched with finger or stick.

And each year certain ritualistic calls, like the sound of the turtle, were heard in our land: "Knuckles down! No fudging! This is for keeps!"

I haven't heard those calls or seen that harvest in many

years. So far as I can find out, kids don't play marbles anymore, at least not in the pervasive, block-by-block, coast-to-coast way they used to.

Of course, there are many other activities of happy memory that kids don't engage in now. They don't seem to spin tops anymore. I can't imagine why. Was there anything more satisfying, after that buggywhip snap of the arm, than to see your whirling top toe-dance around the sidewalk and, with a few spins left, stay steady on its point after your friends' tops had keeled over from exhaustion?

Nor do you see kids these days walking down the street flipping diabolos in the air. You're not sure what a diabolo is—or was? Then I'll tell you: it was a wooden top shaped like an hourglass. You balanced it on a string stretched between the tips of two sticks, one in each hand. Then you tossed it, spinning, as high as you could and tried to catch it on the string when it came down. You repeated this maneuver as often as possible. If you were good at it, you kept it going all the way from Larsen's Fish Market to Our Lady of Lourdes school. (It would be hard, though, to flip a diabolo while carrying a boom box.)

Have you seen a homemade scooter lately? I haven't. I've seen some store-bought scooters, but in my time these were for kids who took violin or dancing lessons. In those days you "rolled your own," that is, you made it yourself out of a two-by-four (the base), an upended wooden box (to support the handles), and the front and back wheels of a roller skate, one pair at each end. You punched tiny vent holes in the side of a tin can to provide air circulation for a burning candle and nailed the can on the front for a headlight. You set the candle inside the can in a pool of melted wax to hold it steady and prayed for an early nightfall.

On deluxe models a door on the open side of the box turned it into a cabinet or safe, in which you kept an oil can and certain personal treasures. A kid out for a good time might be provisioned with his Boy Scout knife (for playing mumblety-peg), baseball trading cards, rare cigar bands, a top or diabolo or both, castinets of dried or polished beef bones, a kazoo, perhaps, and a sack of marbles—in short, a traveling penny arcade. The harsh racket of the metal roller-skate wheels on the concrete sidewalk, amplified to infinity by the wooden box, told residents as far away as Robey Street that a kid of some importance was on the move.

I'm not sure why the diabolo and top, the castinets, the homemade scooter, and other childhood delights have disappeared, but I think I know why marbles no longer bloom in the spring: the soil today isn't right for them.

Consider the requirements of the game as once practiced. You traced the outline of the pot in the center of a flat, bald area, placed the agreed-on number of marbles per player inside it, and then backed off about six feet and "lagged"—that is, you tossed one of your bigger marbles underhand toward the pot. The object was to get as close to it as possible without going inside it. If your lagger crossed the pot line, you had to wait your turn over again and sometimes forfeit a marble. The kid whose lagger came closest to the pot got the first shot at knocking the other marbles out of it. Any marbles you knocked out you could keep—if you were playing "for keeps." Otherwise, you "divvied up" when the game was over.

It doesn't take a graduate engineer to see that for these delicate maneuvers and a minimum of what the classical physicist calls "rolling resistance," you needed a small, flat parcel of barren ground free of pebbles, stones, weeds, and grass. Where did you find these choice properties? Mostly in two places. One was the well-packed, unpaved parkway in front of the smaller neighborhood store, whose owner didn't mind a bunch of noisy kids out front so long as one or more occasionally came inside to buy a Green River soda or a candy bar. You found them also—or created them—on vacant lots, where a spot could be made suitable by stomping it bare with your feet. (Playgrounds, with few exceptions, were out; they were sodded or paved or topped with gravel. Imagine shooting your prize cat's-eye over a bed of gravel!)

Today most commercial parkways are either paved or planted to grass and flowers. As for the vacant lot, when next we mourn the forced retreat of the bison and other wild animals from once-native habitats, let us shed a tear for another migration that was equally a casualty of civilization's advancing tide—the exodus of city kids from once-vacant lots. There was a time, years ago, when properties in old neighborhoods like mine were vacant, not because buildings had been torn down on them but because none had yet been built on them. And although, as Sister Mary Verissima, our sixth-grade teacher, said, the world was created for the service of all humanity, we kids knew that the vacant lot was created solely for *us*. Now, many building booms later, the vacant lots, for the most part, are gone.

But it is not some packed-earth parkway or lot that I think of whenever my fingers itch to shoot once more for a pot of marbles. It is a patch of ground about seven feet square, partly on a back corner of Our Lady of Lourdes boys' playground but mostly on an adjoining corner of the convent yard. It was partially secluded by lilac bushes—and the soil conditions were ideal.

A large catalpa tree provided constant shade, which kept the ground cool and slightly damp (but not too damp). The main playground was graveled, but the pebbles of this little corner of it had long ago sunk beneath the surface, leaving it smooth and perfect for marble shooting.

And Father Shay had made the whole thing possible. It happened, as I recall, like this.

During one afternoon's recess, some of us boys, following the born marble shooter's springtime instincts, allowed ourselves to be drawn to this pristine spot. Not a weed, not a blade of grass, not a pebble—only the cool, flat earth, a great place for growing periwinkle or shooting marbles.

Meanwhile, near the open window of a second-floor classroom, Father Richard Shay, one of our assistant pastors and a great favorite with us kids, was chatting with Sister Mary Veronica (fourth-grade girls). Suddenly, an old, familiar sound, a sound that had once brought great joy to his youth, soared past the window and made his young heart beat faster. It was the unmistakable sound of marbles striking other marbles. Father Shay leaned his prematurely bald head out the window, quickly appraised the situation below, and promptly excused himself.

A few seconds later, down on one knee, he was demonstrating to us kids the shooting skill that several years ago had won him second place in a state-championship marble match and would have won him first, he said, if he hadn't nicked the forefinger of his shooting hand while trying to open a bottle of Green River without an opener.

When at last the bell sounded the end of recess, Father seemed the most reluctant of all to leave. "This is a heaven-sent place for marbles," he said, giving the earth a pat. He spoke the words almost reverently, as if we were on hallowed ground.

Of course, we kids were back shooting marbles during the next morning's recess, and, of course, Sister Mary Amadeus, our mother superior, had to raise her office window at that moment and spot us. We were promptly ordered to keep ourselves and our marbles out of the convent yard forevermore.

We tried for a while to shoot on the gravel of the playground, but it was no use. The pebbles were almost as big as our marbles. We hoped Sister would come to her window again and see what we were up against, but if she did, she gave no sign that it was one of her chief concerns.

Then one Monday morning shortly afterwards, my buddy John O'Donnell brought us unbelievably good news. His parents had had Father Shay over the previous Sunday for a fine dinner of corned beef and cabbage, and when the meal was finished and Father was enjoying his cigar, John, in a general way, brought up the subject of marble playing. Their guest's response was immediate and hearty. Like an old ball-player recalling the highlights of an illustrious career, he took them back through many of his more important meets and replayed, with much finger movement, some of his more remarkable shots.

Finally, John could hold still no longer. "Father, *why* won't Sister Mary Amadeus let us play out back?"

A bit startled by this sudden shift of attention from his past exploits, Father Shay nevertheless brought himself back to the present gracefully and said, "The noise, I suppose. Y'know, you kids can get pretty loud sometimes."

"But some kids in other parts of the playground make even more noise, Father!"

"You may have a point there," Father conceded, "but *your* noise is closer to the convent."

"But," John pressed on, "we'd only be there during recess, and the nuns are in the school then."

"You might have a point," Father repeated, blowing a perfect smoke ring toward the chandelier. "Well now," he added at last, "I'll tell you what I'll do. I'll make a point of seeing Sister this afternoon after Benediction. I'll put the question to her fairly and squarely. After all, Sister is a reasonable woman."

Father called the O'Donnell house that evening. He had spoken to the mother superior as promised. She wasn't exactly wild about the idea of boys playing under the catalpa tree during recess, but if he could guarantee that, in small groups only, they would keep their voices down and not take over the entire convent yard, she would go along with it, on a trial basis. Father was delighted to be held responsible for the boys' good behavior; it gave him the excuse he needed for dropping over often to do a little shooting, too.

It must be remembered here that not many people are perfect in this world, not even marble shooters. When you aim for the last marble, the one that could win the game or lose it for you, and your shooter, fired from six feet away, hits that one marble dead center and sends it flying, you *yell!* You yell louder than any kid in the playground. Or if you're out of marbles and can't play anymore and have nothing else to do, you might climb a certain tree to see what's in that wren house up there. And is it your fault if the wren house, held on by only one rusty nail, falls to the ground and breaks open? What's the big deal? From the looks of it, there had *never* been wrens in it. But does that cut any ice with Sister Mary Amadeus?

"One more trick like *that*—"she says, shooting the words like bullets off the tip of a pointed finger. She doesn't even finish the sentence. She knows she doesn't have to; that pointed finger says it all. You feel that next time it might impale you.

Father Shay's visits to the marble games became more and more admonitory. "I'm catching a lot of static from Sister," he said. "Keep your voices down! Stay off the nun's grass! And not so many of you in here at a time!"

The resolution came, of all times, one Sunday morning at the eight o'clock children's Mass. My mother—the most considerate mother any marble shooter could have wished for—had just made me a new marble bag out of leftover heavy drapery material, with a rawhide drawstring. It had to be the biggest marble bag on our block, big enough for at least forty marbles. It could have held more, but the added weight would have pulled my knickerbockers down.

As I say, don't look for a saint among marble shooters. Why couldn't I have waited to display my new bag until the next day at school? Why did I have to bring it with me to Mass even though I ran the chance of having one of the sisters see me and ask what I was doing with a grapefruit in my pocket? Why? Because I was a born show-off, that's why.

Midway through Father Shay's sermon, I felt sure it was safe to ease the bag out of my pocket and show it to John O'Donnell, sitting next to me. "Midway through" a Father

Shay sermon, I might add, was like midway through a cross-country hike—there was still a long way to go. I noticed several of my buddies dozing off. The sisters' veils seemed to be angled more sharply toward the floor than usual. Even St. Joseph looked uncommonly laid back.

"Here," I whispered to O'Donnell, "look at *this!*" I plumped the marble bag down in his lap.

"Holy Mother O'Malley!" he breathed, calling, as usual, on some obscure family saint. "What a bag!"

He had to see, of course, how the drawstring worked. He opened the bag up, revealing its enormous nest of unhatched marbles. He drew the string taut. The bag closed. He opened it once more—and this time its contents cascaded over his lap, bounced off the kneelers (then unpadded), rattled like musket fire on the hardwood floor, and went chattering off in all directions under dozens of sixth-grade feet dangling from the most astonished, suddenly wide-awake sixth-grade bodies in the archdiocese of Chicago. Some of the marbles may have rolled back as far as the seventh- and eighth-grade boys behind us and as far forward as the fifth and fourth grades ahead of us.

One thing I'm sure of. My prize lagger—a huge marble as black as the darkest midnight, with a tiny cat's-eye, molten bright, burning deep inside it like the fire at the center of the earth—my lagger of all laggers rolled clear across the center aisle into the pews of the sixth-grade girls. I saw several of them drop their prayer books and dive for it. And I saw Mary Bernice McCafferty hold it triumphantly for a brief moment over her head, like a kid holding up a baseball he'd just caught at Wrigley Field.

There was the sound of dozens of kids trying to smother their shocked laughter, the sound of the sisters swallowing their panic. Father Shay stood mute through it all, pale and stricken. When he finally resumed his sermon, you could see he was not the confident marble-shooting champion of old. He looked like a man who would never play marbles again, a man who would never dare to stand up to Sister Mary Amadeus in defense of his marble-shooting young friends. There would be no more marble games under the catalpa tree in the convent yard. I felt it in my bones. And my bones, as always, were right.

I eventually got about half my marbles back. The kids who kept the others probably felt in some strange way that they had won them fairly because the marbles should never have been there in the first place. But I'll say this for my buddy John O'Donnell: he made good on the marbles that were never returned to me.

One more thing. Mary Bernice McCafferty, wherever you are, if you are reading this account, will you please give me back my lagger? You've had it long enough.

Why We Prayed for Obadiah

Sometimes at Mass, during the reading of petitions, I find myself back in Sister Mary Theresa's fifth-grade classroom. We have just finished the Morning Offering; in a moment we will pledge our allegiance to the flag. But meanwhile, there is a new prayer to be said. Sister introduced it just a few days ago.

Each morning a different boy is allowed to name a special intention of his own—"that my mother's cold will get better," "that my dog, Reggie, who's lost, will find his way home," "that I will pass my arithmetic test."

After the petition, the class prays, "Dear Blessed Mother, we confidently ask you to intercede with your beloved Son on behalf of your faithful servant, William [or Harry or John or any of thirty others]. Amen."

So far, the prayers have all been answered. William Devers reports that his mother's cold is much better; Harry Bartlett's dog has found its way home, and, wonder of wonders, John Murray has passed his arithmetic test.

The class's faith in Sister Theresa's heavenly connection is unbounded.

But today it is my turn.

"What is your special intention, Thomas?" Sister asks.

I can't help savoring the moment. No mere cold is involved here, no wayward dog, no arithmetic test, but something dredged from the mainstream of human tragedy.

"Thomas?" Sister prompts.

"That Obie Johansen, my very best friend," I reply, "will not be put out of his home."

There is a shocked silence. Sister feels that this petition needs some clarification.

"Doesn't Obie live with his parents?" she asks.

"No, Sister, he lives alone."

Someone whispers in disbelief, "A kid living all alone?"

Patiently Sister probes further. "How *old* is Obie Johansen, Thomas?"

"Older than my father, Sister."

"I see," Sister sighs in relief. "You should have said so in the beginning." Curious, she adds, "You must tell us about him sometime. Now, class, let us pray."

My friendship with Obadiah Johansen stemmed from my intense boyhood interest in making things of wood, especially model ships. My craftsmanship, however, was limited by the fact that my father's workshop consisted of nothing more than an old card table and a few basic tools. Did I try to build a model yacht? Portholes became a problem. There was no way I could drill them because I didn't have a drill. I burned them in with a small poker brought to white heat in our coal furnace.

None of my ships had more than three portholes because three were all I had time to make before the thick, acrid smoke, drifting up the basement stairs, reached my mother's sensitive nose.

"Junior!" she'd cry down the stairwell. "I smell something burning down there!"

"Portholes," I'd answer. "I'm making another ship."

"My goodness," Mother would reply. "Why don't you simply paint them on?"

(Though I loved my mother dearly, I had doubts about her qualifications as a practical shipbuilder.)

I might have gone on building three-porthole ships indefinitely if it hadn't been for my curiosity about Obie's workshop.

A neighborhood oddity, Obie was a gaunt giant of a man with enormous hands and wrists and a look of implacable sadness. His hair grew down to his shoulders; his beard and eyebrows were as formidable as those of Michelangelo's *Moses*. His eyes were a piercing Nordic blue, the kind you could never look into and tell a lie.

Obie lived alone behind my friend Elmer Wilson in a onetime carriage house that he rented from Elmer's father. For years it had been his home and workshop, a shop said to be fitted with every woodworking tool imaginable.

He had once been a cabinet maker but had since turned completely to the work that Elmer told me he loved best— designing and making toys.

I found it hard to believe that this tall, forbidding, sadlooking man made toys. Aren't toy makers jolly little elflike creatures who sing while they work? But Elmer insisted he was telling the truth.

"When could I see these toys?" I asked Elmer one day.

From the way my friend shook his head I gathered that Obie would swallow me in one gulp if I ever set foot in his workshop.

Most of what we knew—or thought we knew—about this mysterious man we gathered from rumors, the kind that attach themselves like barnacles to individuals who keep entirely to themselves.

Some had it that he was a childless widower whose only company was the memory of a long-ago tragedy. Others claimed that he had never married at all. Some said he was a rich old miser, others that he was very poor. Whatever his background, his grizzly appearance discouraged any personal inquiries. Even Elmer stayed clear of the carriage house. Whenever we boys happened to pass Obie on the street, he would return our timid "Hi, Mr. Johansen" with only a grave and silent nod.

But my curiosity about a workshop filled with toys and with tools that I possessed only in my dreams continued to haunt me as the vision of the Promised Land haunted the Israelites.

The day was golden warm, a day of fat robins and friendly dogs with friendly noses, a fine day for trying a new shortcut as I ran an errand for my mother. Was it my fault that the shortcut took me down the alley behind the old carriage house of Obie Johansen?

And was it my fault that Obie had left one of the great doors open to catch an afternoon's breeze?

I paused and peered into the shadowy interior. I tiptoed closer for a better view.

A room of wonders! Against the far wall was a long, heavy workbench with built-in drawers and shelves, and, hanging above it, row after row of tools. In the center of the floor a broad table held a large dollhouse under construction surrounded by still more tools and pieces of wood. In a corner—

"So!" said a giant's voice behind me. "What brings *you* here?"

I whirled around. Hands on his hips, dressed in a long gray tunic belted at the waist, Obie towered above me as Gulliver once towered above the Lilliputians.

My first impulse was to run. But something in the voice held me. It was a big voice, like the sound of distant thunder—but, oddly enough, there seemed to be no immediate threat of lightning. Obie tried to look fierce and pretended that he had caught me trespassing. Yet there was a look in the blue eyes that made me wonder if they were laughing.

"Why did you come?" he asked, still pretending.

I looked around in vain for an answer. The silence deepened. I had to say *something*. Finally, inspired, I answered simply, "I like to make things too."

"Well now," the giant replied in a softer voice. "Well now." He sat down on a wooden box to bring his head closer to the level of mine.

"What kind of things do you make?"

I told him, lots of things, like a dollhouse for my sister, a bridge and station for my electric train, but mostly ships.

"Ah!" he exclaimed. "You must have a fine workshop too."

"Nope," I said. "I don't even have a drill."

"No drill? Then how do you make holes?"

"I burn them in with a hot poker."

At first the giant may have thought I was being flip. When he saw that I wasn't, the carriage house boomed with his laughter.

"Good for you!" he said at last, wiping his eyes. "Good for you." His voice dropped to a whisper. "Now then, as one craftsman to another, would you like to see what *I* make?" I nodded, speechless in the face of such an offer.

As I followed him around his shop, I wondered how anyone could ever have been afraid of this friendly man. Or had the high barricades of rumor simply kept people from glimpsing the truth?

He showed me the dollhouse he was working on—a house with walls that could be swung out from the four corners to provide access to the interior from any side.

He showed me a boy's top he had turned on his lathe. It was nearly four inches in diameter. You kept it spinning by whipping it occasionally with a short leather thong attached to a wooden handle. In the top's center was a small peg; over this you dropped cardboard discs one at a time as you would position phonograph records on a turntable. As each disc spun with the top, colored dots on its surface whirled themselves into exciting patterns of continuous color.

He showed me toddlers' pull-toys—trains and wagons and animals on wheels, all exquisitely made and left in their natural wood finish. All his toys, he said, he sold through a store downtown.

There was scarcely a day for the rest of the summer that I didn't visit Obie, if only to say hello. Sometimes I brought him things of my own for his critical appraisal. He was always patient and helpful. With his guidance I eventually finished a ship that I could be proud of—with at least a dozen portholes neatly drilled.

He guided me through the wonders of working with wood. He taught me how to use the hammer properly. "Don't *punch* with the head," he advised. "Swing it back in an easy arc and let the fall of its own weight do most of the hammering."

He taught me how to use the plane and the chisel. "See how the grain flows through the wood like a river. Always go with the river, never against it."

And as we worked we talked—not about his past, which he kept to himself, but about my schoolwork, my church and his, the meaning of his prophet's name (servant of the Lord), what I wanted to be when I grew up.

I wanted to be like Obie. He was my friend, my teacher, my confidant.

Once I confessed to him that he wasn't at all the kind of person most people thought him to be. He replied simply, "People created by God are never the same as those created by rumors." Then he added, "But I don't mind what people think. I like to work alone—except, of course, when I can have the company of a fellow craftsman."

The first of the autumn days had come. Lawns were filling

with leaves stricken by the deadly sting of frost. It was the melancholy time of year between the loss of summer and the excitement of the first snow.

I stopped by the carriage house on my way home from school. It was the first time I had seen Obie not busy at some project. He was sitting on the edge of the big worktable gazing dejectedly at the floor. Head still down, he raised only those formidable eyebrows of his in order to look at me.

"I got some news today," he said softly. I knew at once it was not good news. I waited, wide-eyed, fearful.

"I might have to leave this place," he said finally.

"Leave!" I exclaimed in disbelief. "You mean—for good?"

"Yes," said Obie, nodding his head. "Mr. Wilson has sold his home. The new owner may want the carriage house for himself."

"But you'll find something better," I insisted. "I'm sure you will."

"Not in this neighborhood. I know."

"Well then, if you can't find a place, they've got to let you stay!"

Obie smiled at my logic. "I hope you're right," he said.

Clearly the time had come to present Sister Mary Theresa with my own first special intention.

"Dear Blessed Mother," the class prayed, "we confidently ask you to intercede with your beloved Son on behalf of your faithful servant, Thomas. Amen."

I drew a sigh of relief. The problem was now in more capable hands than mine or even Obie's.

I was proud of my self-control when, a few days later, Obie told me it was final; he would have to leave. Just as a precaution, he said, he had looked around for another place in which to live and work and had found one—in a distant part of the city. To me it was as far away as California.

On the day of good-by, he said, "Shake hands." We shook hands solemnly. "We have been good friends," he said at last. "Be glad about that."

I knew I would never see him again.

Sister Mary Theresa will be disappointed, I thought, when I tell her that our prayer for Obie had not been heard. Instead she smiled and said, "This only means that God has something more important for you to pray for."

What on earth could *that* be, I wondered.

Next day Sister had a special intention of her own: "That Thomas will be thankful for the friend God gave him even for a little while—and will some day see that each friendship we make on earth is but a reflection of our lasting friendship with God."

It took a little time, but *that* prayer was finally answered.

Our Old Family Studebaker

Most of the cars my parents owned came to us miraculously covered by a Divine Providence Protection Policy—insurance they could never have done without, not because they were reckless drivers or accident-prone but because my father kept cars to the point where they became rolling hazards.

The trouble was, Dad fell hopelessly in love with each car he bought. For him the sales contract was a solemn promise to love, honor, and cherish, for richer or poorer, in sickness and in health, till death do us—well, maybe not *that* far, but almost. Our family cars were *of* the family as well as *for* the family, entitled to the same status accorded our old collie, the family silverware, the cedar chest that held family records, and my mother's wedding dress.

The longer my father kept a car, the more painful it was for him to part with it. On the rare occasions when this happened, he would proudly point out, "All those years and not a scratch!"—a statement that rang true only because he had scratches, dents, bumps, tears, rips, and crumples repaired immediately after they were acquired.

Our first two cars were touring models, which meant that when it rained, you pulled over to the side of the road, wrestled a roll of isinglass side curtains out from under the back seat, and spent the next twenty minutes matching their snap-on buttons to the studs. We were still struggling with side curtains long after the rest of the world was whizzing past us comfortably in sedans and coupes.

Eventually, however, Mother's insistence on more protective transportation won out, and we acquired a Studebaker sedan—as weatherproof as a Pullman car and almost as heavy. "Solid" was the word my father used to describe it. He would slap door frames and doors and declare to anyone willing to listen, "There's a solid oak frame under that metal! None of your tinny construction in *this* automobile!"

Over the years, the Studebaker developed many idiosyncrasies that only endeared it the more to my father, like its unnerving habit of conking out for no apparent reason, often while crossing railroad tracks.

Fortunately, a neighbor with a flair for mechanics was able to prescribe symptomatic relief. After a stall, Dad would set the shift in second gear, jump out, put his shoulder to the radiator, and, with help from his passengers rock the car back and forth until he heard a loud *click!* somewhere deep under the hood. Then back to our seats and off we'd go, with father vindicated in his confidence that nothing serious could ever happen to us in such a car as this.

The Studebaker's enormous wheels had spokes of wood, a material that worked perfectly for three of them. The fourth, however—the left rear—would squeak loudly after a few minutes in motion. It was then my job, after Father pulled over, to get a gallon can of water we kept under the front seat for the purpose and douse the complaining wheel. The same neighbor had told us that water would cause the spokes to swell and thus crowd out the squeak. This treatment was usually good for a few more miles of quiet running, at which point we'd pull into a gas station and ask a puzzled attendant for a gallon of water.

"Pretty economical car you've got there," one of them once wisecracked.

"The water is for the left rear wheel," my father explained sternly, discouraging any further comments.

"Oh, sure," said the attendant.

Later, another design feature of the Studebaker nearly led to disaster. The car, for all its size and weight, had only two-wheel brakes, the last such model Studebaker made.

Two-wheel brakes, as on our earlier cars, were adequate for their time because everyone else had them too. As long as *all* traffic moved in the leisurely two-wheel brake tempo of a slow waltz, you were safe. But if you were still waltzing when everyone else was doing a stomp, you were in trouble. All too often, what brought us to a stop was the rear end of the car ahead.

Another character trait was that on rainy or snowy surfaces the sudden application of the brakes spun the car halfway around. Many were the intersections we crossed going backwards—to the shrieks of my mother, my sister, and other motorists, who had no appreciation for the fine work being done by my father's guardian angel. We were never harmed. Although apparently unable to prevent the skids, the angel did a masterful job of directing traffic around them.

Heaven only knows how long this state of affairs would have continued had it not been for Sister Mary Therese.

One of my parents' works of charity was to take the sisters of our parish school for a weekly ride through Lincoln Park—"to give those poor women," as my father said, "a breath of fresh air after being cooped up in that convent all week."

Strong at first, the enthusiasm of the sisters for these excursions diminished in direct proportion to the Studebaker's growing unfitness to be on the road. Too polite to refuse the rides, they sat huddled in fear, their fingers nervously working their rosaries.

One day, unfortunately, their prayers fell a little short of their mark. With my father at the wheel, we were following close behind a streetcar—a new model with air brakes capable of stopping it within a few feet, a performance far beyond the capabilities of the Studebaker. The result was that when we came to rest, our radiator, headlights, and front fenders were tightly wedged beneath the streetcar's rear platform, which sustained no damage at all.

At once a burly Irish conductor stepped down, obviously aching to deliver a well-spiced lecture on the stupidity of following so close. But seeing the blanched faces of four terrified nuns, he immediately lost his steam. He put his head in at the driver's window, looked around inside, and asked incredulously, "How can you take an old crate like this out in today's traffic without a Saint Christopher's medal?"

My father retorted that any streetcar that could stop that fast was a menace to traffic and should be banned. What disturbed him most about the whole incident was hearing his pride and joy referred to as an old crate.

In the next few days two interesting and seemingly unrelated events took place. Father had the Studebaker repaired, declaring that he intended to keep it going, and Sister Mary Therese began a nine-day novena. She told my mother that her patron saint, with whom she was on excellent terms, would surely convince my father that, for his family's safety, he must buy a new car.

Mother was skeptical. Her skepticism increased when, a day or two later, Dad remarked that the solution to our driving problems was simply to drive more slowly.

"We're already the slowest car on the road," Mother replied.

Dad smiled tolerantly. "You don't appreciate what a solidly built automobile we have here. They don't make them like that anymore."

"Thank God," sighed my mother.

The ninth and last day of Sister Mary Therese's novena came and went with nothing happening to distinguish it from the day before. My father arrived home from work at his usual time, played catch with me in the backyard, had dinner, read *Riders of the Purple Sage* by Zane Grey, and went to bed.

The next evening, he came home, pitched horseshoes with me in the backyard, had dinner, read *Square-Shooter* by William MacLeod Raine, and went to bed.

The following morning, he announced he had a call to make in the suburbs and took the Studebaker.

He returned at noon with a new two-door Pontiac, a light-footed, graceful dancer of a car that won my mother's heart immediately.

"When did you decide to make the change?" she asked.

"Three days ago," said my father, "but I had to wait for that special spotlight."

My mother did some quick counting on her fingers and smiled. "I love it," she said.

Dad walked to the front, slapped the radiator, and said, "Solid. This car should last us for a long time."

And, with the continuing help of divine Providence, that's exactly what it did.

When Sister Snapped Her Fingers

Among the many talents of my grade school sisters was a virtuosity in the art of finger snapping that I have not seen the likes of since.

Brisk, dynamic, and dependable, the sounds that crackled from those flashing digits had the no-nonsense authority of the policeman's whistle, the fire engine's bell, the judge's gavel. As attention getters they had few equals. They warned, alerted, commanded, summoned, dismissed, directed, and admonished. They had their own gift of tongues.

More efficiently than words, they conveyed a sense of

immediacy. Words you might question (provided you did so politely). But a nun's finger snap? You might as well question a bolt of lightning.

My buddy John O'Donnell (who spoke with authority because his oldest sister was a nun) confided that one of the first requirements for a vocation was dexterity in finger snapping. "If you're no good with your fingers," he told me, "the convent won't accept you." He also said that no matter how expert a novice may be to begin with, she has to take a refresher course in finger snapping before she can make her final vows.

I saw no reason to be skeptical.

Although all the sisters of my experience were great finger snappers, the greatest by far was Sister Mary Mechtildis (eighth-grade boys). Sister was what you might call a finger snapper's finger snapper. Like the gunslingers of the Old West, she could shoot from any position with scarcely a moment's provocation. She was as deadly with her left hand as she was with her right. Her fingers were always loaded, and they never misfired.

What set Sister Mary Mechtildis apart from the rest was the variety of her shots. Her arsenal was awesome. She had different snaps for different occasions, each with its own delicate nuance of sound. In time you learned to distinguish them as you did verbal inflections.

For instance, there was the snap that woke you from your postlunch drowsiness. There was one that said, "Stop whispering to Michael Jennings." One that said, "You're spending too much time at the pencil sharpener." One that said, "Close ranks—one arm's length from the boy in front of you" as you marched to the church on Friday afternoons to practice the hymns for next Sunday's children's Mass. And there were others.

The one I remember most vividly was a snap that I heard but once. It was directed solely at me, and its sound, miraculously, rose one cold and wintry morning above all the traffic noise of a busy city street—and no doubt saved my life.

There were nine city blocks between my home and school—a long walk, especially for my sister Alyce, who was only in second grade. (Second-graders are sprinters: they're not much for distance.)

"Can't we take the streetcar?" Alyce would beg every morning as we set out for school and every afternoon as we set out for home. Taking the Lawrence Avenue streetcar cut the distance by six blocks.

The carfare for me, as I recall, was seven cents; for Alyce, three. If I was lucky enough to have a dime in my pocket, we rode. More often than not, we walked. Even my father's frequent reminder that walking is great exercise gave us no comfort.

For months I had been pleading with my parents for a bicycle. If I only had a bike, going to school would be easy.

"What about Alyce?"

"I'd carry her on the frame between myself and the handlebar. Lots of kids give rides that way."

But my mother was skeptical. "With or without Alyce," she maintained, "riding a bicycle in today's traffic is too dangerous."

"But Jimmy Haggerty rides a bike. So does Elmer Plunkett."

My mother continued to shake her head. I knew it was no use. Jimmy and Elmer had brothers. I belonged to that special and unfortunate breed, only sons.

I may not have had brothers of my own, but, thank heaven, I had my father's brother, Uncle Ed. He lived but a few miles away, close enough for him to observe and question some of the parental restrictions under which his only nephew labored.

"It's high time Junior had a bicycle," he said one day, and within the week I was riding a handsome Ranger two-wheeler.

My parents reluctantly allowed that if Uncle Ed considered a bike safe, there was really no cause for worry. Uncle Ed was a priest. In those days you would as soon question the Sermon on the Mount as an opinion rising out of a Roman collar.

Of course there were certain restraints. For example, I must never, under any condition, ride my bike across Ashland Avenue, the busy thoroughfare on which our parish buildings were located. My sister and I were to dismount and, after getting the nod from Mr. Morgan, the policeman on the corner, *walk* the bike over.

I kept to the order faithfully—well, almost. Some mornings, when we were late and Mr. Morgan had left his post, I would pause at the curb only long enough to appraise traffic conditions; then, standing on the pedals for greater power (bikes had only one speed in those days), pump myself and Alyce across the street.

In time my parents' prohibition grew comfortably faint in my memory. It might have expired altogether if Father Friel hadn't intervened.

Now, you'd think that an assistant pastor of a large parish would have something better to do on a weekday morning than stand gazing out a rectory window at the passing cars and trucks. But Father, a close friend of my parents and Uncle Ed, was apparently a compulsive out-of-the-window gazer. One winter's day, when the streets were slippery from a freezing drizzle, he observed a fourteen-year-old boy whom he knew well pedaling his bicycle across the frozen tundra of the avenue with the boy's tiny and trusting sister perched like a bird in front of him.

I am happy to recall that the trip was made safely with no bad effects except a severe shock to Father Friel's nerves. That evening he phoned my father and told him what had happened. "Junior could have broken his neck," he said, "and his sister's, too. Tom, you've got to put a stop to that."

"You could have broken your neck and your sister's, too,"

my shaken father said to me after the call. "One more caper like that and it's no more bicycle for you! Do you understand?" I understood.

Sister Mary Mechtildis had once said, "We are never tempted beyond our powers of resistance." I leave the accuracy of that statement to the theologians—preferably those who once loved to ride bicycles.

But now I must confess to still another breach of promise.

On the unlikely chance that I will someday be nominated for sainthood (which, Sister said, we should all aspire to) I hope my defenders will point out that there is nothing comparable to the thrill of power a young boy feels in his legs as he stands high on the pedals and propels himself and his passenger across a raceway of hostile cars and trucks.

Besides—and this is probably the most important point—I had an audience. It was the best in the world: Sister herself and most of my classmates on their way to a special feast-day Mass. If I hurried, I would be just in time to join the others on the church steps.

Mr. Morgan was busy talking to some children on the far side. This was my moment. I looked—or at least I thought I looked—up and down the street. Then I pushed off.

That's when I heard it.

Snap!

Without a moment's hesitation I turned back to the curb. There was the roar of a truck's horn and the jolt of its whirlwind passing.

My sister and I dismounted, and after a furious Mr. Morgan finally motioned us over, we walked the bike to the other side, where Sister Mary Mechtildis was waiting for me.

"Don't you ever do such a foolhardy thing as that again!" she cried, white-faced and trembling. "You go into church now, get down on your knees, and thank God you're still alive!"

I was not the high-riding hero I had hoped to be, but I

had sense enough to be thankful—thankful that God had given Sister such a talent with her fingers.

And yet I have sometimes wondered—over all that traffic noise, had I *really* heard the snap? Or did it all relate somehow to Pavlov's theory of conditioned reflexes? Could it be that finger snapping for me had become so closely associated with transgressions that whenever I did something wrong, I imagined I heard a snap, whether Sister had noticed me or not?

I suppose it's futile to pursue the question. Besides, I prefer to recall another snap—one that Sister gave at the end of that feast-day Mass.

"Genuflect!" it said. "On your feet now ... form ranks ... march!"

But she must have put a little something extra into it, because for me it also said, "This is the day the Lord hath made. Rejoice and be glad!"

I rejoiced.

And I was glad.

The Priest
Who Knew All about Boys

Whenever I hear someone argue that priests, because of their celibacy, cannot possibly relate to the everyday problems of family life, I think to myself, "Too bad you didn't know my uncle Ed."

Three of my father's six brothers were priests. Of these, Father Ed in particular showed an understanding of family relationships that I came to appreciate enormously. He could, for instance, spot a pair of overly protective parents five miles away—which was exactly the distance between his rectory and our home.

Uncle Ed had wasted no time in letting my parents know

that he was seriously interested in my development. On the day I was born, when other relatives were celebrating my arrival with gifts of baby clothes and the inevitable silver mug, Uncle Ed gave me a book. ("Don't priests know that babies can't read?" one of my aunts is said to have quipped.) My earliest memories of my mother's voice take me back to the many times she read to me from that book—a collection of poems about childhood by such authors as Swinburne, Coleridge, Wordsworth, and Shakespeare. I have the slim volume still. I'm not sure what became of the silver mug.

In these days of instant entertainment when kids find it easier to turn on television than open a book, it's hard to imagine that some parents could worry that their children were "reading too much." But mine did.

One day somewhere in my twelfth summer, Uncle Ed phoned to see how we all were.

"We're worried about Junior," said my father.

"What's the matter with him?"

"Too much reading."

"Too much—*what?*"

"He's going to ruin his eyes," said my father.

"Nonsense," said his brother.

"But he has his nose in some book or other all the time."

"What sort of books?"

"Anything he can lay his hands on," said my father.

Uncle Ed had seen our library. He knew that, with few exceptions, the only books I could lay my hands on in our house were the slam-bang, shoot-'em-up wild westerns of Zane Grey, William MacLeod Raine, and others—my father's favorite relaxation after a long day in the wholesale furniture business.

I can imagine what my uncle was thinking. "I start the boy off with Shakespeare, Shelley, and Wordsworth and he ends up with potboilers!"

Uncle Ed's response to this cultural calamity (and to my

anticipated eye problems) came on my birthday a few days later. A large carton, almost too heavy for one man to carry, arrived at our front door. It was filled with books that Uncle Ed had hand-picked himself—Conrad's *Heart of Darkness,* Cooper's *Last of the Mohicans,* Stevenson's *Treasure Island,* Defoe's *Robinson Crusoe,* and almost a dozen more—some new, some from my uncle's own library.

I can still remember my amazement at discovering that even without the easy gunplay, the wild gallops in the prairie dust, the showdowns at the old corral, these classics could stir my blood and hold my interest as no books had done before.

One evening, in a fever of enthusiasm for Stevenson's *Treasure Island,* which I had just finished, I begged my father to give it a try.

Reluctantly he set aside the western he was reading. I watched his eyes move over those first riveting words: " . . . I take up my pen in the year of grace 17— and go back to the time when my father kept the Admiral Benbow inn, and the brown old seaman with the sabre cut first took up his lodging under our roof."

"Have you done your homework?" my father asked after a moment.

I went into another room to do my homework, wondering why it never consisted of reading the great old stories. Later, on my way to bed, I saw my father dozing in his chair. *Treasure Island* had slipped to the floor. Awakening to say goodnight, Dad promised he would resume the book tomorrow. But next evening he was back with Zane Grey. I hope now that I understood. I had once loved the wild westerns too.

But it was not only in matters literary that Uncle Ed showed his interest. One day I said to my mother, "I'm the only kid on the block who doesn't have roller skates."

"Roller skates can be very dangerous," she replied. "You could get a bad fall. Better wait till you're a little older."

I don't recall how Uncle Ed heard that I had no wheels for my feet, but one afternoon he arrived at our home with a pair of skates under his arm. "Here, Junior," he said. "It's high time you had roller skates."

Again my mother protested that skates might be dangerous. "Oh, don't worry, Mae." said Uncle Ed. "A spill or two won't hurt him. I've had quite a few myself." He told her how, as a boy in Ireland, he once fell in a well. "But look at me now," he laughed. "Except for a bump on my head that never went down, I'm as good as new."

Yes, there he was, as good as new, a tall, broad-shouldered exuberance of an uncle, an outdoorsman and hunter, the idol of my boyhood years. When I grow up, I used to tell myself, I'll be just like Uncle Ed.

And wasn't it Uncle Ed who had given me my first two-wheeler, the bike I rode my sister to school on? To my mother's protests on that occasion that two-wheelers are dangerous, my uncle had replied, "Ah, yes, two-wheelers. Did I ever tell you about the time when I was driving our two-wheel milk cart down a road in Ireland when suddenly the horse took off like a shot? Maybe a hornet had stung him, I don't know. But I was too young to hold him. Farther on, the road turned sharply and over I went. And yet, except for another bump on my head that won't go down, here I am as good as new."

On a solo visit to Uncle Ed a few years later I remarked that I was the only kid my age who hadn't learned to drive an automobile. Too dangerous. Wait until you're older, I was told again.

"Ridiculous," said Uncle Ed. "Come with me."

Friends of mine who drove had already taught me the basics. The finer points of wheeling a Nash sedan through crowded city streets I learned from Uncle Ed.

"A lesson or two more, Junior," he said at the end of our run, "and you'll be right there with the best of them."

Of course, I couldn't keep my mouth shut. I had to tell

my best friend, who had to tell his sister, who had to tell *my* sister, who had to tell my mother, who had to tell my father.

"Dad," I said after his initial explosion had subsided somewhat, "Uncle Ed said to tell you *he* learned to drive *all by himself,* and except for a bump on the head that won't go down, he's as good as new."

I can't truthfully say that I was the last of my friends to get married. All I remember is that I was so in love that I knew only marriage would make the rest of my life bearable.

But marriage, like roller skates, two-wheel bikes, and driving a car, can be dangerous. How could a young lad my age (26) really be certain he was in love? Besides, hadn't I known this girl only a few short months? To parents whose year-long courtship had often been referred to by my mother as a whirlwind affair, my intentions were as rash as those of Steve Brodie before his daredevil jump off the Brooklyn Bridge.

"How can you possibly marry this girl?" my father asked. "You're not making enough money to support a canary." The canary was always my father's favorite reference point in any comparison of the various stages of financial ineptitude.

It is impossible to describe in detail the arguments that ensued. There were explosions of questions, warnings, lamentations, and prophecies almost biblical in their heroic proportions. Two themes became dominant. One, the economic, expounded by my father with frequent references to the canary, held that a man had no business taking on the responsibilities of marriage without a nest egg to fall back on and a good enough income to make sure the nest egg would never be touched.

The other, more sociological, was developed by my mother with dismal apothegms about the folly of sacrificing my brilliant future (whatever it was at the time) just to indulge some momentary infatuation.

My parents had met Ginny and they liked her—but only as a friend who would someday marry someone else.

As usual in such family crises, they consulted Uncle Ed.

"Junior insists he's going to get married," my mother told him over the phone. She waited expectantly for sympathy and condolences.

"Do you know the young lady?" asked my uncle calmly.

"Yes," said my mother. "She's a lovely girl, but—"

"Good," said Uncle Ed.

"Good?"

"It's high time Junior got married," he continued. "High time indeed. And if you ask me, it's the best possible thing that could happen to him."

Uncle Ed left it at that. There were no stories about his youth in Ireland, no bumps on the head that would apply.

At the birth of Christopher, our first of twelve, when other relatives were celebrating his arrival with gifts of clothes, blankets, rattles, and the inevitable silver mug, Uncle Ed gave him a book.

How Sister Mary Evelyn Found Out

If Jimsey Gurney were in fifth grade today instead of having been there when I was, many of his classroom hours would be spent in "special learning groups." Jimsey learned all right, but not very fast.

In those days, however—at least in Sister Mary Evelyn's class—all thirty-seven of us attacked each day's lessons shoulder to shoulder in close formation and with military singleness of purpose. We never broke ranks. There were no scholastic field hospitals for the wounded or the battle-weary. If someone fell behind, the whole platoon slowed down—

though only long enough to hoist the straggler over our shoulders before resuming our advance. It was all for one and one for all. Sister Mary Evelyn saw to that.

"William Walsh, will you sit with Jimsey Gurney and be his partner during arithmetic?"

"George Crowley, will you sit with Jimsey Gurney and be his partner during geography?"

"Thomas Byrnes, will you sit with Jimsey Gurney and be his partner during grammar?"

If I became adept at diagraming sentences (simple, complex, and compound), it was because I spent so much time helping Jimsey diagram them. (Who was it first said that you can't be sure you've learned something until you can teach it to others?)

There were times, of course, when we resented the delays, times when we wanted to shout, "The answer is 326, Jimsey!... The word is *caravel,* Jimsey!... *Painted* is a transitive verb, Jimsey!... The capitol of Illinois is Springfield, Jimsey!"

But under Sister's disciplinary eye we had to wait until she was sure that Jimsey was hopelessly out of step. Only then would she let one of us come to his rescue. Our forward march would resume until once again it became Jimsey's turn to respond.

Yet in spite of these slowdowns, we managed somehow to reach each day's objective—or so it seemed to me. Perhaps without Jimsey we would have solved one more arithmetic problem per day, parsed another few verbs, or read through another page of our fifth-grade reader. But I can't say that I felt any sense of irreparable loss. Nor do I now. And maybe that's because of what Sister Mary Evelyn pointed out to us one day when Jimsey was absent.

Along with our lessons, Sister reminded us, we were learning something else equally important—the practice of Christian charity. And we were also learning that charity, though sweet, can sometimes be an inconvenience. But then, she went on, the Good Samaritan, who paused to help a man beaten by robbers, also suffered an inconvenience—but one that made him immortal.

Jimsey hadn't been beaten by robbers, but we all knew he had taken several hard punches over the years. His parents had died when he was a toddler, he told us. Since then, he had been raised by a succession of indifferent relatives, most of whom had their hands full supporting their own children. His experiences had not always been pleasant.

By the time he was ready for fifth grade, he found himself with an aunt and uncle who lived in my neighborhood.

Sister Mary Evelyn knew Jimsey's history too. The fact that he was an orphan intensified her resolve to see that he made it successfully through fifth grade. She also knew that if he flunked out, he would be sent to live with another uncle, a severe taskmaster from whose stringent disciplines Jimsey had once run away.

And yet he would have to make it honestly, on his own merits and not through any leniency on her part. Sister Mary Evelyn was straight arrow all the way.

We knew that she often had misgivings. We knew it when she confessed one day that she was offering special prayers to St. Jerome Emiliani, patron of orphans. She felt she needed all the heavenly help she could get.

Tall, shy, ill at ease, with dark brown eyes that looked out suspiciously at the world around him through strands of an unruly black forelock, Jimsey gave the impression that he was always about to apologize for something. That, at least, was the way he looked in class—unneeded and unimportant.

Only myself and three other classmates who lived near Jimsey in the same neighborhood and were his closest friends knew that he had a quite different side to his character. Because of it, we too were determined to see him succeed. We couldn't afford to lose him.

You see, Jimsey, for all his scholastic shortcomings, was

a genius. He was a genius in all things mechanical. He had been born with an Archimedean appreciation for levers, fulcrums, pulleys, wheels, axles, and inclined planes.

By the time he was five, he told us (and we *knew* he was telling the truth), he had taken an aunt's ailing vacuum cleaner apart, corrected the problem, and reassembled all its components. He had done the same with washing machines, clocks, lawn mowers, coffee grinders, and door locks in the various households where he had spent his transient years.

Once on a visit to my home, he noticed that the turntable of our old Victrola wasn't spinning at a constant speed. My parents, also aware of the problem, were going to get it fixed some day when they got around to it. Jimsey fixed it in fifteen minutes. I still remember his satisfaction as he tested his handiwork with a John Philip Sousa record. "See?" he said proudly. "The music sounds real smooth now."

But it was the things Jimsey did for us kids in our do-it-yourself projects that I remember best—things that made him a happy, self-reliant leader of our bunch and that Sister Mary Evelyn knew nothing about.

Did the intricate, hard-to-reassemble coaster brake of your bicycle need fixing? You could try to do it yourself, as I sometimes did, but you seldom got it back just right; there were always several nuts and washers left over. So you called in Jimsey. To him the mechanics of the brake were as simple as the mechanics of a teacup and saucer.

You built yourself a soap-box racer (in the days when there were wooden soap boxes). But getting the steering hookup to work properly could be a problem. Again you called in Jimsey. You sat in open-mouthed admiration as he deftly wrapped the ends of two lengths of clothesline around the broomstick steering post, slipped them through two side pulleys on the frame, and tied the other two ends to the front axle. "There," he would say at last. "It's just that you gotta get the *angle* right."

Who knew how to attach your old roller-skate wheels to a homemade scooter so they would never fall off? Who knew exactly how to dry and varnish beef rib bones to make rackety-rack castanets? Who could scoop a fireplace out of a mound of earth in the vacant lot behind your home and make a flue that drew perfectly? And who knew exactly the magic moment when the potatoes you put in the fire were done to perfection?

Jimsey.

But it was never the capable, self-assured expert who returned to school next day. It was an uncertain, self-deprecating stand-in who felt he had nothing to contribute in the environment of the classroom. And he continued to give Sister Mary Evelyn little reason to believe that he would ever change.

And yet he changed. The change began one midafternoon when William Walsh raced back from the boys' basement washroom with the news that the floor was flooding with water.

I can't say for sure that St. Jerome Emiliani had anything to do with it. Although he founded several orphanages when the plagues of sixteenth-century Europe left so many children homeless, I doubt that he knew anything about modern plumbing. But there are other factors to consider.

For instance, was it merely happenstance that a classmate of Jimsey's and not somebody from another room made the discovery? And was it merely a twist of fate that Mr. Watts, the janitor, was nowhere to be found?

I have no way of knowing. All I know is that suddenly a once shy and apologetic-looking boy rose from his seat at the back of the room and, with the confidence of Webster replying to Hayne, called out, "I'll fix it!"

As if she had known from all eternity that Jimsey would rise at that moment, Sister Mary Evelyn nodded assent. In a flash our friend was gone.

As she followed him out of the room, Sister warned us, "Don't one of you move!"

Nobody moved for what seemed hours. But it could only have been minutes. Then Jimsey and Sister were back. Jimsey's shoes left squishy little puddles of water behind them as he returned to his desk. Yet Sister, who prided herself on having the best waxed floor in the school, didn't mind.

"Tell the class what happened," she directed Jimsey.

Thomas Edison explaining the principle of the incandescent bulb could not have looked more authoritative than Jimsey as he stood up.

"Someone turned a water faucet on too hard," he said, demonstrating the action with a violent twist of his hand, "and the handle broke off. The valve jammed open. I found a wrench on Mr. Watts's workbench and shut the faucet off."

We all clapped.

"Then what?" Sister prompted.

"The floor drain was clogged," Jimsey went on, as if this last detail was hardly worth mentioning, "so I found a plunger and got it going." He said down, smiling.

We clapped again. As far as I can recall, Jimsey was the only classmate we ever clapped for. He was a true hero. And he looked the part. I'm sure the change in his demeanor did not escape Sister Mary Evelyn's notice.

I'm only surmising, of course, but I'm sure that in the light of what happened during the next few weeks, some perceptive spirit (could it have been St. Jerome Emiliani?) whispered in Sister's ear, "Give our orphan Jimsey something to *do*—something that will make him feel important. Give him a chance to *give!*"

Next day, Sister announced, "As you boys know, a lot of things can go wrong in a classroom as old as ours. For instance, right now there are two broken clothes hooks in the cloakroom. Some of our desk tops don't close properly. There's an ink stain on the floor that I can't get off. And Mr.

Watts, our janitor, doesn't seem to have time for such things. So—I'm appointing Jimsey Gurney to be our Chief Maintenance Engineer! He'll be in charge of keeping everything in good repair. All in favor say 'Aye!' "

"Aye!" we all bellowed. The loudest "Aye" of all was Jimsey's.

Can you believe it? Chief Maintenance Engineer! Not just an ordinary, run-of-the-mill maintenance man or janitor but an *engineer*—and a *chief* engineer at that. Oh, I tell you, Sister Mary Evelyn had the touch.

From then on, it was not Mr. Watts but Jimsey we called on to repair a frayed extension cord, check the wiring of the colored lights around the Christmas manger, fix a pencil sharpener, remove ink stains from the floor or chewing gum from under seats, refasten cloakroom hooks, free drawers that stuck in Sister's desk, oil door hinges and folding desk tops that squeaked, rebuild the wobbly floor stand for the American flag, and a dozen other jobs as well.

In time, thanks to Sister's talents as a promoter, Jimsey's range of activity grew to include several classrooms besides our own.

He was kept busy—and he felt important. Nothing gave him more satisfaction than to be able to tell us at the end of a day, "Gotta get here early tomorrow. Gotta fix the door lock in second grade. . . . Gotta stay tonight. Sister Mary Rose's metronome is acting kinda funny. . . . Gotta spent the noon hour fixing the chalk rail on Sister Mary Dominic's blackboard."

If Mr. Watts minded the diminished need for his services, he never mentioned it. Or perhaps he felt he couldn't stand up to the authority of a Chief Maintenance Engineer.

And Jimsey's schoolwork? No longer did he approach a problem with his old, apologetic look. He approached it with the confidence of a proven engineer who knows that problems are made to be solved.

Some problems took a little more time than others, and now and then the platoon had to slow down a bit to let Jimsey catch up. But catch up he did. Enough, at least, to achieve a passing grade at year's end.

Sister Mary Evelyn was very happy about it all. We kids who were Jimsey's closest friends were happy, too.

And so, I hope, was St. Jerome Emiliani.

I Was a
Confession Consultant

"Bless me, Father, for I have sinned. It has been one week since my last confession. In that time I disobeyed my parents four times, missed my morning prayers three times, my evening prayers twice, grace before meals once, grace after meals twice. For these sins I am heartily sorry and ask—"

"No," I said thoughtfully, "it's too much like last time."

"All right then, *what?*" demanded Alyce with all the impatience a seven-year-old would dare show a twelve-year-old brother.

"Sins are pretty much the same," I said profoundly. "It's the *number* of sins they watch. You go in there week after week saying you've disobeyed your parents four times and they think to themselves, 'This kid isn't showing much improvement.' "

"All right!" cried Alyce, exasperated. "*What,* then?"

I was used to these outbursts. Since her first Holy Communion a month earlier, hadn't I been reviewing Alyce's confessions every Saturday on our way to church? But I knew sanctity doesn't come easily, and in conscience I didn't feel that she was quite ready for her first solo flight.

"Let's say that you disobeyed your parents twice."

There was the sigh that women always sigh over the male passion for statistics. "You think he remembers?"

"Father Friel? He never forgets. And he'd think it was pretty fishy if you didn't change things around once in a while."

I particularly admired Father Friel for his rich tenor voice and his stylish way of blessing himself—not with a fly-chasing brush of the hand but with four crisp and rhythmic stabs of his middle finger on forehead, diaphragm, left and right shoulders, one stab each for the Father and Son and the traditional two for the Holy Spirit, who at that time was going under the name of the Holy Ghost.

To tell a man like Father Friel that you had disobeyed your parents four times a week for four weeks running would be an insult to his intelligence. He might forgive you the disobedience but not your lack of imagination.

"All right then," I said with a gentle show of authority, "Let's go over the numbers again."

So over them again we went, over and over, all twelve sins, right up to the top step of the church's main entrance.

I have sometimes wondered if my sister's later proficiency in mathematics wasn't due in part to these weekly penitential drills.

"How was it?" I asked her as we regrouped on the steps for the trek home.

"Oh, fine," she said brightly. "He asked me if I was truly sorry and I said I was and he said, 'Three Our Fathers and three Hail Marys,' same as last time."

I frowned. Same penance as last time? For two sins less? I made a mental note to ask Sister Mary Verissima about this Monday morning.

"Why don't you ever tell me *your* sins?" Alyce asked me once.

"It isn't that I'm interested in your sins as such," I replied. "I just want to make sure your confession sounds believable."

"Is yours believable?"

"Absolutely."

"Then why don't you tell me?"

I pondered this a moment. "Well," I said finally, "I think my sins are too complicated."

Which was God's own truth, as I will try to explain.

My desk in the seventh-grade classroom was at the back between John O'Donnell, on my left, and Frank Cassidy, on my right, an arrangement that, as far as O'Donnell was concerned, filled my days with many delightful distractions. Cassidy was another matter.

O'Donnell was a burly, good-natured, curly-haired, red-faced junior Falstaff, the best catcher the school's baseball team ever had and a lad of limitless humor. He was very good at arithmetic, which I wasn't, and poor at diagraming sentences, at which I was a whiz. If John and I learned nothing else in seventh grade, we learned the importance of Christian charity. Whenever Sister Mary Verissima's back was turned, we practiced it freely.

To liven things up, we concocted a partnership that we named the BO Detective Agency (Byrnes and O'Donnell, in case you're wondering), with offices in all major cities of the world and, oddly enough, a navy of our own that eventually grew (on paper) to three battleships, four cruisers, six destroyers, twelve submarines, and an unlimited supply of munitions. Our slogan: The sun never sets on BO.

For our personal protection we packed imaginary .45s (gats) in our hip pockets and drew them stealthily whenever possible, taking careful aim at the back of Sister Mary Verissima's veil and whispering, "Pow!"

Our clients, unknowingly, were our classmates. Unknowing, too, were the people we shadowed, the priests and nuns of the parish. Let a knock sound on the door and O'Donnell and I would quickly slip our hands to our hips and whisper, "Keep your gat ready! This may be a frameup!"—a remark that was always good for a sputtering giggle no matter who the visitor turned out to be: a six-year-old with a dispatch from first grade; Sister Mary Amadeus, our mother superior; or Father Scanlon, our pastor, a man of enormous size and dignity.

A gentle, trusting lady, Sister Mary Verissima was shocked one day when, turning suddenly from the blackboard, she saw too forefingers pointed at her head and two pairs of lips mouthing an unmistakable "Pow!"

Gentle or not, she knew the time had come to relocate the executive officers of the BO Detective Agency at opposite ends of the back row of desks.

She said firmly, "You boys stop that detective nonsense right now, you hear?"

We were dumbfounded. How did she know? Obviously someone sitting close to us had squealed, and we had a pretty good idea who it was.

Her strategy, however, did not immediately pay off. My partner and I chose to consider the move an expansion of the BO empire. During preclass meetings around the pencil sharpener in the cloakroom, we enrolled all the boys who sat between us as special investigators, sworn to secrecy. Now five hands instead of two went for their guns when someone knocked. There should have been six, but Frank Cassidy declined to join the force on the grounds that he had no time for such nonsense.

Cassidy was going to be a priest. The trouble with Frank was that he sometimes thought he had already been ordained and was on his way to becoming a bishop. If O'Donnell was the perfect conspirator in things surreptitious, Cassidy was the gadfly who kept me on my scholastic toes. Slim and ascetic-looking, dressed always in a starched shirt, he was the boy who always had the right answer. We didn't mind that so much as we did his smug look after giving it.

The nuns loved him, not only because he was a brilliant student but also because he was going to dedicate his brilliance to the service of God. He knew it in first grade. He knew it when he went to Quigley and Mundelein seminaries. And he knew it when he was ordained.

Sister Mary Verissima's altar boys knew it, too, for it was Frank who always won the before-Mass contests in the sacristy to see who could say the Latin confiteor the fastest. Surely there was no more accurate indicator of a vocation than that.

He was also one of Father Scanlon's favorites. On the pastor's monthly visits to our class—which began, as they did in every room, with a hearty "Well, Sister, how are these young people behaving themselves?"—who but Frank Cassidy sensed when the visit was running out of small talk and sprang to the rescue with a pious "Would you give us your blessing, Father?"

Grateful beyond words, Father Scanlon would suddenly look very serious, ask us to kneel down, and then give us the blessing in Latin. To this day I have not discovered a better exit line.

My own status with the nuns was also excellent on the strength of my having three uncles who were priests, one a monsignor and one a canon in Ireland, impeccable credentials for any aspiring student in a Catholic grade school of my time.

As for becoming a priest myself, I wasn't so sure. But I wasn't dumb, either. I managed, from time to time—usually just before report cards came out—to assume the mantle of a troubled pilgrim manfully struggling with the big question of his life. And sister after sister, from grade to grade, impressed, solicitous, and hopeful, assured me she was praying for me and that ultimately God would show me the way. He did.

Now, belatedly, I must give these devoted women the thanks that are their due as I call to mind my twelve children and twenty-five grandchildren. Who can doubt the efficacy of a nun's prayer?

Cassidy was quick to point out to O'Donnell and myself that our BO enterprise was a sin and had to be confessed.

"Why?" we demanded to know.

"Because you're disobeying Sister. Disobedience is a sin."

"So is squealing," I countered.

He pretended not to know what I was talking about, so there wasn't much I could do.

O'Donnell, the more practical member of our firm, told Cassidy he'd punch him in the nose if the subject ever came up again and promptly forgot about it.

I myself laughed it off at first, but every Monday morning Cassidy would ask me if I'd confessed yet. Finally, to shut him up, I told him that I had.

"What did the priest say?"

I had him there. "Ever hear of the seal of confession? It works both ways, you know."

So Cassidy left off, but my conscience didn't. Now I had not only the sin of disobedience to wor y about but also the sinful lie I had told Cassidy. Obviously there was nothing to do but lay the whole matter before Father Friel.

My worries proved to be groundless. Father Friel, that excellent priest, commended me for forming a detective agency instead of something worse (whatever that meant), but since the seventh grade seemed relatively free of crime, wouldn't it be smart to limit our activities to after-school hours? Father Friel put it in such a way that I immediately saw the sense of it.

As for the sin of disobeying Sister Mary Verissima, he gladly forgave me and said the lie I had told to Frank Cassidy was not important enough to be considered a sin.

Lighthearted as only a shriven sinner can be, I broke the news to O'Donnell that our classroom sleuthing would have to cease. We swore we would keep it going outside of school hours; but without the titillating challenge of disclosure by Sister Mary Verissima, the old zing was gone, and quietly, by degrees, our agency, navy and all, went out of business.

At no time was the rivalry between myself and Frank Cassidy more acute than on those Saturday afternoons when we stood in line at the confessional. You may ask, for what prize could we possibly compete while preparing for the sacrament of penance?

You would ask only if you didn't know that the line of penitents had to wind past a large brass candle stand with its battery of votive candles. On those not too infrequent occasions when Cassidy and I found ourselves standing beside each other, the call to battle was irresistible. Which of us could take the longest time to pass a finger through the flame of a burning candle? This trial by fire became such a regular event that you could sense the tension mounting all along the line as my rival and I worked our way up to the flickering lights.

"Now?" I would whisper.

"Now," he would answer.

Back and forth, more and more slowly, our fingers moved through the flame. One afternoon, determined to establish supremacy once and for all, Cassidy actually held his finger still for a second or two as you would roast a marshmallow. I did likewise.

We might have been standing there through Mass the next morning, done to a crust, if two girls hadn't simultaneously screamed and promptly fainted.

His stole flying, Father Friel was out of the confessional like a whirlwind. What he had expected to find I'm not sure, though I have my suspicions, but for a moment there was a look of relief on his face when he saw it was merely two penitents trying to immolate themselves. With a firm hold on our shoulders he propelled us to the door with instructions to get first aid at the convent and not come back for another week.

Each of us claiming victory, we decided it would be better to skip the convent and go right home, even though we knew that suitable punishments would be administered there also.

What a shock it was to Sister Mary Verissima and the

class next morning at Mass to see Frank Cassidy and Thomas Byrnes sitting like statues, forefingers bandaged, while the rest of the faithful went up to Communion. Two class leaders with mortal sins on their souls at the same time!

Only my sister Alyce would speak to me as we set off for home after Mass.

"Just the same," she said loyally, "I know you won."

The Boy
Who Could Only Listen

There was a great feast day of my schoolboy years that you'll search for in vain on the liturgical calendar. But the boys of Sister Mary Verissima's sixth grade knew it well and loved it. In fact, we loved it so much we celebrated it once a week— every Friday afternoon from two to three. We called it the Feast of the Anticipation.

Actually, it was Father Shay, our assistant pastor, who originated the name. He had paid us one of his occasional how-are-the-boys-behaving-Sister visits and found himself in the midst of a variety show. At Sister's invitation, he stayed on, sitting at her desk while she herself, as usual, stood at the back of the room. He laughed, applauded, and shook his head in wonderment as boy after boy—as many as there was time for—volunteered to go before the class and entertain, each according to his talents.

John Flynn, whose voice could soar like a nightingale's, sang "Mother Machree." Ernie Plummer, whose father owned a garage, sketched a diagram of a gasoline engine on the blackboard and explained how it worked. Max Lemon performed a card trick. Henry Meisner played "Smile the While" on his kazoo. Marty Mullen recited, "Who Fears to Speak of Easter Week?"

Aldo Tonelli told a funny story in Italian dialect, and I

told one in Swedish dialect—something I had picked up through close association with several Swedish families in our neighborhood.

Father Shay enjoyed every minute of it. In fact, he seemed genuinely disappointed when the first dismissal bell rang.

"Boys," he exclaimed enthusiastically, "that was wonderful! I'll bet Hollywood doesn't have as much talent as there is in this room."

"And there's more we didn't have time for," Sister said. "You must come again soon and hear the rest of it."

"Indeed I will," Father promised.

But he was curious. He lingered after the class had left to ask Sister what had inspired her to hold these Friday afternoon diversions. I overheard most of their conversation because it was my turn to stay and empty the wastebaskets and clean the erasers.

"The last hour on Friday is the worst time of all for the boys," Sister told Father. "It's so close to their weekend holiday they can hardly contain themselves."

"I know what you mean," Father smiled.

"And it's hard on me, too. I almost have to be an ogre to keep their minds on their work."

"Ah," said Father, beginning to see her thinking—or at least part of it. "So instead of fighting their anticipation of the weekend, you celebrate it."

"Yes," Sister agreed, but she was quick to add, "In a constructive way."

If Father Shay had any doubts about the constructiveness of our afternoon's entertainment, Sister soon dispelled them.

"Every day of the school week," she continued, "the boys are told what to do next—which is right and proper. But I think initiative is important, too. And so is the expression of their God-given talents. Why, some of these boys never dreamed they could do what they're doing. And every time they get up in front of the class I can see their self-confidence growing stronger."

As Father listened, his look became more thoughtful. "So you're not only anticipating the coming of a weekend," he said, "but, in a very special way, the eventual coming of adulthood."

Sister smiled her thanks for the priest's understanding.

"Well, Sister," he said as he turned to leave, "I would like to make a suggestion. You and I know the Church loves celebrations—celebrations of God's bounty. That's why we have so many feasts." There was a happy lift to his voice as he concluded, "Why not call this one the Feast of the Anticipation?"

For the most part, Sister left the choice of material to the boys themselves. And since the class had a remarkable supply of self-starters, one performance was no sooner finished than a flurry of hands assured us of several more.

Each number had to be new. No repeats were allowed except by popular demand, as in the case of Aldo Tonelli's Italian dialect story. At Sister's suggestion, I gave up my budding career as a Swedish dialectician. She felt that my time would be more profitably spent in singing than in trying to be something I wasn't. This cut in on John Flynn's specialty, and he seemed a little miffed by it until Sister pointed out that there should be no feeling of resentment by either of us because John was a high-flying boy soprano and I was a low-flying alto.

Sister was also aware of the shy ones, the contented applauders who were happy to be nothing more than part of the audience. To them she might say, "And what about *you,* John"—or Peter or Frank or James—"is there something *you* would like to do?" If, in an agony of embarrassment, they still shook their heads no, she would take them aside later and question them. If they still had nothing to offer, she'd suggest that they read something from a favorite book.

Usually grateful for this bailout, though nervous as field

mice, they would walk to the front of the room and give us a paragraph or two from "Tom Swift and His Electric Searchlight," "Ralph on the Midnight Flyer," and other classics of our day. Eventually, to Sister's delight, their stage fright would begin to disappear.

Not so, however, with Ollie McPherson.

Timid, self-effacing, too shy even to read something unless he could stand safely moored to his desk, he panicked at the thought of venturing into the vast seascape at the front of the room; if he foundered, forty-five pairs of eyes would watch him go down in disgrace.

One evening after school, when it was my turn to stay and give the blackboard its weekly washing, I heard Sister ask Ollie, "What would you *like* to do?" as if she knew there was some buried treasure there waiting to be discovered.

"I—I don't know," he stammered forlornly.

"Now, Ollie," Sister urged, "there must be *some*thing. Do you like to sing?"

"I sound awful."

"Would you like to draw something on the blackboard?"

He shook his head.

"Well, maybe you could simply tell what you do when you go home after school."

There was a long pause and then a slow response that was little more than a whisper. "I don't do anything. I just— listen."

"You listen?" Sister asked gently. "And what do you listen to, Ollie?"

He looked at her searchingly. He wanted to be sure she didn't think he was trying to be funny. "My grandma," he said at last.

"Your grandma?"

He nodded. "She's very old. She's in a wheelchair. When I come home, it's my job to take her out for some fresh air. We go round and round the block. She talks to me. She says

I'm the only one who understands her or cares. And that's funny because all I do is listen."

"That's a wonderful thing you're doing for your grandma," Sister said.

"Oh, I don't mind," he added lest his teacher feel sorry for him. "I *like* to listen."

Sister was silent for a moment. "How would you like to tell the class about this?" she finally asked. "They'd love to know."

Almost in tears, Ollie whispered, "I couldn't."

"Why not, Ollie?"

"It wouldn't seem right to talk about that. It's just between me and Grandma."

I tried to prolong my cleaning of the blackboard, but Sister finally noticed that I had washed it down twice already. She suggested that I go home now and thanked me for staying. But as I dried the board off and put the bucket and rags away, I heard her try once more to bring Ollie out from beneath his own shadow.

"Tell you what," she said brightly. "*I'll* find something for you, something very special. As a big favor to me, will you read it?"

Sister's animated goodwill was too much for Ollie. He gave a reluctant nod of agreement.

The following Friday, as the afternoon's final performance, Ollie, at a nod from Sister, stood up and, to everyone's amazement, walked to the front of the room. In his hand he held a paper that Sister had prepared for him. He took a deep breath and began to read.

"From Saint Matthew. Take heed that ye do not your alms before men, to be seen of them; otherwise ye have no reward of your father which is in heaven. Therefore when thou doest thine alms, do not sound a trumpet before them, as the hypocrites do in the synagogue and in the streets, that they may have glory of men. Verily I say unto you, they have their reward.

"But when thou doest alms, let not thy left hand know what thy right hand doeth, that thine alms may be in secret; and thy father which seeth in secret himself shall reward thee openly."

That was all a long time ago. I don't know what became of most of my old classmates or if the talents uncovered during our Feasts of the Anticipation ever led to anything more notable than what Sister Mary Verissima intended— the discovery by young and growing personalities of certain powers that lay within.

One of those powers in particular stands fast in my memory—the power simply to listen. And whenever, as François Mauriac says, I "feel the need of being pardoned," I am grateful that there are some, like Ollie, who are so blessed with that power.

My Mother, My Pants

"Growing up isn't easy for kids these days" is a frequently heard comment on the pressures to which youngsters are being subjected: parental pressure to excel in sports and studies; TV pressure to acquire this video game and eat that cereal; peer pressure to wear shirts, jeans, and shoes that carry certain brand labels.

All of which, no doubt, is true.

But life wasn't exactly a bowl of Frosty Crunchies in my early days, either, although the problem was of a different nature. The problem was a peculiar kind of age discrimination. There seemed to be an adult plot, especially among mothers, to keep you from growing up at all. Its outward sign was the type of pants you wore at certain stages of your development—first, short pants, then knickers, and finally, several years later, long pants. Each type marked you as a member of a specific age group as clearly as stripes or pips mark the status of a soldier.

For the most part, you didn't mind wearing the uniform of your rank. But when you felt qualified to move up to the next rank and your promotion was stubbornly delayed, then you felt the icy stab of injustice.

In these days when boys wear long pants from the moment they begin to walk, it's hard to imagine a time when this familiar garment was a badge of honor that you merited only when you were in your teens. It meant the end of childhood days and childish ways. It signified your citizenship in the world of men as the toga had signified citizenship in the world of ancient Rome.

Childhood began with pants that reached only to your knees and were supported by buttons of that much maligned garment, the pantywaist. Over this you wore a tailless shirt or blouse. A drawstring held it snug around your middle, covering the buttons. Every morning you or your mother tied the string in a big bow, which was then tucked under the shirt.

For the rest of the day, one of your major concerns was to keep the bow from slipping out and showing. One of the major concerns of the nuns in the lower grades was to retie strings that had become undone during class. (It wasn't easy for a kid to stay decently dressed in those days.)

Later, in about the third or fourth grade, you graduated to knickers. These were full-cut breeches, supported by a belt. Their legs buckled over your long stockings just below the knees. Now you could discard the pantywaist and wear a shirt with tuck-in tails as your father did—a great boost to your self-esteem.

The change, however, was not made without your mother's misgivings. The belt, she maintained, might constrain your innards and thus impede your growth.

This, you knew, was only a dodge. What your mother really feared was that you were growing up before your time and would never be her little boy again.

Eventually, of course, you got your belt. You wore it with pride, with swagger, with your thumbs hooked into it, and, as I recall, with no unfavorable side effects except an occasional reminder from your parents to "pull up your pants, Junior."

"Look, Grandma, I'm wearing a real leather belt!"

"My, aren't you growing up!"

You were indeed growing up—growing up so fast that in another few years you were too old even for knickers.

You were ready for your first pair of long pants.

Your mother, however, wasn't so sure—particularly if you were an only son, as I was. To her, long pants meant that you might leave home any minute and never be seen again.

Unfortunately for me, Sister Mary Mechtildis (eighth-grade boys) felt the same way.

"The children aren't young for long any more," she said to my mother one day. "It's sad."

"It *is* sad," my mother readily agreed.

"Every morning I see another boy coming into my classroom wearing long pants. Why, it seems only yesterday when boys wouldn't *dream* of wearing them until well into high school."

She was right. The age limit for long pants had been moving steadily downward. Both Sister and my mother saw this trend as a sinister conspiracy by the garment industry to force-grow the country's young, and they were united against it.

"Of course, it's just a silly fad," said Sister. "I'm glad to see there are parents strong enough to resist it."

My mother nodded and smiled her thanks for the compliment. I could tell by the look in her eye that with such support she would stand her ground for several more years.

But the problem would not go away. It billowed forth one day on the stage of the school auditorium in full view of the assembled student body and several adults.

A special program had been prepared to honor the school's safety patrol, of which I was a member—boys who at noon recess and dismissal time shepherded the smaller children across the main intersections near the school.

Twenty or so strong, wearing our patrol-boy version of the Sam Browne belt, we were lined up before the priests and nuns of the parish, our parents, and our peers. One by one we were to step forward and shake hands with Father Scanlon, our pastor, and Mr. Keene, our alderman, who had just given a spirited talk on the fine safety record being set by boys like us the city over.

I was not so much aware of my patrol-boy importance as I was of my patrol-boy appearance. I was the only kid on stage not in long pants—a fact that I hoped would not escape my mother's notice.

At last it was my turn. I took one step and hesitated. An unmistakable feeling of looseness had developed just below my right knee. It could only mean one thing: a buckle had become unfastened.

But I couldn't just stand there. I had to move. I took another step—and immediately the right leg of my knickers dropped down to my shoe. It dropped with all the dramatic impact of a final theater curtain.

Many in the audience laughed. Some of my friends whistled. Others applauded.

Frantically I tried to yank up the sagging leg. It rose forlornly to half-mast, then dropped again. More laughter, more whistles, more applause. To stop, bend over, and refasten the buckle would have only intensified the awkwardness of the moment. Burning with shame, I shuffled forward.

"Pay no attention, Thomas," Father Scanlon smiled as I finally managed to shake hands with himself and Mr. Keene.

Nobody could ask for the impossible like Father Scanlon.

Our dinner table was always the place where important family matters were settled. Here my parents decided whether or not to buy a new car, to redecorate the house, to increase their insurance, to replace the old furnace. Here it was that my mother had for a time stalled my promotion from short pants to knickers.

And here it was, after my humiliation at school (and with considerable urging from my father), that she at last faced up to the fact that indeed I *was* growing up. I must soon have my first pair of long pants.

"Soon" to my mother meant somewhere in the sweet by-and-by. To my father, fortunately, it meant next day. Father won out.

And so, late the following afternoon, accompanied by my parents and younger sister (Grandma and Grandpa had wanted to witness the great event, too, but they both had colds), I appeared in Foley's Department Store for my first trousers.

Mr. Alvin Gummerson was the salesman. I note this fact for sentimental reasons. It was he who had fitted me for my first pantywaist and for just about every piece of clothing I wore thereafter. He was one of the last of a vanished breed—the salesman who takes such a personal interest in his customers that they eventually become his friends.

Mr. Gummerson was a tall, thin, and thoughtful man. A stubborn fringe of graying hair that had laid siege to the top of his head for years but had never scaled the heights gave him the look of a benevolent philosopher. He spoke in low, measured tones and never exaggerated. My parents liked him because, as my father, a salesman himself, put it, "He never gives you any of that salesman's guff."

"Well now," Mr. Gummerson said after the usual greetings, "what's it to be this time?"

"Pants for Junior," said my father.

Pants? Mr. Gummerson paused. From habit he had already turned toward the knickers table.

"Yes," said my mother, who knew a poignant moment when she saw one, "I'm afraid the knickers are gone forever."

"Ah," said Mr. Gummerson. "Ah," he said again. The first "ah" was an *ave atque vale* to an innocent age now departing; the second was a reluctant salute to the inevitable.

Long pants, appropriately enough, were on the floor above knickers. Like many salesmen of those days who had their own following, Mr. Gummerson was free to sell in any department of the store. In the slow and wobbly elevator he and my mother explored every possible variation of the theme "They do grow up, don't they?"

I'm sure it was Mr. Gummerson's most trying sale. Pair after pair of pants were brought out and tried on. My mother considered each pattern, color, and fit with the dogged deliberation of Pasteur studying his microbes. After each of her rejections, Mr. Gummerson would excuse himself and return with another armload of offerings.

At last—after my father was heard to mutter, "I could have outfitted the whole neighborhood in half this time"— Mother decided on a pair of plain grays. The tailor was called in to make some small adjustments.

"Don't you think," asked Mr. Gummerson, "that he should have at least two pairs?"

My mother considered this idea for a moment. "No," she temporized, "let's see first how these work out."

It was clear that if they didn't "work out," I'd be back to knickers indefinitely.

Sister Mary Mechtildis was busy writing at her desk when I entered the room. She returned my "Good morning, Sister" pleasantly but without looking up. It was only later when she called on me to stand and give a book report that she noticed.

"*Thomas!*" The word was a shocked whisper.

"Yes, Sister?"

She looked at me silently with a faltering smile of gentle sadness—as Hannibal might have looked on the gates of Rome before giving up his siege of the Eternal City. The last of Sister's children had left her for good.

"Continue, Thomas," she sighed at last.

I've been wearing long pants ever since.

My Tipperary Confession

By the time I was thirteen, my father could no longer turn away from a great longing to see once more the hills of Tipperary and the brothers and sisters he had left behind when he was scarcely twenty.

So off we sailed to Ireland, my father and mother, my sister and I, to Thurtles, Bansha, Latin, and Glenban; to Aunt Annie, who showed me how to ride a horse and milk a cow; to Aunt Mary, who had me sing "Kathleen Mavourneen" over and over to her neighbors, who declared I was another John McCormack surely; to Uncle Paddy, who played handball with me in the long evenings behind the cowshed and who secretly dropped a sovereign in one of my shoes during the night as consolation when I had lost—Paddy, who had inherited the ancestral farm, where I slept in the bed my father was born in.

Much of our time was also spent with Uncle James, the canon, at his rectory near the country town of Bansha. You wouldn't play handball with Uncle James any more than you would play it with St. Patrick, but he offered many other delightful diversions. There was a two-wheel, horse-drawn wicker buggy that he would let you drive when you and he were alone. And there was a bicycle that he would let you ride once you'd learned to ask permission correctly.

"Uncle James, can I ride your bicycle to town?"

"Whether you can or not depends on yourself, Junior, but as far as I'm concerned, you *may*."

We had not been long with Uncle James when he queried me about my spiritual habits. Did I say morning and evening prayers faithfully? Evening prayers most always, morning prayers sometimes. But I assured him I would try to do better. Sunday Mass? Of course. My parents saw to that. Holy Communion? Every Sunday—and confession every Saturday.

Then I choked.

"What's the matter, Junior? Are you sick?"

I was sick and I was terrified, for it had suddenly come to me that there would be no one to confess to next Saturday but Uncle James himself. And how can you tell your own uncle that you had disobeyed your parents, entertained an irreverent thought or two, and laughed at questionable jokes?

A handball-playing uncle might understand, perhaps, but not one who reacted so visibly to the incorrect use of the verb *can*.

I got out of my immediate predicament by pleading a sudden stomach cramp, which my mother, who was present, promptly attributed to all the shortbread I had devoured at afternoon tea.

Through the rest of that week my feelings of entrapment boiled like the storms of Aran. Had I been brought all the way to Ireland, home of my ancestors, to experience the worst humiliation of my young life?

Then, as suddenly as the crisis had struck, it evaporated.

"I think," my father said casually at Friday dinner, "I'll take Mae and the children to see the city of Tipperary tomorrow."

"Good idea," said the canon, who immediately understood the real purpose of the trip. "There's a train leaving Bansha at eleven o'clock." Then he added, "If you see Father Kilpatrick, give him my best."

The church in Tipperary seemed as old as the Irish faith. Slender Gothic columns, gray with years, rose rapierlike from patches of glass-stained sunlight and arched away into the dark upper reaches of the nave as if trying to touch eternity. As I waited my turn, my father behind me, I began to examine my conscience. Gradually a disturbing suspicion began to loom among my transgressions. Even though my father had been born here, Ireland to me was as yet a place of unfamiliar landscapes, customs, and faces. It's possible, I reflected, that even the sins they tell here are different. Maybe the priest won't know what I'm talking about or he'll think my faults are too grievous to be mentioned in this land that my father frequently called Ireland of the saints.

"Go ahead, Junior," my father nudged me. "It's your turn now." I hadn't even noticed that the penitent ahead of me had left the box.

"You want to go first?" I offered.

"No, I'll wait."

Father Kilpatrick heard my faltering confession in attentive silence. Occasionally he gave me what I took to be a reassuring nod. When I finished, he gently suggested that I find strength against temptation in more frequent prayer, assigned me my penance of three Our Fathers and three Hail Marys, the same I had often received at home—and then settled back for a friendly chat.

"Well now, lad, where are you from?" he asked, knowing that my speech did not originate in Tipperary.

The worst was obviously over. I gave a belly-deep sigh of relief. "Chicago, Father."

"All the way from the States, is it? And where are you staying?"

"In Bansha, Father."

"And who do you know in Bansha?"

"My uncle, Father, Canon James Byrnes."

"Glory be to God, so you're Jamie's nephew, then?"

Apparently the worst was *not* over. My reverend uncle had now been clearly linked to this miserable sinner who had crossed the Atlantic to disgrace him. "He sends you his best," I said feebly.

"Indeed he would!" exclaimed Father Kilpatrick, his voice warm and friendly. "Isn't Jamie one of my dearest friends? Now tell me about yourself."

On further reflection, I decided the worst *was* over, my sins as quickly forgotten as they had been forgiven.

Mindful of my father waiting outside the confessional

and no doubt wondering what his son had to tell that should take so long, I tried to race through a brief account of my visit. But my confessor was in no hurry.

Did I know the McNultys on the west side of Chicago? No? A pity. Fine people, the McNultys. Sean, the husband, was born in this very town, but the wife came from Kerry. Her sister had married a Finerty from Athlone who was supposed to be very big in Chicago politics. "But then you're a bit young for politics, I suppose."

"Yes, Father."

Was I enjoying my stay? "So you learned to ride a horse and milk a cow, did you? Good for you."

Had the canon taken us yet to visit his namesake, James of the Glen, a distant cousin reputed to be ninety-five years old with a beard down to his waist? "Not yet? Make sure you meet *him,* lad. In his prime he was one of the great hurlers of all Ireland."

I walked out of the confessional at last, past the wondering stare of my father, who, I learned later, was to enjoy much the same cozy kind of conversation.

The Ireland rushing past me on the train back to Bansha was no longer a strange and unfamiliar land. Sins were much the same here as in Chicago, at least in my age bracket. Forgiveness was the same. Human curiosity and gentleness were the same.

And the doctrine of Communion of Saints—communion between the faithful on earth and the blessed in heaven— must have been the same, too; this was easier for me to understand in later years because I had intimately experienced its first state, communion among the living members of the pilgrim Church itself—no matter how long the way to Tipperary.

The Rehabilitation
of a Choir Boy

Recently, at a Sunday Mass sung by an adult choir, and at another, a "Guitar Mass" sung by young adults and teenagers, I found myself wondering, as I have wondered often—where have all the children gone? I suppose some parishes still have children's choirs, but I haven't heard one in a long time, though I have attended Mass in many churches.

My wondering stirs memories of my days in Our Lady of Lourdes parish school where singing was a way of life. The nuns saw to it that you began singing in first grade, and you continued to sing through final graduation—"with grace in your heart to the Lord," as St. Paul says.

The whole school was a children's choir. Every Sunday, whatever your age, you sat with your class at the eight o'clock children's Mass and sang the old hymns. Eventually, as your voice steadied and began to do what you asked it to do, you might be selected, if you were a boy, to sing in the elite boys' choir, which was recruited from the sixth, seventh, and eighth grades. You then sang not only on Sunday with the rest but also at the Solemn High Masses of Christmas, Easter, and special feasts.

And—can you believe it?—at the eight o'clock *daily* Mass.

There were appearances, too, for individual singers. If you had a good voice, you'd be called upon from time to time to serenade one of the lower grades. Sister Mary Verissima might summon you to her desk and whisper, "I told Sister Mary Grace you'd sing something for her class this afternoon. Now might be a good time, don't you think?"

So away you'd go to the fourth-grade room, knock on the door, put your head inside, and say, "Sister, I've come to sing something for you."

"How delightful! Come in, come in!"

Books would close, pencils and papers would disappear in a chorus of bangs as desk tops dropped shut, and the class would warm you with the reverential attention reserved for the young gods from the upper grades.

One of these performers was Frank Fahey. If there was ever an individual who did *not* fit the conventional mold of the cherubic choir boy, it was Frank. His schoolroom deportment and scholastic performance were such that, on the average of once a month or more often, his mother would have to appear before Sister Mary Amadeus, the principal, and show cause why her son Frank should not be expelled.

A well-ballasted, broad-shouldered woman of impressive girth, wearing an enormous flowered hat set on a mop of black curly hair, Mrs. Fahey would emerge from her car in the get-ready crouch of a boxer who knew he was behind on points but was determined to make up for it in the next round.

When Frank was in the lower grades and still small enough for his teachers to handle, these visits by his mother were usually in outraged protest against the punitive actions of some nun Frank had tried beyond the limits of forbearance. But as Frank grew in size, if not in scholastic aptitude, even the most exasperated nun thought it wise to adopt a hands-off policy and seek satisfaction through the more diplomatic channels of teacher-to-principal-to-parent. Gradually over the years, however, Mrs. Fahey saw the sense of directing her anger not at the nuns but at her son.

What transpired in Sister Mary Amadeus's office during these later visits was no secret thanks to the reports of passers-by on their way to and from the boys' washroom. Mrs. Fahey would tongue-lash and sometimes slap her offspring into a forlorn promise to reform. Frank managed to look so penitent on these occasions that Sister Amadeus was always moved to give him another chance.

Although his father was a police captain, Frank seemed to have little respect for law and less for order, an attitude that showed up with depressing monotony in his grades. He was by far the oldest boy in the school, having spent much more than the usual time getting acquainted with each year's curriculum.

He was a first-run copy of his mother except that he was much taller. His black hair curled in the same tangle of ringlets that, when he slept, must have made him look like a Botticellian seraph.

In class Frank would sit quietly for the first hour or so, after which time some dormant gene, tracing back perhaps to Conn of the Hundred Battles, would stir restlessly in the depths of his marrow. Hearing the call of a distant battle horn and frustrated at being hemmed in by the syntax of sentences, the time tables of arithmetic, the tenets of the Faith, he would pinch the neck in front of him or slide a foot across the aisle, kick his neighbor in the shins, and dare him to complain.

Detected by Sister, he would then spend the rest of the day in the principal's outer office, forbidden to speak, condemned to reading one of his school books. We estimated once that seventy-five percent of Frank's education was acquired in this way. Why he was still in school by the time he reached sixth grade can only be ascribed to the nuns' saintly conviction that no boy is ever a total loss. Someday, they prayed, Frank would settle down.

Then it was discovered that Frank had a voice. It came to light one afternoon when Mrs. Emmet, the church organist, on one of her periodic visits to the sixth grade to recruit talent for the boys' choir, asked Frank to sing. He sang "Mother Machree," a favorite of Sister Mary Amadeus, who was also present. He was in.

Frank went on to become the choir's leading soloist. Almost miraculously, his classroom demeanor began to improve. He never quite reached the level of decorum expected of the rest of us, but with Frank *any* improvement bordered on the miraculous. The visits of his mother became less and less frequent. The sisters were ecstatic. Their prayers were being answered.

Then almost overnight, and about two years before anyone else's, Frank's voice changed. By the time he reached seventh grade, his soaring soprano had plunged to a deep baritone, or, as some maintained, to a bass, and Frank began to shave.

Since the boy sopranos carried most of the solos, Frank was relegated to the general chorus and told not to sing so loud, a restriction that galled him. In retaliation he began to grow a small goatee, which eventually Sister Mary Amadeus ordered him to cut off. Although in this instance he obeyed, he was soon back to his old ways. Rubber bands once more zipped through the air; blobs of glue were dropped on seats temporarily vacated; bent pins were fired from a sling formed by a rubber band stretched between two widespread fingers; and Frank's sawed-off peashooter (its length shorted for easier concealment) made an extended return engagement.

These activities usually took place when Sister Mary Verissima was busy at the blackboard, her head turned away from the class. Unfortunately for Frank, however, she became adept at spinning around unexpectedly, even in the middle of an arithmetic problem or a sentence diagram, and off Frank would go for another day in the principal's office, his rubber bands, pins, and peashooter confiscated.

Replacing the peashooter became a bore for Frank until he realized one day that Sister, after class, simply dropped it in her wastebasket. An immediate arrangement with whatever boy had the after-school job of cleaning erasers and emptying baskets that week assured the prompt return of the peashooter to its original owner.

The beginning of the end of Frank's shenanigans came one memorable Monday morning during the daily eight o'-clock Mass. John Flynn, who had superseded Frank as leading soloist, was singing the *Agnus Dei*. Slowly, somewhere deep in the ranks of the chorus, a peashooter was raised to firing position, aimed at the back of John Flynn's neck. The *Agnus Dei* ended abruptly in the singer's loud "Ouch!" followed by gasps of shocked surprise and the inevitable giggling, all of it clearly audible to priest and congregation below.

Even over the tearful promise of Mrs. Fahey that the incident would never be repeated, the long-deferred dismissal of her son was announced that afternoon by the pastor himself after a careful review of Frank's record. We had our farewell glimpse of our embattled classmate as his mother propelled him vigorously toward their family car.

Depressed even more than Frank and his family, I'm sure, were the nuns, who had prayed so earnestly for his reform, particularly Sister Mary Amadeus, whose supplications to St. Jude, patron of difficult cases, had apparently brought no response.

For a while, we spoke of "good old Frank" with that odd mixture of envy and awe reserved for the maverick you see as yourself in your dreams and to whom you will always be grateful for the excitement he brought to your otherwise orderly years. But by degrees the memory faded, and by the time we graduated from eighth grade, Frank was no more a presence than if he had disappeared into the Amazon jungles.

But he hadn't.

One afternoon almost ten years later, driving home from downtown in my parents' car and drawn by who knows what antic burst of nostalgia, I decided to have another look at my old parish school. The time was 3:15. As I drove past, the front doors swung open. I parked, got out, and watched.

The children began leaving in the familiar single file down the sidewalk past the church. There, on a signal from one of the nuns standing guard, they were allowed to break ranks and go their separate ways home.

But they were in no hurry to go home this day, for at the curb, handsome as General BlackJack Pershing astride his charger, sat someone on a motorcycle, someone they obviously knew and liked.

It was Frank. He was dressed in the rakish cap, black leather jacket, gauntlets, and gun holster of the motorcycle police. I moved up closer behind him. Some older boys were making him promise that he'd attend their baseball game with St. Margaret Mary's next Friday. A young girl, in about fourth grade, jumped up and down for attention, wanted him to know that she had won a spelldown that day. Two younger boys begged for a ride. "Nothing doing," said Frank. "You be good kids and someday you'll have a motorcycle of your own."

I stepped in and asked my former classmate if he remembered me. He did, though his face clouded momentarily as if he suddenly remembered other things, too. Then he slapped me on the arm. "I'm glad I ran into you," he said. "I want to invite you to a concert."

"A concert?"

"Tomorrow night at the Community Hall. Ever hear of the Aeolian Singers?" I had. "Well," said Frank, "I'm a member."

"Great!" I said.

"I'll leave a ticket for you at the door. Maybe two, eh?" He winked. I promised to be there. Then he added with studied nonchalance, "I have a couple of solos."

Another moment and he gunned his machine, swung expertly away from the curb in a graceful demonstration of Hogarth's famed curve of beauty, and, with a blast of power, roared off after a motorist who had dared to coast through the corner stop sign.

As I drove home, I thought of Sister Mary Amadeus. And I wondered if St. Jude had once been a singer, too.

When Preaching
Was Really Preaching

Whenever our Sunday homily is longer and less inspiring than I feel it should be, I think of the young man Eutychus, who sat in a window of a room where St. Paul was preaching to the disciples and where, the Bible says, "he continued his speech until midnight" (Acts 20:7–12). Heavy with sleep, the youth lost his balance, "fell down from the third loft, and was taken up dead." The saint, however, gathered him in his arms, prayed over him, and restored him to life—a service that should be provided, but isn't, I'm sorry to say, by certain preachers of my experience.

Memory could be playing tricks, but I don't recall any perceptible need during my schoolboy days for the priests I knew to resuscitate members of their congregations. True, some worshipers fainted now and then, but only from pre-Communion fasting. An alert corps of ushers got to know the chronic swooners and were ready at the first *thump* to carry them outside, where they usually recovered in time for Holy Communion. The whole business only underscored the importance then of being as empty of food as of sin before going to the rail.

I remember most of the priests of those years as fair-to-excellent preachers—some, of course, less histrionic than others, but all of them capable of keeping the faithful from toppling over in the pews.

Perhaps the old Latin Mass had something to do with it. Once on the altar—except for brief now-you-see-me-now-you-don't whirlarounds to bless the people (or, as my friend John O'Donnell said, "to make sure they're still there"), the priest retained holy privacy, screened by the back of his chasuble and by the mystery of the Latin liturgy, which, no matter how fast you read your missal, invariably outdistanced you by several pages. But sooner or later the celebrant had to come to the pulpit and address the people face-to-face in English. Perhaps we paid attention simply out of gratitude for the change, which O'Donnell called the "halftime break."

As I recall, priests in those days didn't "give homilies." They "preached sermons." The distinction, if I read the Catholic Encyclopedia correctly, is that the homily is essentially "a commentary on Sacred Scriptures," whereas the broader term "sermon" can be applied to homilies and other forms of religious discourse as well: instructions on matters of faith, morals, and liturgical practice, panegyrics, eulogies, and several others it would take a sermon to cover. We got them all back then.

Arriving home from the children's Mass on Sunday, I would invariably be asked two questions by one or the other of my parents: "Who said the Mass?" and "What was the sermon about?"

"Father Scanlon said the Mass, and the sermon was about eternity and how long it is," I might reply.

"How long is it?"

"Well, Father said to imagine an iron ball as big as the earth, and every hundred years a little bird comes along and gives it a peck. How long will it take the little bird to destroy the iron ball? A long time, right? Ha! When that happens, Father said, eternity will just be getting started!"

I remember thinking that Father Scanlon may have known a lot about eternity but he sure wasn't up on the life expectancy of your average bird. Nevertheless, the image of that tiny creature assaulting an earth-size iron ball every hundred years was enough to keep you thinking for days.

On Monday mornings the nuns, too, asked you about the sermon, even though they had heard every word of it. This was simply to see if your thoughts had been where they were supposed to be and not on the next baseball game with St. Margaret Mary's.

Frankly, I have always had trouble with the word *homily*. It's too close for my devotional comfort to two other words, much less edifying. One is *homely*. The other is *hominy*—which, I understand, is an Algonquian term for hulled corn.

I have heard the homily described as a "civilized, familiar discourse made by a pastor of souls to the members of his flock." Its method is usually gentle. It examines, interprets, renews, reminds, invites. The sermon, on the other hand, at least the sermon as I recall it, pushed, shoved, commanded, exhorted, threatened, and often intimidated. The difference I observe between today's homily and yesterday's sermon is the difference between a sit-down chat in the rose garden and the annual Super Bowl Game.

The old-fashioned sermon was made for thunder and lightning, and there was plenty of it around in those days. It was a time when oratory was considered one of the fine arts. You worked your way into it through grade school elocution lessons ("Thomas Byrnes will now recite 'Gunga Din,' by Rudyard Kipling"). In high school and college, where oratorical contests were almost as common as football pep rallies, you studied and often memorized such philippics as Robert Emmet's "Speech from the Dock," Patrick Henry's "Give Me Liberty or Give Me Death," Webster's "Reply to Haine," and many more.

You went to hear orators speak as you went to see Rogers Hornsby swing his bat, and with an accomplished speaker on the stand the suspense was often comparable. My father took me one night to hear a favorite son of Illinois, Senator J. Hamilton Lewis (J. Ham to his friends), who was campaigning for reelection. (My mother stayed home. She couldn't stand the senator's pink whiskers.) As usual, J. Ham was in fine form. He arrived at the hall half an hour late, moved at a deliberate, thoughtful pace to the platform, took a minute or two to find a suitable place for his pearl-handled walking stick and Borsalino hat, and then gave his full attention (as the audience gave theirs) to the finger-by-finger removal of his gray doeskin gloves.

Every heart in the place was pounding, including mine. When finally he raised his right hand high, as if commanding the very gods to be silent, and thundered, "My fellow Americans!" the shouts and cheers of his adoring followers could have been heard across the state. He had said nothing, and yet he had said it all.

J. Ham knew all the ploys. At one point, a voice from the audience (a plant, now that I look back on it, pretending to be a heckler) asked him how he stood on a certain ticklish issue of the day, where one verbal misstep could have lost him many votes. As boldly as Perseus facing the Gorgon Medusa, J. Ham straightened to his full five-feet-five height, thrust his pink whiskers heavenward, and bellowed, "Sir!" (Long pause.) "Sir!" (Again.) "I shall *speak of it!*"

That's all the audience wanted. The senator had answered the challenge; he would speak of it. They cheered, whistled, and stomped their approval—and nobody seemed to mind when, an hour and half later, he left the hall without having mentioned it again.

Gestures were once as much an adornment of the old sermon as they were the old oration. They were an essential part of your earliest elocution lessons, taught, in my case, by Miss Elsie Plummet, an "outside" teacher who came to our parish school once a week to coach us in diction, stance, expression, voice projection, and gesturing. Her precepts gave us fine criteria for judging the pulpit performances of our parish priests. I remember Father Scanlon, our pastor, as being the loudest. A giant snow-capped mountain of a man, he had by far the most commanding presence. His gestures were commanding, too. He was a perfect example of Miss Plummet's dictum, "If you're bringing a hand down for emphasis, don't start the gesture above your head unless to express extreme agitation." It seems to me that most if not all of our pastor's gestures started above his head. But that was all right, because he was usually in a state of extreme agitation over something or other—people coming to Mass late and leaving early, whispering during Mass, not using their missals, not showing up for the parish bazaar, not going to Communion more often, not contributing enough money to the fuel collection, and other trespasses the shepherd of our flock found it difficult to abide.

Father Friel, on the other hand, had what even the youngsters in the lower grades recognized as exceptional class. His voice was golden, his movements were controlled and flowing, and whenever he spread his arms out in an all-embracing gesture, he remembered to keep the two middle fingers of each hand together for a more graceful effect—exactly as Miss Plummet had advised us kids to do.

Father Shay was the youngest of our three priests and, though never boring, was the least assured as a public speaker. That is, he seldom made little shivers run up and down your spine as the others were capable of doing.

His problem was that, in a day when speaking from a prepared script was considered unthinkable and speaking from notes was frowned on, Father Shay needed notes. He tried to conceal them in the sleeves of his alb, among gospels and epistles, in corners of the pulpit, but everyone knew they were there. The tip-off always came when he lowered his head for a closer look and his glasses rode down to the end of his nose. But he was a pleasant man, sincere and devout, and people didn't criticize him too harshly; they only pitied him for his lack of self-confidence. The nuns said special prayers for him to St. John Chrysostom, patron of preachers and orators.

Then one weekday morning we discovered we didn't have to pity him any more.

It was Father's turn that week to say the daily eight o'clock Mass, at which the celebrant always gave a mini-sermon. My friend John O'Donnell and I were the servers.

Slipping into his alb, Father was suddenly motionless as if trying to remember something. With the alb still about his neck, he went through all his pants pockets. He went through them again. No luck. "Holy Saint Anthony," he whispered, going directly to the heavenly specialist in finding lost objects.

Another moment, his face turning pale, he said to me, "Tommy, run over to the rectory. Ask Mrs. Bailey to look in my room and see if I didn't leave some notes on my desk. Hurry now, please!" I thought for a moment he was going to run back to the rectory himself, but there wasn't time. It was just a minute or two before eight. With cassock and surplice flying, I raced across the busy street to the rectory.

Mrs. Bailey took her time answering the doorbell. She took her time whatever she did. A heavyset woman with many years of housekeeping behind her, she had trouble with her feet, as everyone in the parish knew. Always in large bedroom slippers lined with lamb's wool, she walked with the pushing motion of a tired but determined cross-country skier.

Having delivered my message, I discovered that our immediate concern was not to find Father Shay's notes but to find Mrs. Bailey's spectacles. She carefully explained to me that Father's room was upstairs, and that was the problem—not that she needed her glasses to go *up* the staircase, mind you; she needed them to come down. Without them she might misjudge the steps, and I wouldn't want her to fall, now, would I?

No, I wouldn't, so I helped her check every likely surface from parlor to kitchen. A glance at a mantel clock told me that Father Shay was now well into the eight o'clock Mass.

"Maybe they're upstairs," I suggested.

She paused for moment, weighing this possibility against the hazards of descending the stairs without them if they were *not* upstairs.

"I'll help you downstairs if we can't find them," I offered.

Grateful for this assurance, she plodded up the steps,

saying that I reminded her of her cousin Julie's boy, although, to be truthful, he was a speck older than I, and his hair wasn't quite as red. She wanted to know my name, my mother's maiden name, and if there were any priests in the family. When I told her my father had three brothers who were priests, she blessed herself three times and looked as impressed as if they had been the Holy Trinity.

She led the way along the upstairs hall to Father Shay's room in back, turned in at his open door, and immediately cried, "Glory be to God, there they are!"

Father's notes? No, Mrs. Bailey's spectacles. She remembered now. She must have set them down on Father's dresser while straightening up after he left for Mass.

We never found the notes. But as I turned to leave, a question popped into my mind that I couldn't hold back.

"If the spectacles were up here, how did you—?"

"How did I get downstairs to let you in, is that it?" She sighed. "Ah, Tommy," she said, "my memory's not what it used to be. I keep forgetting to be careful."

Father Shay was following John O'Donnell off the altar as I burst into the sacristy. He was a man at peace with the world. There was laughter in his eyes when I told him his notes were nowhere to be found. "Don't worry," he said. "I must have accidentally thrown them away." Then, under his breath, he added, "High time."

"It was the craziest thing," John O'Donnell told me as we crossed over to the school. "He got up to speak without his notes. He closed his eyes for a minute as if praying. Then he talked about putting your faith in God, especially when you are in deep trouble. No need to look anywhere else for help. Go direct to the Top. I had a funny feeling up and down my spine."

Father Shay never used his notes again.

I've been told by experts in such matters that it was the

"intimacy" of television that brought about the end of the old oration, the old-fashioned sermon. Possibly that and the fact that we've grown too sophisticated for the projected voice, the grand gesture—except, of course, at political conventions. The norm now is TV's one-on-one situation, where someone cozies up to you in your living room to sell you insurance, toothpaste, and a million other products. I doze through a lot of it as I doze through some homilies.

But I know what would wake me up in the latter instance and keep me awake: a well-prepared address delivered with the freshness and excitement of St. Paul bringing the good news to the Gentiles. And may the priest be not afraid to raise his voice now and then above the level of a chalk talk on mortgage financing, and may he be not afraid to open his arms once in a while in an all-embracing, love-one-another gesture—not forgetting, of course, that business about the middle fingers.

I Remember Piano Lessons

Every so often I conduct a modest survey among my piano-playing grandchildren to see if I can detect any significant change in the classic child-piano relationship of my early years. I also do it to show the kids how lucky they are to have a grandpa who really cares, even though some of the less dedicated wish I'd mind my own business.

At one time or another all my grandchildren take piano lessons, whether they want to or not. Their parents believe, as did *their* parents, that piano lessons are as critical to a youngster's development as good food and booster shots. The lessons are mandatory for much the same reason that going to school is mandatory—to increase awareness of the lovely things available to us mortals on this amazing planet.

Even if Johnny or Mary develops no more than a nodding acquaintance with the Muse, the effort is never considered a total loss.

Sometimes, however, impressed by an offspring's unexpected flash of dexterity in getting a difficult chord just right, parents might feel that a genuine talent is about to surface, a talent that may someday lead to immortality. But most of these hopes gradually fade as Mom and Dad begin to wonder if the parents of, say, Paderewski had as much trouble getting young Ignac to within striking distance of the keyboard as they've been having with Junior.

Because some of my grandchildren wanted to play in their high school marching band, they switched from the piano to something easier to carry, like the clarinet, the French horn, or the saxophone. Others have switched from the piano to football, baseball, hockey, weight lifting, and bike riding, to name but a few of the favorite pursuits of ex-piano students. When this happens, battle-weary parents console themselves with the thought that "Junior can never say we didn't give him a chance, can he?"

Oh, *can't* he! He may not use those precise words, but it's a self-deluding parent who thinks in later years Junior will blame himself for not being able on occasion to sit at the piano and charm a roomful of guests with the brilliance of his virtuosity. Most likely, he'll skulk into a corner and mutter, "*Why* didn't my parents try harder to make me practice?" Why? Because they knew that if they did, they'd be picked up for child abuse.

Lack of interest is the reason cited most often when youngsters give up on the piano. "Johnny just doesn't have a feel for it" is a common parental excuse. Okay—but I wonder how many kids who eventually graduate from eighth grade start out with a "feel" for long division, subordinate clauses, and the date of the Boston Tea Party. I still don't have much of a feel for compound fractions.

I think some kids are turned off by the weird titles

composers often give their pieces. I had a fourth-grade friend once who swore he was learning a number called "The Tree Surgeons' Polka." Only later, when he became almost as adept at reading English as he was at reading music, did he realize that the title was really "The Three Sturgeons' Polka"— which to him, for some odd reason, made more sense.

I myself suffered through several years of piano lessons and such titles as "The Merry Meadow Mouse," "O See the Busy Bumble Bee," "The Lapwing's Lullaby," and others of similar alliteration. The only piece I was ever truly fond of was "The Fire Brigade March," a thunderous lightning ball of big, booming chords that seemed to portray in furious succession an explosion at the gas works, the sounding of the alarm, the roar of the engines, the clanging of the bells, and finally, for good measure, another explosion at the gas works. For a fifth-grader, playing the ma ch was the closest thing to working out on a heavy punching bag that the world of music had to offer. I went at it with unrestrained juvenile gusto, especially when I played for my grandfather, who was hard of hearing. I think I'd be a piano player yet today if "The Fire Brigade March" had been the only piece I ever had to learn. My parents, however, insisted that my teacher, Sister Mary Grace, start me on a new piece that wasn't such an out-and-out bell ringer. Sister answered that she *had* given me a new piece, a bouncy little morsel named "Hop O My Thumb," but I had been too busy riding on the fire engine to learn it.

My efforts to master "Hop O My Thumb" were somewhat constrained by my inability to figure out what the title meant. I still haven't figured it out—which may explain why I still can't play it. (I can, however, play a few bars of "The Fire Brigade March," if anyone cares to hear it.) Eventually Sister Mary Grace convinced my mother that there really wasn't much of a future for a one-composition pianist and that I'd better drop my lessons because I obviously didn't have a feel for the piano. When I hung up metronome for good, my mother sighed and said to my father one evening over a fine dinner of corned beef and cabbage, "At least he can never say that we didn't give him a *chance!*"

"No," my father agreed, "he can never say that."

I must tell you more about Sister Mary Grace; she deserves better than the grace-note mention I've just given her.

According to the schoolboy legend woven from scraps of adult conversation overheard at home, Sister had once been a promising concert pianist. But a call stronger than that of the concert stage had finally brought her to the convent, to Our Lady of Lourdes school, and to her little music room at the end of the second-floor hallway, where she would spend the rest of her life teaching the piano to others.

If you studied with a lay teacher, who taught in her home or yours, your lessons were something apart from the rest of your education, something extra that required extra effort.

But if you studied with Sister Mary Grace, you studied in the atmosphere of the normal school routine, even though, on some days, your lesson might be scheduled for after school hours. Unless you were hopelessly unmusical or your parents couldn't afford the extra two dollars a month for the lessons, the piano was as normal a part of your life as the Baltimore Catechism. Its music, heard clearly through Sister's half-open door, even accompanied you on your trips to the washroom.

Seeing Sister day after day sitting in her chair beside the piano stool, a figure of saintly patience, some of us who were familiar with her legend were inspired to invent a romantic fiction that may or may not have been close to the truth—a distinction that bothered us not a whit.

She's *waiting* for something, we told ourselves—a Talent (probably a girl), a Someone who may in time live out Sister's unfinished dream of being a celebrity.

Whether she was waiting for such a visitation or not, it arrived. It came from Cleveland, as I recall, at the start of my eighth-grade school year, and its name was Andy Dombrowski.

Andy was a tall, intense kid with the general physique of a buggy whip. Whenever we saw him bent over the keyboard, his blond hair down to his nose, his hands flashing like firecrackers over the keys, we knew that we were indeed in the presence of a real talent, a *God-given* talent, according to Sister Mary Grace, which, as every parochial schoolboy knows, is the very best kind.

Often when my lesson was scheduled to follow Andy's, Sister would invite me in to listen as she kept him playing well into my allotted time. I was never sure whether she did this to inspire me or to delay as long as possible the cultural shock of coming down from Andy's performance to another go at "Hop O My Thumb" with T. Byrnes at the keyboard.

More than once I heard her tell Andy, "You have a great future in store, but you must work hard and not let anything—not anything—interfere with it. You must practice, practice, practice. That is the only way to thank God for the great gift He has given you."

Father McNamara, however, had other ideas. Manager of our school's baseball team, he vowed every spring that "this year for *sure*" we'd win the championship of the Catholic grade school league. In fact, "This year for sure!" became our team's rallying cry.

Father was well qualified for his job. It was no secret that once he had pitched in the minors and had gone as far as the Triple-A League before, as he put it, "The head umpire threw me out of the game and into the seminary."

We kids liked to think that Father Mac was waiting for something, too—another great talent, a youngster who would one day live out our coach's unfinished dream of fame on the diamond.

I was present the day when, waiting for it or not, he found it.

It was an early spring afternoon. All the kids who hoped

to make the team were at the nearby park for tryouts and first practice. As I remember, someone was knocking fungoes to the outfielders; someone else was directing a pepper game. Off to one side, Father Mac, in baseball cap, old sweater, and catcher's mitt, was taking the throws of two or three would-be pitchers. And standing nearby was a tall, skinny kid with the look on his face of Moses gazing on the Promised Land.

I knew he had just come from a late piano lesson. No doubt he was about to follow Sister Mary Grace's advice to go right home and continue practicing when he came upon our team workout.

Father Mac soon noticed him, assumed he was there to try out, and asked him his name.

"Andy Dombrowski, Father."

"What position do you play, Andy?"

"I like to pitch, Father."

"Have you played much, Andy?"

"Quite a bit, Father."

"Okay, then. Joe, let Andy use your glove for now. Andy, go down there and throw me a few."

Right foot on an imaginary rubber, Andy cradled the ball almost lovingly in his glove, set his long fingers expertly around the seams, and announced, "A curve."

Father seemed a bit startled. His other pitchers were content merely to get the ball up to him and within arm's reach.

In one continuous, graceful motion Andy wound up and threw. He ended his delivery with a whip-snap wrist action that sent the ball spinning far to the right, then at the last moment brought it back to dead center for a strike. Father whistled—a low, soft whistle. "Beautiful," he whispered.

"A fast ball," Andy announced next. The ball popped like a rifle shot as it hit the pocket of the catcher's mitt.

"Did you ever see such a natural pitching motion?" Father asked of no one in particular. He was obviously the happiest priest in the diocese, and to us it was clear that we were in the presence of still another God-given talent.

Many pitches later, Father said, "That's enough for now." We could tell what he was thinking. He was thinking, *this year for sure!*

Our coach didn't object to Andy's piano playing as long as it didn't interfere with his pitching. Sister didn't object to Andy's pitching as long as it didn't interfere with his music. But there were times, Andy told us, when he wished he'd been somewhere else when the talents were handed out.

Father might say, "Andy, you missed practice yesterday."

"Had an extra long piano lesson, Father. Sister gave me a new piece to learn."

Or Sister might say, "Come back after school this afternoon, Andy. I'd like to go over that sonata with you again."

"Gee, Sister, Father McNamara's expecting me. He's showing me how to throw a sinker."

It was inevitable that tension should develop. But one day, to keep the peace, Father paid a special visit to Sister Mary Grace.

"Sister," he said, "I want to extend a special invitation to you. This afternoon we're playing St. Jerome's on our home field. Andy is going to pitch. I think you owe it to yourself to see this young man in action."

Without blinking, Sister replied, "Why, thank you, Father. I'd love to—on one condition. Andy will be here for a lesson any minute now. I'll have him play for you. I think," she added, smiling, "you owe it to yourself to see this young man in action."

Father laughed and agreed to stay. He knew a good fast-ball hitter when he saw one.

And so it went for the rest of that spring. Sister had her pupils pray to St. Cecilia, patron of music, that Andy would eventually give up baseball and turn his full attention to his

God-given future in music. Father Mac had his team pray to St. Sebastian, patron of athletes, that nothing would deter Andy from his God-given future in baseball. The battle of the saints was on.

I am happy to report that by the close of the school year, it ended in a tie. For the very first time—with Andy pitching, of course—our school won the championship. And for the very first time, a music student from our school won a coveted music scholarship to high school.

But Andy turned it down—as he turned down Father McNamara's sponsorship of him to attend a summer baseball camp for young teenagers. It seems that someone on the sly had sneaked in a few prayers to St. Alphonsus, patron of vocations. Andy would be going to Quigley Preparatory Seminary.

And I am happy to report, after my latest survey, that there still seems to be no significant change in the classic child-piano relationship. Those with a God-given talent for music pursue it to the full—unless other and seemingly more important things interfere. Those with no "feel" for the instrument simply give it up—with great sighs of relief from themselves and their parents.

As for me, I skulk into corners at parties where some show-off is rattling the ivories and ask myself, "Why—*why*—didn't my parents try harder to make me practice?"

My Grade-School Sisters' Secret Lives

I'm glad I have seen the day when so many nuns wear conventional dress and sign magazine articles, books, and report cards with their baptismal names and surnames. I am also glad that when I was a schoolboy all nuns wore the old, traditional habits and bore the names of their patron saints. I have known the best of both worlds.

The best of the old world was that the nuns were women of mystery—and every kid worth a hot lunch cherished a good mystery. In my school not only were the sisters' ankles, ears, hair, foreheads, and necks concealed from view, but so were their family ties and ancestry.

Expert at lighting the shadowy corners of long division, the irregular verbs, and historical treaties, they were equally adept at keeping the source of that light under wraps of heavy black wool serge. We knew more about Betsy Ross than we did about the nun who introduced us to her.

The only exception I recall was Sister Mary Bridget (third-grade boys), who at least gave us a good fix on her native heritage. When driven to the limits of her classroom patience, she would exclaim with eyes flashing, "Watch out or I'll get my Irish up!" The first time I told my parents about her, my father, a Tipperary man himself, wondered from what part of Ireland her "Irish" had come. I told him I would ask her, but at the last minute I lost my nerve. I felt it would be like asking the Holy Father to name his shaving cream.

Even the nuns' religious names told us little about themselves. What similarity was there, for instance, between Sister Mary Joseph's dimpled, cherubic face (which was about all of her you could see) and the long-bearded, heavy-browed figure that gazed down on us from a side altar, or between tall, angular Sister Bernadette and her diminutive namesake in the church's grotto? We felt their names were simply meant to throw us off the track.

But, like nature itself, the schoolboy imagination abhors a vacuum. What we didn't know about our teachers and their backgrounds we all too readily made up—sometimes with remarkable abandon. In fact, that's why we appreciated them so much—they were a constant stimulus to our creative powers.

Young Sister Mary Edith, when she thought no one was looking, never walked down stairs, but tripped airily, turning at each landing with an exuberant half-spin like a ballerina. We decided she had once been a professional dancer—and a ballet dancer at that. Even her good-natured denials when word finally leaked through to her failed to quash the rumor.

And there was Sister Mary Mechtildis (eighth-grade boys). At final dismissal time it was her job to patrol the line of kids as we walked single file down the sidewalk past the church. There, at her signal, we were allowed to go our separate ways home. As with whoops of joy the last of us broke ranks, Sister would gaze after us wistfully, then slowly make her solitary way back to her now silent and empty classroom—one of the many deserted cells from which we had just escaped. At that poignant moment, with her black veil fluttering dejectedly about her shoulders, was there a lonelier-looking human being in all the world than she?

Such a forlorn figure, we felt, could have had nothing but a lonely, even tragic past. We didn't know what it was, so we improvised.

Sister Mary Mechtildis learned about it one day when Freddy Bassett's sister, Marcie, a serious, wide-eyed, fluffy little tot in second grade, came to the eighth-grade room to wait for her brother, who had been detained to finish an arithmetic paper.

Marcie, her big blue eyes riveted on Sister at her desk, suddenly began to cry.

"What's the matter, dear?" asked the teacher.

Between sobs Marcie managed to say, "I'm sorry . . . about your . . . father and mother."

"My father and mother?"

"Freddy told me all about it. And I'm sorry your sister died in the orphanage fire."

Sister Mary Mechtildis couldn't help it; she began to laugh.

"But," said Marcie, brightening, "I'm glad *you* escaped!"

The nun laughed till the tears came.

And then there was Sister Mary Grace, who taught piano.

What else but a former career as a concert pianist would do for Sister Mary Grace—and one as a former grand opera star for Sister Mary Clare, who led the hymns at the eight o'clock children's Mass on Sunday?

There was also Sister Mary Evelyn, who had taught me in fourth grade and remained one of my all-time favorites. For her the only background that seemed appropriate was baseball. Whenever an interscholastic ball game was played in the park near our school, Sister Mary Evelyn was there— our most faithful and most outspoken fan. Her cheers could often be heard above those of the other spectators, to the delight of us players and the embarrassment of Sister's companions.

But even to *our* fertile imaginations a baseball career seemed a bit too much. How could this gentle nun have ever been a ballplayer?

I found out how.

A seventh-grader at the time (Sister Mary Verissima's class), I played center field for our school's team. I was pretty good at catching fly balls that came my way but not so good at knocking them out there. In the ninth inning of a particularly emotional contest with St. Margaret Mary's, our arch rival, I found myself at bat with the score tied, two out, and a runner on third. What a storybook opportunity to become a hero!

But even with a miraculous medal in my hip pocket (standard equipment) I ingloriously struck out.

Among the boos, moans, and general commotion I distinctly heard a single, piercing "Oh, no!" that could have come from no one but Sister Mary Evelyn. As I slunk sheepishly to the bench, I sneaked a furtive glance in her direction. She was shaking her head in disbelief.

"Thomas," said Sister Mary Verissima the next day, "Sister Mary Evelyn would like to see you in her room right after school." No need to ask her why. Sister Mary Evelyn was going to give me the worst dressing-down of my brief baseball career.

After the dismissal bell, I waited for my classmates to leave, then went down the hall to Sister Mary Evelyn's room.

"Come in, Thomas, and shut the door," she said.

To my amazement, I received a smile that exuded forgiveness, confidence, and determination.

"Now, look," said Sister, "there's no reason on earth why you can't be a good hitter." She picked up her blackboard pointer and held it like a baseball bat. "But you're not swinging correctly, and I'll show you why."

She set a geography book on the floor and stood beside it in a batter's stance. "Here's home plate. Out there," she continued, pointing toward the back of the room, "is the pitcher's mound."

I looked toward the pitcher's mound. A statue of the Little Flower looked back noncommittally.

"Watch closely now," said Sister Mary Evelyn as she took a practice swing with the pointer. Willie Stargell couldn't have looked more professional.

"Here comes the pitch! Here you are, swinging!" She swung. "See what you did wrong?" she asked.

It was quite obvious what she—or rather, I—had done wrong. Instead of moving my left foot forward into the pitch as I should have done, I had drawn it back defensively toward third base, thus weakening my swing.

Said Sister simply, "You're stepping into the bucket."

"The bucket, Sister?"

With the matter-of-fact calm of an old pro she explained. To break a timid batter's habit of stepping away from the pitch, old-time managers often placed a water bucket behind his forward foot. Unless the foot moved directly forward, it either tipped the bucket or went into it. After a few such batting sessions, unless he was a hopeless case, the batter usually showed improvement.

"Just imagine there's a bucket behind your foot next time you go to bat," said Sister.

I thanked her wholeheartedly and took several swings, careful to move my left foot straight forward.

"You've got the idea," she said at last. "Just try not to be afraid of the ball."

As I was leaving, she said firmly, "Remember now, this batting practice was just between you and me."

But how could a *nun* possibly know so much about baseball? The question remained unanswered for another year, during which time, I'm happy to report, my hitting noticeably improved. Not until my graduation did she finally tell me—too late, I realized, for me to pass the news around the school.

Yes, she had played baseball—with her twin brother and four other brothers on their family farm. She had played it when she was scarcely more than a toddler; she had played it well into her teens. She knew the game from backstop to outfield and loved every strike, every line drive, every pop-up, every home run of it. "But," she said with a smile, "I just didn't think I had a future in it."

Besides, the day came when other inclinations began to stir.

And so in time she became a nun, while her twin brother went on to play for the New York Yankees—who probably never knew what a talent they had lost to the convent.

And then, of course, there was Sister Genevieve. . . .

III.   HAPPILY EVER AFTER

"Let's Wrestle, Daddy!"

A popular bumper sticker asks the question "Have you hugged your kid today?" If that sticker had been around when my children were small and we lived in the big old farmhouse, I would have answered, "I sure have. In fact, I *wrestled* with my kids today."

I felt then, and still feel, that there is no better way to get close to your offspring—two or three at a time, if you have them—than with a friendly combination of half nelson, hammerlock, and toehold.

It all began one evening when Kip, our firstborn, was five and his brother David was three-and-a-half. Both were asking the familiar question of childhood "What's there to *do?*" Finding nothing better to stir their interest, they turned to each other like lion cubs and were soon rolling on the living-room floor in a noisy tangle of arms and legs. Their simulated grunts and groans told me they were no strangers to the bogus theatrics of television wrestling.

Quite a show, I thought as I looked up from a book I was reading. Two-year-old Nina thought so, too, and promptly joined her brothers on the floor.

This, I said to myself, could be fun, a lot more fun than the book. An idea began to sprout, nourished by echoes of my wife Ginny's frequent reminder that we must find more time to spend with our children, more time having fun. "All they want," she said, "is *us*."

I put the book aside, slipped out of my shoes, got down on all fours, and did a fair imitation of a big cat stalking its prey. Before the kids had time to react, I pounced!

"Gotcha!" I cried, encircling them with my arms.

Their initial squawks of surprise became screeches of delight as they realized that Daddy was going to play with them.

"You'll never get away," I growled. "Never!"

"Oh, yeah?" the boys responded, thrilled at having found a common enemy.

Nina, ever solicitous, attempted at first to defend her father but soon found it was more fun to be on the boys' side.

"I've got Daddy," she announced, sitting on my head.

We rolled, tumbled, squirmed, twisted, squeezed, threatened, bluffed, yelped, and hooted—we may even have hugged—until at last Ginny suggested we declare the contest a draw and take a well-earned rest. I was ready to comply. The children, however, pulled themselves away with obvious reluctance. It was all over—and so soon.

But they need not have worried. A tradition had been born—as much to my delight as theirs.

The sport, as we came to practice it, followed procedures as simple as they were unorthodox. At some point almost every evening, one or the other of the kids would call out, "Let's wrestle Daddy!" Any hesitancy on my part, no matter for what reason, would draw cries of "Daddy's chicken!" And so I would quickly stretch out on the floor in a deceptively helpless position and dare my adversaries to keep me down.

"Charge!" they'd yell, and hurl themselves at me in slap-happy abandon.

The purpose of this initial attack was to overwhelm the old man and render him immobile. If successful, it would have been more of a shock to them than to me.

Their next move was to back off and regroup—or try to. If successful, this strategy would also have been a disappointment to all parties. It was much more fun to be caught suddenly in a leg lock, a head lock, or any other kind of lock I could come up with. The more desperate their situation, the sharper their exhilarating sense of peril.

Through it all they kept up a steady cross fire of threats, taunts, and strategic commands to each other.

"You'll be sorry, Daddy!"

"Grab his foot, Dave!"

"I can't. He just grabbed mine!"

"Daddy, you're tickling me! That's not fair!"

They were right. Tickling wasn't fair, but now and then I wasn't above cheating a little, if only to hear the laughter mount higher and to let them know they were engaged in mortal combat with a foe who was absolutely ruthless.

Of course, there were moments when I purposely relaxed my various holds and let them think that I was no longer equal to their superior numbers and skills. All three would then sit on me and demand unconditional surrender.

"You give up, Daddy?"

Never! With a sudden lunge I would again have them in my clutches, and the battle would seesaw back and forth until, by mutual agreement, we called it quits.

"We'll get you tomorrow, Daddy!"

As the years raced by, there were times when, one by one, the older children sensed they were getting too big for this kind of rough-and-tumble, too big for Daddy to handle them all at once, and so they stepped aside for their younger brothers and sisters coming up. I must say, Daddy appreciated their thoughtfulness.

But with the head count of kids steadily rising to an even dozen (where it finally stabilized), there was always plenty of fresh talent around. They were around—and so were the older ones—one memorable Sunday when two strange figures suddenly appeared at a living-room window.

I had been working hard all weekend to finish an important writing assignment in time for a Monday deadline. Whenever Daddy found himself in one of these last-minute crunches, the children knew they must hold their spirits in check and keep the noise level down to a minimum—an effort that caused considerable strain for all members of the family. This particular weekend had been the most trying of all.

By midafternoon, however, I was able to burst from my room and shout, "It's finished!"

The tension release was immediate and uproarious. Life could resume again!

"This calls for a celebration!" someone cried. Ginny made cocoa and popcorn for the kids, a highball for me. Within minutes our living room took on the look of a three-ring circus.

At one end, some of the older girls were showing their mother a new dance step. The record player was blaring. The girls were singing at the top of their lungs and doing an energetic imitation of the Rockettes. Two of the boys with gymnastic inclinations had pushed the coffee table to one side and were demonstrating handstands in the center of the room. At the other end I was on the floor, tumbling with some of the younger ones and one or two others who should have been disqualified for being in the wrong weight class. From time to time I found it necessary to add to the din by shouting, "Stop throwing those sofa pillows!"

In the midst of it all, I became uncomfortably aware that we were being watched. I looked up. Framed in a nearby window were two adult figures, an elderly, well-dressed couple, whose faces reflected a mixture of astonishment, disbelief, and what might have been a growing urge to run for their lives.

I broke free of the wrestling match and hurried to the door.

"Hello!" I called.

Without moving from the evergreen hedge outside the window, the man apologized. "We rang your bell, but I guess you didn't hear it. We were worried about all the noise and thought—"

"You thought a riot was going on," I filled in. "A perfectly natural conclusion. But won't you come in?"

Behind me now in the doorway were Ginny and the children, some of them still showing annoyance at having our celebration interrupted. To the strangers this phalange must have looked as impenetrable as Caesar's Tenth Legion.

"We're the Wingates," the man continued, still unwilling to move until all the facts were clear. "Your pastor, Father Egan, suggested we look you up."

"Now you've *got* to come in," said Ginny, slipping out past me and taking our visitors in hand.

The tide of kids parted like the Red Sea. The Wingates moved inside. The sea closed in behind them and swept them along into the living room.

Ginny apologized for the room's appearance and explained that we'd been celebrating a special family event. Mrs. Wingate apologized for having disturbed us and explained that she and her husband, old friends of Father Egan, were thinking of buying the Brooks house down the road. I thought, If the Suttons are hoping that a visit to the Byrnes home will convince these people that this is a nice, quiet neighborhood to settle in, they're due for a big surprise.

Although we did our best to make our guests feel welcome, their obvious sense of guilt for having interrupted our family revel continued to hang in the room like a blue mist, a situation not relieved by three-year-old Monica's repeated question, "Are we going to wrestle again, Daddy?"

At last, after skimming the surface of a few easy conversational topics, Mrs. Wingate looked at her watch and expressed alarm at how late it was.

"We had no idea!" she exlaimed. "We really must be going. And thank you *so* much."

"Well," said Ginny, after they had left, "they were nice people, but I don't suppose we'll ever see them again."

"Too bad," I said. "Father Egan will feel we let him down."

But they came back. Mr. Wingate came back first—one Saturday afternoon a week later, alone.

"We're buying the Brooks house," he announced, "but I want to clear something up. It may have seemed rude of us to leave as abruptly as we did last Sunday when you were doing your best to make us feel at home. You probably thought we couldn't understand the noise, the confusion, and the excitement. But we did—completely. That's why we wanted to leave you to yourselves. We've had four kids of our own, and some of our happiest times were spent rough-housing as you were. Our living room was always upset. But we loved it."

He paused and wiped a speck from his glasses.

"A lot of our neighbors," he continued, "were so proud of their spotless living rooms they wouldn't let their children play in them. Can you imagine? Not playing in the living room?"

He smiled this last question at some of the children who were ringed around us on chairs, couch, and hassocks. "Gosh!" one of them said in disbelief.

"You understand now why we left? So you could get on with your fun."

When he finally stood up to go, he said, "What they really want more than anything else is *us*."

At the door he paused. "And if the truth were known," he added, "what *we* want more than anything else is *them*."

"Amen," I said.

Eventually the time came when, even with twelve children, there were no small ones left to wrestle with. The hugging continued—and does to this day—but there are no more daily wrestling cards at the Byrnes Family Arena.

And yet, old wrestlers never die. They just climb back into the ring with their grandchildren.

"Let's wrestle with Grandpa!"

The cry brings a stampede of tiny feet, a crush of young bodies, starbursts of yells, battle orders, feigned protests, and laughter.

"Grandpa, you're tickling me! That's not fair!"

And I'm still as ruthless as ever.

A Prayer, a Priest,
a Puppy

My wife insists that our moves over the years from the city to the suburb to the country were made to provide more room for our growing family of children. I sometimes have the feeling, however, that they were made to provide more room for our growing family of children's pets.

We began our married life in a city apartment. No pets allowed. Mr. Schusler, our landlord, was rock firm on that point. A thin, worrisome man always in search of a problem, he told us once that as a boy he had been nipped in the ankle by a hyperthyroid Sealyham and would never forget it—nor forgive the Sealyham. "Trouble with dogs is," he often said, "they can't be trusted." His disaffection for dogs extended also to cats, gerbils, canaries, and budgerigars. He didn't trust them, either.

Children he could tolerate—barely. He tolerated four-year-old Kip, our firstborn, and two-year-old Dave, our second, but the arrival of Nina, our third, put us well beyond Mr. Schusler's breaking point. "Trouble with kids is," he said one evening near the end of our relationship, "they make too much noise. That is," he had the grace to add, "for apartment living."

We had to agree. Nina at the moment was giving full-lunged notice that she was ready for another feeding. From the kitchen came the rumble of wooden kiddie car wheels on the linoleum floor and a two-year-old's imitation of an air horn. In the bathroom Kip was playing with the hot water faucet. Turned to a certain position, the handle generated a series of booming discords that rattled the pipes from basement to roof and gave Kip a heady sense of power.

Mr. Schusler sighed and wagged his head. "Y'see what I mean?" he asked over the noise.

Yes, it was time we acquired a house of our own. It was time to give the children more room to play in, to run in, to shout in, to cry in, to be children in.

And to have a dog in.

Ginny and I had first discussed the need for a dog shortly after Kip was born. Or maybe it was the same day. We agreed that no child, especially a boy, should be without one for long. A dog, we felt, is as necessary to a child's development as vitamin supplements, inoculations, potty training, and storybooks. A dog helps build a child's character and sense of responsibility. A dog provides a child with necessary affection—in case the parents back down, I suppose. And yet, here we were, four years after the birth of Kip, and still no dog. Incredible! Obviously, there was no time to lose, although we had to admit that Kip, so far, had been developing quite well without one.

But first, where would we settle? In a far suburb, of course, where the air is fresher, the skies sunnier, the yards more spacious. And where dogs look happier.

In time we found both suburb and house. We could at last think realistically about getting our first family pet.

A purchase of such importance, however, is not made lightly. You don't buy a dog as you would a loaf of bread. You read up on dogs. You study the relative merits of the various breeds, from Chihuahua to Irish wolfhound. You check the ads. You talk to friends and relatives.

And you talk to St. Francis of Assisi.

It was our new next-door neighbor, Irma Foley, widowed matriarch of the neighborhood, who suggested that St. Francis might help us find a dog. "Remember how fond he was of animals," she reminded us the day we moved in. (She had come over with a welcoming gift of home-baked bread.) "I like to think it was St. Francis who helped me get Franz."

Franz was her ubiquitous dachsund, who at the moment was checking out pieces of our furniture as the movers carried them in.

"Why don't you have the children say a prayer to St. Francis? It couldn't hurt."

No, it couldn't hurt. But a plaque bearing his beautiful prayer, "Lord, Make Me an Instrument of Thy Peace," had hung conspicuously in our apartment, reminding us, among other things, that it is in giving, not getting, that we receive. I wasn't sure that St. Francis was the saint for this job. Besides, isn't St. Rosco the patron saint of dog lovers?

Nevertheless, we agreed to try St. Francis. Although Mrs. Foley recommended that we leave the choice of breed up to the saint's discretion, Kip and Dave were not above ending their evening prayers with "Please make it a German shepherd."

We were only three nights into our petitions to St. Francis when the telephone rang.

"Tom," said a strange voice as if its owner had known me for years, "this is Monsignor Shannon. Welcome to St. Mary's!"

"Thank you, Monsignor," I replied, surprised that he already knew of our arrival.

"You uncle Dan just called from Chicago," Monsignor continued. "He tells me you're looking for a nice dog for the children."

My thoughts spun back to a wondrous summer afternoon when I was little more than a toddler and Uncle Dan, then a young assistant priest in a nearby parish, stood beaming at our front door. "Junior," he said, "happy birthday!" In his arms was a brown and white collie pup, my first dog.

"Danny and I are old friends," Monsignor was saying. "He's delighted that you've found a place in St. Mary's parish and so am I."

"Thank you again, Monsignor," I said. "We're looking forward to meeting you."

"Good. Could you come right over?"

I wasn't sure I understood. "This evening, Monsignor?"

"Yes. You see," he explained, "I have a dog I'm sure you'll like."

It was almost nine o'clock. There was no time to scout up a baby sitter, so Ginny stayed with the children while I went to see our pastor alone.

Monsignor Shannon proved to be as congenial as his voice over the phone. A smile, warmed by many years of welcomes, greeted me in the rectory parlor.

"Do sit down," he said. "I'll fetch the dog in a moment."

I wondered at this, for there was already a dog in the room—a handsome, full-grown Kerry blue.

"This is Tip," said Monsignor proudly. "Isn't he a beauty?"

"A beauty," I agreed.

After politely sniffing my hand, Tip moved in to be scratched behind the ears.

"You can't beat a Kerry blue," said Monsignor.

"How can you stand to part with him?" I asked.

"Oh, this isn't *your* dog," my host quickly explained. "Yours is in the basement. Sit still now, Tom, and I'll bring him up."

I sat still—as still as you can sit in the same room with a Kerry blue. Having accepted me as a qualified ear scratcher, Tip must now test me as a ball tosser.

But in the rectory parlor? The rubber ball that Tip had brought from behind the chair lay waiting at my feet. I stalled for time. The blue backed up, panting, anticipating, commanding, threatening.

"Play ball!" he barked with all the impatient authority of a big-league umpire.

Before I could be penalized for delay of game, Monsignor Shannon returned to the room. He was holding a reddish-brown, wiry-haired, bright-eyed imp of an Irish terrier in his arms. The dog, scarcely out of puppyhood, was lathering Monsignor's chin in delirious thanksgiving for being released from the basement.

"This is Clancy," said Monsignor. "Isn't he a beauty?"

He was a beauty.

"You can't beat an Irish terrier," said Monsignor.

The moment Clancy saw Tip he broke loose with a joyous yelp of recognition and landed on the floor as sure-footed as a bird. In the twitch of a tail the two dogs agreed on a fast game of cops and robbers, Tip the pursued, Clancy the pursuer. For every turn the blue made the terrier made two more. They sent scatter rugs scattering, they bumped into chairs, they rocked end tables, they repositioned floor lamps.

"Go, go, go!" they yelled at each other.

"You see what I'm up against?" laughed Monsignor Shannon as he finally captured and contained Clancy.

What he was up against was his love for dogs, a love that had tricked him into saying yes when a parishioner, moving to an overseas assignment, had offered him the terrier.

"How could I refuse?" he sighed. As he rumpled Clancy's whiskers, he added regretfully, "But two wild Irishmen in the same house—that's one too many. Here," he added, holding the terrier out to me, "he's yours if you want him."

It's one thing to consider dogs as dogs, to weigh objectively the merits of one breed against another. But the pup for you is the one you happen to be holding in your arms at a given moment. I'm sure St. Francis would agree.

Clancy looked up at me and stretched for my chin.

"Let's give it a try," he whispered.

"You can't beat an Irish terrier," I admitted.

"You're so right," murmured Clancy, snuggling down.

Next day there was a call from a Mrs. Erlich, who, she said, was a dear friend of our neighbor, Irma Foley. Irma had told her we wanted a dog. Mrs. Erlich's German shepherd, Brunhilde, had just had a litter of pups, and Mrs. Erlich would like us to have one. No, she didn't want any money, she just wanted a loving home for the dog.

Well, why not? After all, *two* children had prayed to St. Francis. And, as Kip suggested, "The terrier can be Dave's, the shepherd mine." You can't beat that kind of logic.

More years later, after we moved to the country, our assemblage of animals included three dogs, two horses, numerous cats, rabbits, ducks, gerbils, and parakeets, two roosters named Art and Fred, and a billy goat named Herb.

That's a lot of animals. But then, twelve children are a lot of petitioners. And who can resist the earnest prayer of an innocent child?

Not, apparently, St. Francis.

What My Father Said about Baptism

At the baptism of our twenty-fifth grandchild I was not surprised to find myself in a statistical frame of mind. I didn't need a pocket calculator to tell me that with all those grandchildren, plus 12 children of our own, my wife Ginny and I had so far attended 37 baptisms in our immediate family alone.

To these I added at least a dozen more where we had been either godparents or guests. That put the number, conservatively, at 49.

In addition, however, there were the monthly baptisms—usually 4 or 5 simultaneously—that for the past 6 years we had witnessed during the 12 o'clock Mass in our parish church.

Six years of monthly baptisms at, say, 4 babies each and we have a total of 288, which, plus the others, comes to 337, give or take a few drops of holy water.

Of course, we don't *have* to attend the noonday service. We simply find it more congenial to our lazy Sunday morning mood than the earlier Masses. Besides, when the baptism service is concluded, just before the offertory, there is the fun of clapping out a joyous welcome to the new arrivals in our parish community. How often do you get a chance to clap in church?

I also feel that there is a kind of noblesse oblige involved here. What would the newborns think if only a few of us showed up to celebrate their entry into the Mystical Body? Some club *we* joined, they might complain, and who could blame them?

I am thankful for this extended exposure to the baptismal ritual. It has enabled me to appreciate more fully than I otherwise might the beautiful fact that though there have been changes in certain related customs, they are all woven through with an unbroken thread of continuity, a thread that was first spun in the waters of the Jordan and still today binds one generation to another and all generations to the faith. The thread has become a mantle that envelops us all, as the baptismal garment, so often a family heirloom, envelops the child.

It even envelops that delicate period after the childbirth when the two families, though feigning neutrality, eye each other warily as they ask the new parents, "What are you going to *name* the baby?" This is but a paraphrase of the deeper question "Whose side are you on, anyway?"

Fortunately, the Church herself remains noncommittal. She asks only that the child be given a name with Christian significance, usually the name of a saint, to symbolize life in Christ and entrance into the Christian household.

Some parents try to dodge this face-off between grandparents by bestowing a name unknown in either family—or by deserting the New Testament entirely and coming up with something like Clancy, Lance, or Dirk, which seem to be very "in" these days. In deference to the Church's wishes, a saint's name is usually slipped in behind it, never to be seen again except on a diploma or driver's license.

I'm glad my father's time was up before such names became the vogue—my dear father, whom I almost lost when I told him that we were christening our firstborn Christopher. He thought we were naming the baby after Chris Chrispopolous, who ran a neighborhood vegetable stand. No, we said, we're naming him after a saint.

"What's the matter," my father answered, "aren't the old Irish names good enough for you? What's wrong with Patrick or Dennis or John or Phillip or your *own* name?"

I didn't think it was the time to tell him that my own name and most of the others were hardly the exclusive property of the Irish. We had named the baby Christopher to keep any one side of the family from being mad at the other. Instead, though we hadn't planned it that way, we succeeded in making both sides mad at *us*—at least until they had an opportunity to hold Christopher in their arms. A few years later, however, my father had a namesake.

The same kind of problem exists, naturally, when the newborn is a girl. Here the maternal grandma's name is the odds-on favorite—unless the baby has an older sister already bearing the name. Since even the most devoted mother would draw the line at calling her girls Gertrude I and Gertrude II, an aunt, a cousin, or an old school chum is the most likely honoree. Seldom have I seen a female firstborn named after her mother's mother-in-law.

I notice, too, that some of the old baptismal fables are fading away. For instance, years ago, when a baby cried or howled during the ceremony, it was supposed to mean that he or she would grow up to be what was called then a "militant Catholic," one who would man the trenches, so to speak, for the Faith, who would be eloquently outspoken in spreading the good news.

Unfortunately, some parents took this to infer that babies who slept peacefully through the service would be equally lackadaisical in matters of faith and morals as they grew older. I knew a godfather once who confessed he was sorely tempted to pinch his sleeping godchild's bottom just to bring him over to the militant side. I doubt that the question will ever be settled until a future research expert finds a way to determine whether certain prelates of the Church howled or slept through their baptisms.

From what I observe, most babies today are baptized

when they are from two weeks to a month old. Some, judging by their size and lung power, are even older than that. When I was young, the rule was "the sooner the better." I myself was christened after one week—the result of a compromise between my mother, who wanted to wait another week, and my father, who wanted me baptized the day after I was born, as he had been.

Few things vexed my father more than some relative's slowness in bringing a new family addition to the baptismal font.

"What's the matter with those people?" he'd ask my mother. "Are they lazy—or don't they care?"

"Of course they care. The baby was born only last week."

"But they haven't even set a date! I bet it'll be at least a month before they get around to it. In the meantime," he'd add darkly, "*anything* could happen."

On more than one of these occasions, Father would remind us that he himself, born on Christmas Day, was bundled into an open buggy on St. Stephen's Day and taken to church over several wintry miles for *his* baptism. "That's the way they did it in Ireland," he'd say proudly. "They took no chances."

"Took no chances!" my American-born mother would exclaim, trying vainly to follow my father's logic. "Think of it! Childbirth in a drafty old stone cottage with only a peat fire for warmth and no doctor anywhere around—wasn't that chance enough without exposing the poor baby to the rigors of a hurry-up Irish baptism?"

To which my father would calmly reply, "But think of the head start it gave me in receiving the graces of the supernatural life. Maybe that's why I've always been so healthy."

He may have had a point there. I never knew my father to be ill except from a wrenched back he suffered once from trying to lift a large bookcase without first removing the books.

"As for a doctor," he'd continue in defense of the old way

of life, "haven't I told you a dozen times I had a doctor—eventually?"

About a week after my father's birth, according to family legend, Dr. James Slattery, a crusty old all-purpose doctor and the only one within miles, stopped by on one of his infrequent visits.

"And how's everyone here?" he is reputed to have asked.

"We're all fine, glory be to God," he was told.

Seeing the new baby in its mother's arms, he exclaimed, "Another one, is it? Well now. I might as well have a look as long as I'm here."

He examined my future parent and pronounced him as healthy as a young colt, a simile that sprang naturally from his long experience with livestock.

"He was a great doctor," my father would reminisce. "After telling my mother simply to continue with whatever she was doing for me—feeding me, I suppose—he went out to the barn and performed a successful tracheotomy on an ailing horse."

For some reason, my mother always shuddered at this point in the story, but it was the part that I liked best.

"Even with an opening in his windpipe—a special tube the doctor implanted—the horse lived to a happy old age, although whenever he moved faster than a trot, the tube would whistle."

This was my cue to ask, "Show us how the horse whistled, Daddy." Whereupon he would purse his lips and blow the first few bars of "The Harp That Once Through Tara's Halls."

No doubt about it, James Slattery must have been one fine doctor.

I don't think my experience with family baptisms is yet over. Some of our married twelve will no doubt have more children. Two of the twelve are still unmarried. So there is much to look forward to.

I hope I'm still around to see whether they howl or sleep through the baptismal ceremony.

A Father's Day Memory

I fell in step behind two boys, no more than seven years old, on their way to Sunday Mass. It was Father's Day.

"*My* father," said one, "can take a watch apart and put it back together in five minutes."

"*My* father," said the other, "can take a *car* apart and put it back together in half that time."

"Oh, yeah?"

"Yeah!"

"Well, *my* father—"

They were quoting the familiar Gospel on Fathers, According to Their Young Sons, Chapters One to Infinity. I had contributed a few verses to that gospel myself.

"Now listen, boys," I wanted to say, "*my* father . . . "

There were many occasions during my early boyhood when I knew that my father was a man apart. One of them was the time he demonstrated that he could read the mysterious writing on Chinese laundry tickets.

Once a week I had the responsibility of taking my father's shirts and collars to Choy Chan's laundry two blocks away. Before doing anything else, I had to bring the claim check, or ticket, directly home, where Mother or Dad would slip it under the bread box for safekeeping. I had the chilly feeling that if the ticket were lost, my father would go shirtless for the rest of his life.

If curiosity is the beginning of learning, as wise men say, my education took a giant step forward one day when, laundry ticket in hand, I began to wonder what its bold, splashy markings could possibly mean. I asked my father.

To my delight, he gave my question his full attention. Turning the tiny slip of paper upside down once or twice, he cleared his throat and finally said, "Each ticket is lettered with an old Chinese proverb. This one says—let's see, now— it says, 'The strong man stands firm against the dragon.' "

"It really *says* that?" I asked, scrutinizing the paper again.

"Indeed it does. It means we must never let bad luck get us down."

"Gol-*lee!*" Was there another man in the whole world as smart as my father?

Nevertheless, I wondered what the dragon had to do with my father's shirts. In answer to my puzzled frown, Dad said, "Choy Chan writes this same proverb on the package of my finished laundry. He searches until he finds it among all those bundles on his shelves."

I marveled at Choy's imaginative, though somewhat roundabout, way of doing business.

My father had learned Chinese, he told me, from an old laundryman he met when he came to this country from Ireland. "I was young then," he explained, "and picked things up fast. Besides," he added, "you can't beat the Irish when it comes to mastering Chinese."

I was quick to spread the news of my father's linguistic skill among the kids of the neighborhood. They were gratify- ingly impressed. *Their* fathers could sell insurance, build houses, operate stores, but could they read Chinese laundry tickets? Not a one.

My father was a whiz at medicine, too. I was sure he could have practiced it if he'd had the time. I knew this because of what family legend had told me about how he cured my colic when I was an infant.

Those were the days, I gather, when burping the baby was not the essential denouement of the feeding ritual it later became, and I suspect that much of my wailing was caused by nothing more than a few air bubbles waiting to surface.

For these crises my father had a remedy that never failed. He would pour out a scant teaspoonful of Irish whiskey, set fire to it, "to burn out the alcohol," dip the corner of a fresh handkerchief in it and then encourage me to suck on it, whereupon he would put me over his shoulder and march from one end of the house to the other. He marched in time to the stately cadence of his own strong baritone reciting lines from his favorite poem, Sir Walter Scott's "Lady of the Lake." He especially like the opening canto, which begins, "The stag at eve had drunk his fill. . . . "

I can think of no better conditioning for a future writer than to be carried as an infant on a tall man's shoulders, rising and falling to the rhythmic chant of iambic verse.

My father was a Tipperary man. Tipperary men were known as "stone throwers"—in tribute, he said, to some long-ago victory over a neighboring chieftain, whose forces were sent scurrying under a hail of stone and rocks before they could get within shillelagh distance of the Tipperary lads. This, my father solemnly assured me, was the first known use of heavy artillery.

Dad was a stone thrower, too. One of our favorite diversions was pitching stones at tin cans we'd set up on an old milk crate in the vacant lot behind our home. Dad's accuracy became a legend among the neighborhood kids. Older boys who challenged him soon learned, to their amazement, not only that he could outpoint them at twenty paces but that his eye grew sharper and his aim more true the farther back he stood. Wally O'Leary, a good friend of mine, once observed, "Your old man should be pitching for the Cubs." It didn't take long for the rumor to get around that my old man *had* pitched for the Cubs.

One of my father's proudest moments, I'm sure, was my debut as an altar boy. In those days our parish had two weekday morning Masses, one at six o'clock, the other at eight. To be assigned by Sister Verissima to serve the six o'clock Mass for the coming week was the highest of honors. It stamped you and your fellow server as dependable, rugged individuals who cringed not at the prospect of trudging to church through the dawn-quiet streets while the rest of your classmates lay snug and warm in their beds.

For me it was an eight-block journey. When the weather was bad, my father drove me to the church, attended Mass, and drove me home. There, before my mother and young sister were awake, he would cook breakfast for the two of us, regaling me with his experiences as an altar boy in Ireland.

"Did I tell you about the time Hennessey's goat wandered up the aisle just before Mass and Father Flanagan himself had to pick it up and carry it out? And when he gave his little talk, he said he was glad to see that at least *one* member of that family had come to church."

Nothing stirred more panic in a freshman altar boy than the growing suspicion that his partner wasn't going to show up and he'd have to serve alone. I faced that panic for the first time one evening when Johnny Furlong's mother called my mother to say that Johnny appeared to be coming down with something awful and wouldn't be able to serve the six o'clock Mass with me tomorrow. She hadn't bothered to find a replacement because good old Johnny had told her I would have no problem.

I didn't sleep well that night, and when my father woke me in the morning, pains in my stomach and head told me that I too was coming down with something awful. And it was too late to find a stand-in.

"Now there'll be nobody to serve," I moaned. I could see Sister Verissima's altar boy demerits flying around the sixth-grade room like snowflakes in a blizzard. I buried my face in the pillow.

"Well now," I heard my father say, "it can't be all that hopeless."

"But what can I *do?*"

"You just stay in bed and get well. I'll go."

"*You'll* serve Mass?"

"Why not?"

"You *will?*"

"Father Friel will be tickled to death."

He moved toward the door. I sat up. There was something more he should know. "The cards with the Latin responses," I said, "are on the altar steps next to the bells."

"Don't worry," he replied—and he smiled reassuringly. "I won't be needing them."

I lay back on the pillow and fell blissfully asleep.

Yes, I remember my father. I remember him insisting, when I was a preschooler—no matter how tired he or I was—that I say my evening prayers at his knee. That's where I learned the Our Father and the Hail Mary and where, with Dad at the helm, I sailed into the deeper waters of the Apostles' Creed, the Confiteor, and the Act of Contrition.

I remember him giving me an Indian tent for Christmas, big enough for the two of us. Because the snow was deep outside, he set it up in the parlor, using large safety pins to secure its edges to the rug—after first persuading my mother that it was a perfectly natural thing to do. Any Indian, he said, would have done the same.

There have been fathers who left more impressive achievements behind them—who built bridges, discovered new life-saving medicines, led armies to victory. And their records will long be remembered.

But not in the way I remember *my* father—as a father *first.* Did I later realize that he was fooling me when he pretended he could read Chinese; that he cured my colic not by his secret potion but by carrying me on his shoulder as he marched through the rooms of our home; that he knew full well that the Romans with their catapults were far ahead of his ancestors in the use of "heavy artillery"?

Later still, I could ask, What does it matter? The important thing is that he took the *time* to fool me—as Hans Christian Andersen took the time to fool generations of children with stories that will live forever because they never lived at all. He took the time to give me what at my age I wanted most—a hero. A personal hero whose exploits, real or imagined, were the joy of my early years and filled me with wonder and pride as they fill me now with choice memories.

He took the time to throw stones with me, to erect a tent in the parlor with me, to pray with me, to play catch with me, to pitch horseshoes with me, to do any of a hundred other things—*with me.*

In short, he knew not only that I was his, but that *he* was *mine.*

The Clock That Never Stops Running

"Look, Grandpa, Mummy taught me how to tell time!" My young grandson pointed proudly to the mantel clock in his parents' living room. "See? The little hand is on two and the big hand is on twelve. That means it's two o'clock. When the big hand gets to three, it'll be a quarter past two. When it gets to nine, it'll be a quarter to three, and then three o'clock. Tomorrow I'm going to learn how to read the calendar."

He knew from the congratulations heaped on him that this must be an important turning point in his life—and it was. He had entered a world where time is identified by the numbers of clock and calendar, different from the world where his days were metered solely by an internal clock, whose hands were set by familiar events and the activities of familiar people, a clock that told him with surprising accuracy what period of the day and year he was in. When he is older, he will marvel at how long that clock, powered by rich associations from the time zone of childhood, will keep on running.

My Aunt Laura taught *me* how to tell time. The two of us had been sitting in Grandma's kitchen one November afternoon sipping cocoa and playing "My father owns a grocery store" while the old grandmother's clock on its corner shelf sounded the quarter hours.

At some point in the game, the resolute bongs of that ancient instrument must have reminded my young aunt that time is fleeting; that her nephew, though willing to spend the rest of his life playing "My father owns a grocery store," was meant for bigger things; and that knowing how to tell time would be a great help to him. Inspired by the clock or not, she put the groceries aside and was suddenly talking about minutes and hours, short and long hands, and how they work together to get you from one day to the next.

Someone once said we never forget the car we learned to drive in. It's certainly true that I never forgot my family's old Studebaker—and I never forgot the clock I learned to tell time by. Ask me today what time it is and I'll check my wristwatch, but the watch is no more real to me than the memory of that stately old Seth Thomas, its face yellowed and spotted with age, its hands moving serenely through the circle of my childhood hours.

It would be unfair of me not to mention that it was Aunt Addie, my mother's other sister, who shortly afterwards taught me to read the calendar—a skill that, like telling time, I have since found to be enormously useful. We were in the same kitchen (one of my favorite haunts) drinking cocoa and playing "I see something in this room."

"I see something in this room," I said, "and it begins with *C.*"

Predictably, Aunt Addie answered, "Calendar." A huge one, compliments of St. Lawrence Church, colorfully illustrated with scriptural scenes, hung in full view next to Grandma's stove.

"It *is* the calendar, isn't it?" Aunt Addie pressed.

I savored the moment as long as I dared. "Nope," I said smugly.

A little nettled, my aunt went through curtains, cloves, cleansers, coffee grinder, and chair ("Nope" to all of them).

"All right," she said at last, "*what* then?"

"You give up?" (Protocol must be observed.)

"I give up."

"Church!" I exclaimed triumphantly.

"Church? Where?" she demanded.

I pointed to a tiny silhouette of St. Lawrence Church in a corner of the calendar's November page, which was dominated by a high-tension picture of Archangel Michael in fierce and fiery combat with the lost Lucifer.

Aunt Addie laughed. "You think you're pretty smart, don't you? Well now, we'll see just how much you *do* know about the calendar."

It quickly became obvious that I didn't know much, but an hour later I was able to surprise my parents, who lived downstairs, with the news that the days of the week have different numbers in the same month, which makes for a lot of numbers because there are twelve months altogether. Would they like me to draw them a picture of November? I began with the two angels because they seemed far more important than the numbered squares beneath them. For me, November would forever be this winged triumph of good over evil.

Ask me today what the date is, and if I don't know it, I'll probably consult a businesslike pocket or desk calendar, but rarely does my memory fail to add those biblical adornments that so richly illuminated the Gregorian divisions of the year in Grandma's home.

And the clock keeps running. As a child, I knew it was time to get up when I heard a series of familiar clicks in the nearby kitchen. It was the sound of my mother's wedding ring striking the glass milk bottle as she turned it end over end (in the days before homogenization) to mix the cream, which had risen to the top, with the rest of the milk she would soon be pouring over my oatmeal or cream of wheat.

I remember it all because in some secret morning place, deeper than the inner ear, I sometimes hear that wedding ring on glass.

The sounds of a piano come to me faintly from a distant room, and I am back in the old two-family house, where my grandparents and aunts lived upstairs. I am a frequent visitor there—*too* frequent, my mother thinks, now that Aunt Addie has a beau who calls on her regularly. So a signal has been arranged between my aunts and me. If I hear "With Someone Like You" being played, I know Aunt Addie is at the piano entertaining my future Uncle Tom and I am to stay put. But when I hear "My Old Kentucky Home" (by either aunt), I know the coast is clear and I am welcome to come up for a wonderful evening of songs, recitations, or just friendly talk. In any case, though I may have visited them just that afternoon, I am made to feel that I am the most important person in the house.

Today, even though I am a father and a grandfather, when evening comes, a moment of childlike peace—gentle as a mist, brief as an amen—rises from the past, brushes me softly, and is gone. It is the time of day when *my* father came home from work and the family was joyously rebonded, the time when, in early dusks, Louis the lamplighter, a tall, skinny kid in an overcoat that reached down to his shoe tops, tromped up Dorchester Avenue with his long pole to set the gas lamps glowing—in honor, I was sure then, of my father's return. It is the time when I spread my father's newspaper on the floor to read the funnies and *Little Benny's Notebook,* the time when I felt in my marrow that no matter what had happened during my father's absence, all was now well with the world.

When I enter a church today, kneel down, and bless myself, why do I immediately, without hesitation, begin to say the old Apostles' Creed? Because "the clock" tells me it's time to say it—a clock set by Sister Aurelia in third grade. Why she insisted that our first prayer in church should be the Creed I'm not sure—possibly to keep our Lord from wondering too long whether or not we were true believers.

I see that same clock running in my children, now grown. It tells them that today is a very special day. It is the day after Christmas. One of our married daughters has come to help straighten up our home after the family gathering of yesterday. She gazes out the window with a long-ago look in her eyes and says, "They'd be arriving about now, wouldn't they?"

I know what she is seeing: a car pulling into the dooryard of the old farm where we once lived. There are three men in the car, with smiles as broad as the car's bumpers. One of the men is Uncle Willie. Our mob of children, our two dogs, and a cat named Eloise run out to greet them. We have very savvy animals. They know who our true friends are.

The living net of children envelops our visitors, and with joyous shouts, hugs, and kisses the day's catch is drawn across the snow-filled lawn toward the house.

Uncle Willie is a Jesuit priest—William J. Finnegan, S.J. His companions are Jesuit Brothers Farr and Kessick. Between the three of them and St. Robert Francis Romulus Bellarmine, they do a bang-up job of running the Bellarmine Retreat House in Barrington, Illinois. I have known Uncle Willie since college, when he was dean of Loyola University, Chicago. He has always had a special gift for making friends, and a special gift for keeping them. He treats them as if each is the best friend he has, and all of them—and their children—call him Uncle Willie.

"Uncle Willie! You have to see my new electric train!"

"You have to ride my new sled!"

"You have to hold my new doll!"

"You have to play my new hockey game!"

The cries sparkle like snowflakes blowing past a lighted window. Uncle Willie and his companions, their arms full of packages, enter the house to the strains of "When the Saints Go Marching In," which one of the older children has put on the record player. "Uncle Willie's Day"—the *real* name for our day after Christmas—has begun.

Presents are exchanged, games are played, songs are sung around the piano, stories are told before the open fire, marshmallows are roasted, a Christmas play is staged by the younger children, Brother Farr reads his poetry, and dinner is served. Then at last there is the dreaded moment when Uncle Willie looks at his watch and says, "It's getting late."

The long, reluctant good-bys; Uncle Willie's final wave: "God bless you! I love you all!"

My married daughter turns away at last from the window, smiling, as the car drives off into yesteryear.

Today, others of my grandchildren are learning to tell time. Later they will learn how much time has to tell *them*. I hope their internal clocks keep running, too—reminding them to thank heaven for bountiful moments with meanings far beyond mere numbers, for days and hours that once were filled with special graces bestowed by their Creator.

In his beautiful play *The Skin of Our Teeth,* Thornton Wilder has his hero, George Antrobus, describe how he survived the loneliness of wartime sentry duty. "I used to give names to the hours of the night"—names of the great philosophers, whose works had nourished him in his youth, and names of books of Holy Scripture. Nine o'clock was Spinoza; ten o'clock, Plato; eleven o'clock, Aristotle.

Midnight was Genesis: "In the beginning God created the heavens and the earth; and the earth was waste and void; and the darkness was on the face of the deep. And the Lord said let there be light and there was light."

So *much* light . . .

Our First Thanksgiving
on the Farm

"You know, dear," my wife said one evening as we sat with our nine children, elbow to elbow, around the dinner table, "we need more room."

She was right. The old table that had served us well for many years was no longer adequate.

"Okay," I said, "a new table. We'll start looking tomorrow."

Ginny finished cutting a lamb chop for Gael, our youngest. "I'm not talking about tables," she said patiently. "I'm talking about houses."

I should have known. My wife seldom thinks small.

It took me about a week to shift gears from tables to houses, but in the end I had to admit that she had a point. No matter how you stack them, shift them around, or talk about togetherness, nine children can be a bit much for a suburban home originally designed for a family closer to the national average of 2.2 than ours.

So we began looking—not in the same area but farther out, in the country, where we had always hoped to live someday. In time we decided on a friendly old farmhouse with ten acres that had once been the heart of a dairy farm. It offered us country living, good schools, and the reassuring presence of not-too-distant neighbors.

But however practical our reasons for moving, leaving old friends for the unknown was a depressing experience, especially for the kids. Their feelings of loss were intensified because the break occurred just a few days before Thanksgiving. To them we were the Pilgrims leaving home for an alien shore.

"Don't worry," I tried to reassure them. "We'll find plenty of friendly Indians—just as the Pilgrims did."

The younger ones weren't sure that Indians would be the answer.

To their credit, once we moved, they all did their best to look happy. "We love it here; we really do!" they repeated frequently as they explored the barn's dark, empty hayloft, tramped the length of the meadow out back, and climbed the trees of the small orchard. But between bursts of enthusiasm there were sudden calms, and I knew what they were thinking: "I wish Marcie and Anne were here, and Jerry, and Ted, and Emily. . . . I wonder what the new school will be like . . . what the new kids will be like. . . . "

"Bless us, O Lord," we prayed at the Thanksgiving table, "and these Thy gifts, which we are about to receive from Thy bounty. . . . "

"And let us be thankful for our new home," Ginny added. "And for our new life in the country. We're going to be very happy here." A circle of solemn faces nodded slow agreement. She held out her hands to the two oldest girls, who sat on either side of her. In a moment the handclasps encircled the table like a halo.

"Cheer up," I said as I started to carve the turkey. "In no time at all you'll have more friends than you can count."

"Sure hope so," they answered.

After dinner, Ginny and the older girls went for a walk. The older boys went out to explore the barn once again. The two youngest disappeared upstairs for an afternoon nap. I thought this was an excellent idea and did the same.

About an hour later, I was awakened by a cry from below. "Daddy! The schoolhouse is on fire!" It was eleven-year-old Nina.

I snapped upright. "The *what* is on fire?" I gasped.

"The schoolhouse! Hurry, Daddy! Mummy called the fire department!"

I could hear the mournful wail of the fire whistle in the distant town summoning the volunteer firemen.

But why all the urgency? Wasn't the nearest schoolhouse, an old, abandoned structure, more than a mile away?

Then suddenly I remembered—and raced down the stairs. The "schoolhouse" was no more than twelve feet from our back door!

A former owner had converted an ancient one-car garage into a study by substituting a wall and window for the main doorway and by installing a smaller door on the side facing our house. He had crowned the peaked roof with a picturesque cupola and bell. That was all the children's imaginations needed. To them it was ever after the schoolhouse.

Streamers of pink-tinted smoke were drifting out the building's side door. Crouching low, I peered inside. Flames danced along the edge of a tattered grass rug near a rusty oil stove. Flames also sputtered behind the stovepipe. I stepped over the threshold—and promptly tripped over someone's leg. Lord, I thought, one of the kids has been overcome! I grabbed the leg and pulled.

"It's all right, Dad!" sixteen-year-old Kip sputtered. "I think we have it now!"

Flat on his stomach below the smoke, he was aiming the nozzle of a pumplike contraption at the flames. His younger brother Dave, also on his stomach, was working the pump handle furiously.

Kip was right. The flames were reluctantly giving up. Another few shots of water and they died completely. "Everybody out of here!" I shouted.

Out they staggered, coughing, their faces smeared with soot. One of them held a primitive pesticide sprayer, which they had filled with water. "You shoulda seen this place a few minutes ago," Dave said triumphantly.

From over a nearby hill came the sound of sirens.

In another minute the farmyard was filled with vehicles and people: two rural fire engines—a pumper and tanker—each carrying four or five men; a sheriff's squad car with the sheriff, his deputy, and two men they had been having coffee with in Olson's Cafe when the alarm sounded; an emergency truck from the electric company with the driver and two friends; and at least six cars packed with neighbors, their parents, children, aunts, uncles, and whoever else had been celebrating Thanksgiving with them when the engines roared past their homes.

I apologized to the fire chief for bringing him out on Thanksgiving Day. "No strain," he assured me pleasantly. "I needed a little fresh air after all that turkey."

What, he wanted to know, had been the problem? Dave supplied the details. "I went out to the schoolhouse, see? It was real cold out there." (Why, I fumed silently, hadn't he returned to the main house if it was so cold out there? This was the first of several questions I intended to ask the boys later.) "So I decided to light the oil stove. Boy, is *that* an old relic!" (Why had he decided to light the oil stove if it was such an old relic?) "Before I knew it, some oil leaked out on the rug and caught fire. I called Kip and we found an old fire extinguisher in the basement, but it fizzled out." (Why hadn't he called *me?*) "Kip found this old sprayer, see, and we filled it with water and put the fire out." (Just like that.)

"Good work," said the chief, who knew a first-class fire-fighter when he saw one. He gave Dave and Kip a congratulatory slap on their shoulders. (Maybe I'd forget the questions.)

Neighbors were now coming up to Ginny and myself and introducing themselves. Their children sought out our children.

"Thank heaven it wasn't serious." "So *you're* our new neighbors; we wondered who had bought the old McArthur place." "Been dying to meet you folks. If there's anything you need ... "

Many of them had been frequent guests in the old farm-house and knew it better than we did. Ginny invited them in.

Grateful for the quick response of the volunteer firemen

and the others, I invited *them* in. They were delighted—and curious, like the rest, about how a four-bedroom house could accommodate a family with so many children. I explained that plans had already been made for an addition. Ginny and the girls set out cookies, crackers, cocoa, and coffee. I found the makings for some highballs. We sat on chairs, couches, stairs, windowsills, and the floor. Our eight-year-old Tony found someone his age who was also a model railroad buff, and together they stretched several feet of track among the tangle of legs and feet in the living room. The sheriff's deputy invited Tony to come over some day and see *his* layout.

The fire chief asked what I was going to use the schoolhouse for. "A study," I said. "A place to write."

"Ah," said the chief, brightening, "so you're a writer."

I was, and so, it seemed, was he. "I haven't sold anything yet," he admitted, "but maybe you'd like to look at some of my stuff." I told him I'd be happy to.

One of my daughters and a neighbor girl decided the party needed some background music, so they went to the piano and played "Chopsticks" over and over until the chief, trying to outline a story idea he was working on, asked them to cool it.

Somebody's grandfather told me he had helped install the new heating system in the house when it was remodeled a few years ago. "Come on down to the basement," he invited me, as if it were his own. "I'll show you what to do in case the furnace doesn't kick in right away. There's this little button, see?" Five or six of us followed him down. "Watch your heads," he warned us as we went down the stairway. While he showed me what button to push, one or two of the others checked the wiring and found it safe. "You never know about these older houses," one of them said. Someone else demonstrated how I should fit a protective screen around the sump pump to keep it free of debris.

"Now then," said the grandfather, "let's see where you're

going to put this new addition." Eventually he approved our plans, and we returned to the living room.

Ginny and the kids were paddling around contentedly on a sea of advice, suggestions, cautions, and recommendations, all offered with the best of goodwill to make us feel more at home.

They all had their favorites: the best doctor, the best dentist, the best pediatrician, the best hairdresser, the best vet, the best druggist, the best roofer, the best well digger, the best tree surgeon, the best fence builder, the best man for the septic tank.

We learned (to our surprise) that we must never close the door of the downstairs bedroom in winter. That would interrupt the circulation of heat, and we would freeze to death on cold nights.

We should get a cat. There were a lot of field mice out here in the country. Better yet, get two cats. And the best place to get cats was the Hildebrand farm. Hildebrand cats were notorious mousers.

The grade school teachers were okay. Miss Bemis was their favorite—she had a great sense of humor. And she didn't load you down with homework as some of the others did. Miss Bemis was "neat."

The high school teachers were okay, too, especially Mr. Ryan, who taught algebra and coached the football team. Mr. Ryan was also "neat."

The tide of information and good fellowship continued to swell: the best grocer, the best butcher shop, the best restaurant, the best hardware store, the best dry cleaners, the best service station, the best shortcut into town. . . .

And, as the children said afterwards, "The best Thanksgiving of all!"

Thanks to those friendly Indians.

Sister Jean-Marie
and the Junior Prom

Our fascination with country living sprang from a firm belief that this was the only way God intended us to live. City-born like ourselves, out for a Sunday drive, we felt the heavenly tug every time we passed a CATTLE CROSSING sign beside a rural blacktop.

In the country you'd be closer to nature, if not to your orthodontist. You'd be closer to the race memories of a lost Eden, if not to your pediatrician, your piano teacher, and the supermarket. This last inconvenience would be of no consequence, of course, if you grew your own meat, vegetables, and laundry detergents.

The air in the country was fresher than the air in the city or suburb, and so were the eggs—once you'd found a chicken farmer within a reasonable drive from your home, say, seven or eight miles down the interstate. And in spite of the traffic roaring along your county roads, where the posted speed limit then was 65 MPH, the country was generally held to be safer for children than urban areas, where the limit was only 30.

This was a period when books like *Five Acres and Independence* were immensely popular, and Elizabethan tavern–style signs, swinging from whitewashed gate posts, declared their adjoining plots, however modest and devoid of agricultural buildings, to be "farms"—a euphemism that persists to this day. In short, the country was the place for recapturing Adam's lost harmony with the birds and the bees, the gray garden slug and the horsefly.

And so, as I noted earlier, we moved to the spacious old farmhouse with a few surrounding acres that had once been part of a dairy farm. There were newer homes within hailing distance on land that had once been grazed or tilled, but much rural atmosphere remained. From our upstairs bedroom we could see silos and barns that told us, Never fear, real farmers are not far off.

I must admit that, all in all, it was a good life—if you didn't mind having to spend so much of it behind the wheel of your station wagon. It was a rewarding life, too, even though one of its greatest rewards, at least for the younger ones, was an hour-and-a-half train ride into the city. It was also an exhilarating life (part of what I called the Elysian Syndrome)—and it took a high school junior prom to bring our view of it into more realistic focus.

Our three oldest children attended a Catholic coeducational high school located in the nearby town and staffed mostly by nuns. One of the school's major social events was the Junior Prom, held near the close of each school year. Some may wonder where in a rural town like ours did the juniors find a facility big enough for a dance band and scores of dancing feet. The answer is easy, and it's easy because there was only *one* answer—the high school gymnasium. The town had no hotel with a ballroom, only a six-bedroom-two-bath affair over a haberdashery shop and the First National Bank.

Gavin McGafferty, a prosperous farmer in the area, had once offered the dance committee the free use of his big dairy barn. "We held a swell barn dance there last year," McGafferty said, by way of inducement.

The committee was enchanted by the offer until they checked it out and learned that all during the dance a sixty-head herd of prize Holstein cows, healthy in all their bodily functions, would be quartered in their customary stalls just below the floor.

The only other possibility was the Midland Hotel, located in a town too distant to be considered for more than a few seconds, which was all the time it took Sister Eulalia, the school's aging principal, to nix the idea.

So year after year the brave kids of successive decorating committees took up the challenge of converting the austere, sweat-soaked gym interior into a one-night teenage dreamworld. They were armed, as always, with little more than a few rolls of colored crepe paper and the sobering suspicion that no matter what they did, their efforts were foredoomed. Moreover, their only reward would come, traditionally, at the start of the Prom evening when, with only a few first arrivals present, the band leader would call out, "Let's hear it now for the decorations committee! They've done another great job!"

Between dances the kids sat on the same folding chairs they sat on for weekly assemblies. The big difference now was that instead of being out on the floor, the chairs were pushed back flat against the unfinished brick walls. The drinking crowd balanced their cokes on their knees.

The eagerly awaited high point of each Prom was Sister Eulalia's nine o'clock decision to retire for the night. This meant that Father Toomey, our young assistant pastor, could bring the overhead lighting down from its full basketball-game candlepower to a slightly more romantic level.

After the dance, most of the kids went for something to eat at Murray's Restaurant on the edge of town. Murray's was where their fathers often went for lunch and where the food, though not "fancy," was known to be "good, down-to-earth stuff." Besides, Murray's, being so close, was highly recommended by the parents.

By the time David, our second oldest, reached his junior year, Sister Eulalia had been succeeded by the much younger Sister Jean-Marie. Born in France, she still spoke with a charming trace of her homeland accent and, once her mind was made up, acted with the vigor of her ancestors storming the Bastille.

Sister Jean-Marie soon heard about the previous proms from Father Toomey, and, in her French tradition of doing things with élan, she resolved that from now on the Junior Prom would be a "celebration, not an end-of-the-year wake."

She organized a Parents Committee—well named because she saw to it that the parents of nearly every junior were on it. It was formed to implement her thesis that helping the kids to have a happy Prom night should consist of more than a warning not to stay out late.

"The only place for the Prom is still right here in the gym," Sister told the assembled committee at our first meeting. "That's a fact of life we can't change. What we *can* change is the gym itself."

A few heads nodded in agreement. I knew what they were thinking. They were thinking, We'll go all out this year and get a dozen more rolls of crepe paper.

"First," Sister said, "the Prom must have a theme, a setting, a personality all its own. Don't you agree?"

A personality all its own? What in the world did *that* mean?

"Well, *don't* you?" Sister pressed. It was obvious she didn't get to be principal by waiting around for slow-wits like us to catch up with her.

We all agreed. We could find out later what a "personality all its own" meant.

"Suppose we pretend it's a French café," Sister charged on.

The committee voted unanimously for a French café.

"Suppose we call it, 'The Cafe of the Students'—or, in French, 'Café des Étudiants.'"

The committee voted unanimously for Café des Étudiants.

"Next," said Sister in her French tradition of practicality, "we must form a finance committee to raise funds. We will need money—not too much but not too little."

A finance committee was immediately formed. So was an art committee, a construction committee, a lighting committee, and several others it would take a committee to keep track of.

"And remember," Sister said in conclusion, "this must all

be a big surprise to the juniors. From now till Prom night, the gym will be closed to everyone but committee members. The rest," she added, in her French tradition of graciousness, "is up to you. God bless you for your help."

Thus instructed and thus blessed, the various committees went to work.

Over the years, the gym had seen countless basketball games, indoor track meets, gymnastic contests, bake sales, rummage sales, and parish bazaars. But to the committee members, all of it together seemed little more than a yawn compared to the whirlwind of activity that began to build as parents with skills in design, painting, carpentry, wiring, and other crafts pushed the transformation forward.

"By George!" one of them remarked near the finish of the work. "It *does* have a personality all its own!"

Here is the Prom Night setting the tired workers finally left behind them, the setting that greeted the first couples as they arrived only minutes after their parents left.

An entranceway elegantly flanked by tubs of topiary trees. You almost had to touch them to see that their leaves were tufts of green crepe paper expertly fixed in spherical webs of chicken wire.

An antiqued sign that looked as if it might have swung in the winds of a hundred Paris summers and winters. It said CAFÉ DES ÉTUDIANTS.

A colorfully lighted bandstand at the far end of the gym with an eight-foot-high backdrop of hand-painted panels depicting such Gallic trademarks as the Eiffel Tower, the Arc de Triomphe, an enormous French poodle, French taxicabs, gendarmes, the tricolor, and much more.

Two life-size kiosks, papered, like much of the wall space, with posters provided by a parent in the travel business.

Large free-form discs of heavy cardboard, coated with glitter and suspended like pancake clouds to conceal the basketball backboards and the steel ribbing of the ceiling. With all light concentrated below the level of these "floating" discs, the dark vault above them might well have been the springtime sky of a Paris night.

Cloth-covered tables around the perimeter of the dance floor, and on each table a small vase of flowers.

A bistrolike bar that dispensed soft drinks, its youthful bartender resplendent in pencil mustache, pomaded hair, arm bands, and apron.

And the lighting! Securely taped to the walls, an elaborate network of tiny Christmas tree lights that sparkled like stars in the soft, diffuse glow of make-believe post lanterns.

And when the band began to play and the first dancers moved to the floor, those parents who had gone home to clean up and were now back as chaperones were amply rewarded for their efforts when their kids drifted past them and dreamily whispered, "Neat! *Really* neat!"

Mrs. Zollar, an old fan of Sister Eulalia, feared the lighting was too subdued and remarked about it to Sister Jean-Marie.

"In the cafés of Paris," Sister replied, "it is even darker than this. In fact, it is so dark you can hardly find your way around."

Mrs. Zollar raised her eyebrows in a "How do *you* know?" look but let the matter drop.

After the dance, the kids thanked the chaperones for "the best evening we ever had" and bade their parents good night. It was assumed that, as in years past, they would then go to Murray's Restaurant for a late supper of the good, down-to-earth stuff.

I know some did. I also know some did not.

At an hour long past the time when our David would have easily made it home from Murray's, I heard a car pull slowly into our yard as if its driver hoped to arrive unnoticed. There was a careful closing of the car door and a soft tiptoeing up the front steps. I heard it all because I already had our front door open.

"Have car trouble?" I asked calmly. I thought this was as

good a question as any for openers. "How was the flight down to Rio?" would have been another, but I didn't think of it in time.

"Gee, Dad," David exclaimed. "I hope you weren't worried. But y'see, a bunch of us decided at the last minute to go to the Villa Maurice. What a band! What a dance floor! What food! You shoulda been there."

The Villa Maurice? The Villa Maurice that was barely outside the city limits of Chicago?

Yep. Same Villa Maurice.

But *why?*

"Why?" David repeated slowly, giving me time to see the stupidity of my question. "Because," he said finally, "it's *big* town. It's where the action is. Dad, you *know* there's nothing doing out here in the boonies. It's dullsville!"

For a moment I thought of reminding him that the air is fresher out here in the boonies. But for some reason I changed my mind.

That was a long time ago. Our twelve children are now grown. All but two are married and have families of their own. Only one of them lives in the country. Some of the rest live in big cities. Some, like David, his wife, and their six children, live in a town that is almost as big as a city and, in fact, calls itself a city. I had lunch with him not long ago.

"How are things?" I asked.

"Not bad," he answered. "But we're getting pretty crowded at home. We need a lot more room."

"I know the feeling," I said.

"We've been thinking," he continued. "With the kids growing up the way they are, wouldn't it be great if we found a nice place out in the country?"

"The—country?" I managed.

"I think it's where God intended us to live," said David solemnly.

"Where the air is fresher," I added.

"Exactly!"
"And the eggs, too."
"*Now* you've got it!"
"Great idea!" I said.
I'm glad I remembered the eggs.

How Did We Ever Manage?

"How did we ever get along without it?" is a frequently heard tribute to such modern indispensables as the office copier, the microwave oven, the VCR, and the instant television replay of close calls at second base.

I don't suppose any of us would be comfortable going back in person to the "good old days," but I believe that an occasional glance in their direction tends to sharpen our faith in the intrepidity of the human spirit. For the truth is, we got along quite well, as I remember my boyhood years. Blissfully unaware that we would someday have the silicon chip, the word processor, and the space satellite, we followed our modest stars and were content to wonder how we ever got along without the radio, the electric vacuum cleaner, and the safety razor, much as our ancestors must have wondered how they ever got along without the safety pin. As St. Thomas More said, the times are never so bad that a good man can't live in them.

There were many good men and many good women in those times, including my parents and grandparents. We all lived together comfortably and, for the most part, happily in our two-family house, and every so often some new product of man's creative genius made us wonder how we ever got along without it.

My father wondered how we ever got along without the self-starter in the automobile. Mother wondered how we ever got along without the electric washing machine and thanked the saints for it—much, I'm sure, to the surprise of that heavenly body. Grandma thanked them for the Singer sewing machine and the Gold Dust twins. Grandpa and I were grateful, especially on Saturday afternoons, for Pearl White in "The Perils of Pauline," but we didn't think it appropriate to thank the saints for that particular beneficence.

Our family members saw a lot of each other—to everyone's delight. I guess the simplest explanation is that we liked each other. We would have roared with laughter had anyone predicted that someday one room in the average home, and one room only, would be designated "the family room"—as if some new and captious etiquette considered socializing as unseemly as pole vaulting and trap shooting in all but specified areas. Yet even in this room that is supposedly dedicated to familial pleasures, the omnipresent TV set, that marvel of mass communication, stands ready to serve those who prefer not to communicate with others no matter what room they're in.

In my home, family rooms were all over the place. The parlor was an excellent family room. So was the dining room. So was the front porch. So, for that matter, was the back porch. But in my view the best of all was the kitchen.

We didn't just cook in the kitchen; we congregated in it—as we did in church—in affection and friendship and with a sense that we were participating in an ancient sacramental rite. As the meat juices sizzled leisurely in the roasting pan and the vegetables dispatched their steamy odors to the four points of the household compass, we talked about whatever came to mind; no subject was too big or too small for our attention. And there was no microwave bell to tell us our time was up.

Kitchen conversations were a warm, aromatic part of our daily lives, flavored as they were with the pungent smell of cumin, the bold fragrance of curry, and the sunny summer bouquet of rosemary, marjoram, tarragon, and thyme. And if the conversation lingered like a guest loath to leave, there was always time for more of it over the dishpan—for we hadn't yet discovered that we couldn't get along without the automatic dishwasher.

The basement laundry area became another tip-top family room after my mother got her first electric washing machine. It was called the Easyway, a name its manufacturer must have given it in a frenzy of irresponsibility. The Easyway was to the housewife what the first Model T was to the motorist—a headstrong, uncanny, unpredictable contrivance of dark and desperate origins.

It arrived, as I recall, asking no quarter and thoroughly prepared to give none. Its operating directions had been lost in shipment—which was just as well, for the machine seldom operated in the same way twice. It preferred to make up its own mind as it went along, free to exercise any of its numerous options for doing mischief.

In the days when a copper wash boiler, a pair of zinc laundry tubs, and sliced-up bars of Fels Naptha soap were Mother's only tools for doing the wash, she did it single-handedly. But after witnessing the Easyway's trial run, my father insisted that she never go near it unless he or I, and preferably both of us, were present. There were times, I felt, when he wished the local fire department could also have been present, for the electric motor, mounted in an open framework beneath the tub, often caught sprays of sudsy water, which made it spark, hiss, crackle, and smoke. When this happened, we ran for the backyard, where we stayed until the smoke cleared; then we came back and replaced blown-out fuses.

The washer had no agitator for stirring the clothes about in the tub. The tub itself was the agitator. Its design was Early Oil Drum, and it lay horizontally on an uneasy bed of gears, levers, and pulleys, which rocked it like a cradle gently or violently, depending on their mood. Sloshing action, I believe it was called.

"Don't stare at the tub," my father wisely cautioned us once. "It could make you seasick."

A power wringer rose above the edge of the tub as uncompromisingly erect as the Statue of Liberty. Like that noble lady, it promised new freedom to the poor "huddled masses" who once wondered how they ever got along without the *hand*-operated wringer.

We wrung clothes from the washing machine to a rinse tub and from there to a clothes basket. In summer we hung the clothes in the yard to dry. In winter we hung them in the basement. As yet there were no automatic dryers, or at least we didn't have one.

If Mother caught a finger in the wringer, she promptly hit a safety lever with her free hand to release the pressure. If she caught both hands in the wringer, as she did a few times, she needed her young son, alert and quick as a squirrel, to hit the lever for her. The blow always totally disassembled the rollers. Only the son's mechanical expertise got the machine working again. Except for pinched fingers, Mother's hands, thank heaven, easily survived these trials.

The vaporous, saunalike intimacy of the basement laundry intensified our pioneer feeling of mutual support, especially when Grandma and Grandpa came down to keep us company. That in itself was reason enough for my mother to thank the saints for her new washer. As for me, I had the warm impression that, like an Indian boy on a buffalo hunt, I was contributing importantly to family survival—in my case, survival through another engagement with the Easyway.

Yes, we got along.

We got along, too (can you imagine it?), without the computer—more specifically, the computer in the classroom. We didn't have one, but we did have Sister Mary Verissima. Sister taught forty-eight sixth- and seventh-grade boys in the same room and was the farthest thing imaginable from an electronic, programmed, push-button piece of hardware. But she was the *closest* thing imaginable to an inspirational, creative, caring, and at the same time strict and savvy stand-in for the Blessed Mother—which is exactly what she felt she had been called to be. Her students felt the same way.

"Forty-eight kids in the same room?" educator friends of mine have asked incredulously. "Are you *sure* it was forty-eight?"

Yes, I'm sure, and I'll bet with a little concentration I could supply most of the names on request.

"Are you sure there were *two* classes in the same room?"

Of course I'm sure. On one side of the center aisle sat Paul Biebel in sixth grade; on the other sat his brother William in seventh. The Biebels were smart kids. *They* knew what grades they were supposed to be in.

"But it must have been *bedlam!*"

Well, it wasn't a rest home, but it wasn't bedlam. There were sounds, to be sure, sometimes quite loud, but they were the normal sounds of young boys as they "increased in wisdom and stature and in favor with God and man," to lean a bit on St. Luke. I think the veil had a lot to do with it— almost the same veil we could find in the old prints of Mary on the way to Bethlehem and, again, at the foot of the cross. Bedlam didn't stand a chance with a veil like that around.

"Pencils down in seventh-grade!"

The seventh-graders, who had been busy with a written assignment, were now quizzed orally or sent row by row for a turn at the blackboard to explore the mysteries of long division or to diagram sentences.

"But how could the kids in one grade concentrate on their writing while the kids in the other grade were reciting?"

As one who once worked in a newspaper's city room, I can truthfully say, "I don't know. But it's done all the time. Maybe it strengthens your powers of concentration."

"Diagraming sentences is old-fashioned," a grammar school superintendent once said to me, referring to that classic horizontal line we drew with segments for subject, predicate, and object and with slanting offshoots for articles, adverbs, and adjectives. Like an X-ray, the diagram laid open the bare-bones structure of a sentence and showed how its various parts related. If you could diagram a sentence—simple, complex, or compound—you clarified all mysteries. Sister considered diagraming as indispensable to a knowledge of syntax as a course in anatomy to a knowledge of the human body.

I was surprised when I reached high school to find that the freshman English course included a review of basic English grammar. I was even more surprised when I found that *college* freshman English also included a review of basic English grammar—as if up to now we had communicated mostly in basic Aramaic. More than once I was sure I heard the voice of Sister Mary Verissima whispering, "Remember, Thomas, you heard it here first!"

Meanwhile, on the sixth-grade side of the room, pencils were busy drawing maps, outlining catechism or history lessons, or scratching through the endless business deals of those two arithmetic book heroes, Mr. A and Mr. B. My friend John O'Donnell maintained that the deals must have been pretty shady, else why did the two principals maintain such spartan anonymity? Nevertheless, these two indefatigable traders went on year after year exchanging the same bushels of corn, oats, peas, beans, and barley in an unsung effort to give each new class certain fundamentals of arithmetic.

But what I remember best about Sister Mary Verissima as a teacher was her strong emphasis on creativity.

"Pretend you're a bargeman on the old Erie Canal and write a paper on what your life is like. You'll also be marked on penmanship and neatness.

"Make up a story to tell before both classes during the Friday afternoon story hour. And *please* don't repeat the one about the holdup victim who flashes his scapular medal at his attacker and converts him to the true faith on the spot.

"Prepare a speech on why Ashland Avenue should or shouldn't be widened. Be ready to give it before both classes

Monday morning. You must get used to speaking before others. Think up appropriate gestures. The first boy who puts his hands in his pockets will have to write an essay on 'Why God Gave Me Hands.'

"Draw a picture. Draw houses or horses, archangels or archbishops—but draw. The best drawings will get gold stars and will hang for three days on the bulletin board.

"Draw a musical clef and try to make up a one-line melody. Be prepared to sing it for the class.

"*Discover yourselves!* Each of you is unique and very special in God's eyes. Find the blessed talents he has given you so that you may use them *ad majorem Dei gloriam!*"

Somehow we got along. Modest though our pursuits may have been, there had to be something inspiring about the age—something greater than the age itself—for out of it came the minds that gave us the marvels of these electronic years.

I think if Sister Mary Verissima were still alive, she would compose a small prayer about those marvels:

"May they lead us not into temptation; that is, dear Lord, not away from each other, not away from our made-to-the-image-of-God identities, and, most of all, not away from remembering that all things, old or new, great or small, bear witness to your forever unfolding creation of the world!"

"Amen."